Separation of Powers in Practice

TOM CAMPBELL

Stanford Law and Politics

AN IMPRINT OF STANFORD UNIVERSITY PRESS

STANFORD, CALIFORNIA

2004

Stanford University Press
Stanford, California
www.sup.org

Library of Congress Cataloging-in-Publication Data

Campbell, Thomas, 1952–
    Separation of powers in practice / Tom Campbell.
        p.   cm.
    Includes bibliographical references and index.
    ISBN 978-0-8047-5027-1
    1. Separation of powers—United States.   2. Separation of powers—United
States—Cases.   I. Title.
KF4565.C36 2004
342.73'044—dc22   2004006012

Original Printing 2004

Last figure below indicates year of this printing:
13   12   11   10   09   08   07   06   05   04

Designed and typeset at Stanford University Press in 10/12.5 Palatino.

SEPARATION OF POWERS IN PRACTICE

I dedicate this book to my wife, Susanne, and to my parents, Marie Campbell and Judge William J. Campbell, chief judge of the United States District Court for the Northern District of Illinois.

Contents

THIS BOOK CONSISTS of a series of case studies and essays illustrating clashes between the branches of the American government. The separation of power between the three branches of federal government, and between federal and state authority, allows each level of government to apply advantages unique to itself. The arrogation of power by a branch in a manner crossing over those divisions exposes the comparative disadvantages of the arrogating branch and calls for vigorous resistance by the branch upon which the encroachment has occurred. Such encroachments are more common than the comparative silence of the branches would indicate, as a result of which, comparative advantages of the branches have been distorted and lost.

I do not advocate any specific policy outcome in any topic. In the examples developed in this text, I do, strongly, advocate that the Court stick to interpreting the intent of Congress and the vindication of constitutional principle; that Congress spend its time determining and upholding the policy preferences of the people, while not forgetting that its members, too, are bound by an oath to uphold and defend the Constitution; and that the president utilize the flexibility of the executive branch to fit statutory and administrative law to practical circumstances, while ceasing to encroach on the powers explicitly given to Congress, as in declaring war. The federal government, as an entity, needs to recognize the plenary power vested in the states, reaching, for example, the issue of life's beginning and end, as well as the specific powers reserved to the states under the Constitution, including regulating militia. I reach these conclusions independent of the policy outcome that I or any reader might prefer, asking only whether resort to a particular branch or level of government is more appropriate than resort to a different branch, from the point of view of the inherent structural advantages of each. If that is the case, then it is my hope that the branch inappropriately engaged will desist, or that, if necessary, the other branches or levels of government will be able to force it to desist, in order that the matter be resolved through the apportionment of responsibilities intended by the Constitution and most consistent with the abilities of each branch.

I was on leave of absence from my position as professor of law at Stanford University to serve as a U.S. congressman from 1989 to 1993, as a California state senator from 1993 to 1995, and, again, as a congressman from 1995 to 2001. I commenced preparing these materials while I was a professor of law at Stanford, and I completed the manuscript while dean of the Haas School of Business at the University of California at Berkeley. The examples are drawn from issues with which I personally dealt while in public office.

Over the years I taught courses in this subject area, my law students at Stanford Law School and my college students at Stanford in Washington, D.C., provided me many valuable insights. I was also privileged to have many excellent research assistants who helped with the preparation of these materials, most important, David Graubert and Jeff Negrette of the Stanford Law School and Cameron Doolittle of the Boalt Hall School of Law and Haas School of Business, University of California at Berkeley. My new colleague, Jesse Choper, provided many valuable comments on—and corrections to—the manuscript.

John Hart Ely gave me the chance to become a law professor at Stanford, and Paul Brest made it possible for me to serve in public office while maintaining my position on the faculty at Stanford. I owe them each a profound debt of gratitude.

SEPARATION OF POWERS IN PRACTICE

CHAPTER 1

Introduction

IN THIS INTRODUCTORY chapter, the substance of the examples used throughout the text is summarized, and the basic advantages of each branch or level of government illustrated through those examples are described. The American system of government separates power. It thereby achieves protection for its citizens against the potential of tyranny. The separation also can call forth advantages that each branch possesses for the efficient disposition of issues of public policy and private dispute and to enhance the public's confidence in the fairness of the process that led to those dispositions. In a government with no formal separation, a sacrifice is necessarily made of at least some of these advantages. A danger exists also, however, of too severe a separation. Where one branch fails to undertake a task for which it is the best suited, it willingly permits another branch to usurp that authority. The consequences often include a compromise in the efficiency of the branch assuming the power from the branch giving it up.

In these materials, I present several different issues in recent public policy. The analysis is not attempted to derive what the best outcome, substantively, on any one of them might be. Rather, I attempt to demonstrate how the resolution of these issues came about, highlighting the advantages of each of the federal branches and, in some cases, of the states as compared with the federal government in reaching those resolutions.

My hope is that students of American government, and especially those who serve in government, will see in this analysis a guide of when to abstain and when to seize upon an issue presented to them. Attorneys representing private parties will, and should, look to all three branches of government as potential sources of redress. For their purposes, this analysis might assist such an appeal when it is demonstrable, along the lines I propose, that the branch to whom appeal is made is the best suited, institutionally, to handle the issue. Similarly, the private party seeking to prevent a particular result might raise the kind of objections outlined here to an adversary's seeking relief from a branch of government inappropriate for the particular request. Overall, my hope is to turn the direction of at least some discourse from how a policy advocate can obtain a particular outcome to what is the body of government most appropriate to be engaged in a question of the kind at hand.

The opening sections deal with the process of how Congress passes laws and how courts interpret them. Chapter 2 offers a brief outline of the structural advantages of each branch. Chapter 3 deals with the legislative process, presenting several examples of how the rules of the U.S. House of Representatives allow, and impede, the people's work to be done. The practical workings of today's Congress are essential to understand before forming a judgment as to the inherent advantage of Congress in deciding questions of competing policy.

In considering how individuals serving in government carry out their functions, to what extent should we demand that our legislators, and our president, independently assess the constitutionality of what they pass, sign, and do? If we absolve them of that responsibility, we are tolerating violations of the Constitution, since so little of what those branches do ever is submitted to the Supreme Court. If we are serious about standing up for the authority of each branch of government, then each branch of government should be responsible, in return, in what it does, to abide by the Constitution's strictures, even when there is no other review. This issue is discussed in the second part of Chapter 3, dealing with the constitutional obligation that all federal and state officers take an oath to uphold the federal Constitution.

Touching on examples to be developed in the following chapters, the text next focuses on how courts go about their traditional function of interpreting statutes written by Congress. The Court often slips, in carrying out this function, from interpreter to creator of public policy. The Court will often say that Congress has "acquiesced" to its interpretation of a statute. Chapter 4 analyzes the rules of statutory construction, including acquiescence, to try to separate what the Court should do and does well from what the Court should not do: take power from Congress.

There is a constraint that the judicial branch imposes upon itself, a constraint not shared by the other branches. Presidents change policies between, often even during, administrations. So also does Congress, which changes every two years anyway. These are strengths of each institution. By contrast, the Court purports to avoid such frequent changes through the doctrine of stare decisis. In reality, it has very seldom actually so bound itself in recent years; and that is a good thing since stare decisis, when it has force, binds the Court to do what the Court believes to be wrong—a concept impossible to square with the Court's fundamental role to identify and uphold constitutional principle. These issues are addressed in Chapter 5.

I then turn to the following ten specific clashes between the branches.

Obnoxious Speech

In Chapter 6, I deal with the prosecution of an individual for publicly burning a U.S. flag at a political convention, the reversal of his conviction (and the statute in question) by the state appellate court, affirmance by the U.S. Supreme Court, the subsequent passage of a new statute by Congress, and the eventual overturning of that statute as well.

In this flag-burning example, the executive branch shows its advantages, and disadvantages, in choosing whom to indict and under what statute. As the Texas Court of Criminal Appeals held, the police and prosecutor could have proceeded simply under breach of the peace if the goal were to prevent the immediate flag burning.[1] So another purpose was at work. The choice of statute gives us a clue that a hortatory purpose was involved: the prosecution wanted a conviction for flag burning, not for breach of the peace. This exercise of authority is undoubtedly within the discretion reserved to the executive branch, here, a state's executive branch. No branch other than the executive possesses this power, to initiate criminal prosecution.

The story actually begins much earlier, however, with the passage of the anti-flag-burning statute by the Texas legislature. The state was expressing a sentiment through its elected representatives in Austin. The message was broader than a desire to prevent danger of riot or setting fire to property. The legislature has an advantage in being the closest representative of the people's will. In choosing to pass a criminal statute, rather than a nonstatutory resolution regarding the flag, the Texas legislature made use of the discretion it alone possessed.

The U.S. Supreme Court and the Texas Court of Criminal Appeals both held the Texas statute unconstitutional. The inherent advantage of the courts—and especially the federal courts, which are insulated from popular sentiment by life tenure and nondiminution of salary—is to uphold fundamental rights. It was appropriate, therefore, for each court to measure the statute against the First Amendment's guarantee of freedom of speech. In performing this function, the courtlike method of analysis was to reason from previous cases interpreting the First Amendment, so as to convey the impression that the conclusion was to be expected from what had gone before.

This attribute has both advantages and disadvantages. The advantage is that the Court's claim to consistency vitally defends against its characterization as a mere policy-maker. If the Court becomes policy-maker, it is inferior to the legislature in both design (ability to gather the relevant facts and take testimony) and legitimacy (if preference, rather than principle, is to govern, then the people's preferences are more clearly expressed through their representatives whom they elect than the justices they do not). The disadvantages are two. The first is that the Court is hampered from moving away from earlier errors by the need to appear consistent with earlier opinions. Neither the legislature nor the executive has a similar disadvantage. Second, the Court, in crafting a ruling, has to rule by creating a broad category, then applying that category to the case before it. To rule only on the basis of the one case is not to announce constitutional principle. This becomes disadvantageous when the category for analysis sweeps more broadly than the Court might have intended, leaving dangerous precedent that later cases must distinguish.

The action of Congress in connection with this episode in recent American history shows how it can communicate rather directly to the U.S. Supreme Court. It created a statute and, in that same bill, obliged the Court to hear an appeal of any conviction under that statute on an expedited time schedule. Congress came close, in this instance, to obtaining an advisory opinion; it might have been better if it had been fully advisory, in that at least one individual had to go through indictment, trial, and conviction in order for Congress to obtain a response to the question it was asking the Supreme Court. The fundamental ability of Congress is to use words precisely fitted to the problem at hand. In this instance, we see Congress's attempt to use that ability so as to appeal to one specific justice who held the swing vote on the U.S. Supreme Court. Congress has other powers not in evidence here and significant by omission. The fact-finding mechanisms available to Congress are superior to those available to a court, particularly for the ascertainment of sociological facts about America. These powers could have been used to determine what threats flag burning actually posed and, in so asking, to obtain guidance on what statute would work most effectively to allay them. The other congressional institutional advantage started but not completed in this case was an effort to amend the Constitution. A constitutional amendment offers a way to define and vindicate principle, much as a court does, but without having to rule by broader category than the immediate concern or having to show consistency with earlier holdings.

At the end of Chapter 6, I consider the American Nazis' march through Skokie, Illinois, a village heavily populated with Holocaust survivors. The federal court protected the demonstrators, with a discussion in a separate opinion about the possibility of private insurance solving a problem that the First Amendment prevented the village from solving on its own.

Exclusionary Rule

The Rehnquist Supreme Court is in the process of undoing what the Warren Court set in place regarding the exclusionary rule. This is a difficult process, since the premises for establishing exclusionary rules for evidence obtained in violation of the Fourth and Fifth Amendments were constitutional. Exposing the inherent disadvantages of the judicial branch, the Court is now attempting to allow for exception after exception to the exclusionary rules, without explicitly overruling the decisions that originally held the exclusionary rule to be required by the Constitution. It is a process that shows, as clearly as any of these materials, the weakness of the judicial branch. Once freed of its constitutional moorings, the exclusionary rule continues as a judge-made and judge-supervised process for deterring constitutional violations. The decision to deter a constitutional violation, however, should be a legislative one. It is not, itself, a constitutional decision. Whether society should spend resources making Fourth Amendment violations less common (by the cost of reversals and retrials) or highway accidents less common (by the cost of more frequent repaving) calls for the weighing of interests, at which the legislative branch, not the judicial branch, excels.

The exclusionary rule was first applied to the states under a rule of principle; namely, that the use of illegally obtained evidence constituted a denial of due process. A general rule of exclusion would apply; exceptions could then be considered along the lines of whether the judicial process was unconstitutionally tainted by admission of the evidence, given the circumstances of the particular case. Completely defensible ignorance of a new constitutional rule, for example, might be sufficient—as when the Court adopts a new constitutional interpretation or strikes down a facially valid statute that authorized the search in question. Also possibly allowable as an exception would be evidence so far removed from the original constitutional violation as to satisfy a rule of attenuation.

That approach would permit the judicial branch to show its own inherent advantages, including the U.S. Supreme Court's supervisory role over federal courts. The essential starting off point, however, had to be that the Constitution compels exclusion as a general principle.

As that principle has eroded, however, the Court has assumed a nonjudicial role for the exclusionary rule: one of estimating what kinds of exceptions to the rule will induce more police misconduct. The Court has arbitrarily assumed that only misconduct by police is to be deterred, not misconduct by prosecutor, magistrate, court employee, or judge. The Court has engaged in relatively poor social science inference in a sham effort at "balancing" likelihood of future violations against society's law enforcement needs.

By contrast, Congress and state legislatures have much the better institutional advantage here. To the extent each wants to devote public resources to the goal of deterring constitutional violations, the legislative branch can hold hearings on what kinds of steps (for example, *Bivens* actions, personal fines, disciplinary actions, or exclusionary rule) are most likely to deter governmental misconduct.[2] The cost of each alternative in terms of legitimate prosecutions forgone could then be estimated, and a weighing of interests, the function the legislative branch performs best, could ensue.

The role of the executive is the most underplayed in this area. No use of illegally seized evidence could go forth, of course, without the prosecutor, an agent of the executive branch, desiring it. If we are not speaking of a constitutional requirement, then any governor (or district attorney or attorney general, depending on who holds the executive power to prosecute under the state's constitution) or president could instruct whether to go ahead with the use of specific evidence. It might be that the interests of law enforcement almost always trump, but there would be the occasional egregious case where the executive branch official, reflecting community standards, might opt not to use evidence in a prosecution.

Finally, this subject introduces an interesting interplay between Congress and the Court regarding the *Miranda* rules. The attempt by Congress to undo *Miranda* statutorily was rejected by the U.S. Supreme Court, in an opinion written by Chief Justice Rehnquist.[3] In dissent, Justice Scalia accused the majority of creating a new category of binding precedent: a constitutional rule. Such a rule was not to be found in the Constitution itself, but it could not be reversed by Congress. If Justice Scalia's criticism were warranted, it would be a devastating indictment of the intellectual integrity of what the Court does. The Court binds Congress only because it purports to announce what the U.S. Constitution requires, not because it has the right to make up useful rules short of constitutional compulsion.[4]

Affirmative Action: The Use of Race by Government

The inherent advantage of the judicial branch is in defining the contours of constitutional rights. In *Regents of the University of California v. Bakke, Grutter v. Bollinger*, and *Gratz v. Bollinger*, the right of state universities to make use of race in their admissions policies was considered.[5] In so doing, the Court showed an institutional disadvantage: ambiguity in its ruling. There were three major different positions announced by the Court in *Bakke*: four justices held that any use of race by the state required the highest kind of justification, four justices held that most uses of race with a remedial purpose were permissible, and one justice (Powell) allowed race for purposes of diversity in education only, and then only as a plus factor, not as a determinative factor. In *Gratz* and *Grutter*, almost the same kind of split resulted, with only two justices (O'Connor and Breyer, and only the former explicitly) embracing the middle ground. A statute by Congress or a decision by the executive to terminate federal aid would not have such potential ambiguity.

The inherent advantages of the judicial branch include an ability to monitor an enforcement decree. If the use of race is appropriate in a remedial context, judges can and have kept jurisdiction over cases for years, watching the outcomes and, in some cases, eventually terminat-

ing the litigation when the discrimination complained of has been erad-
icated. In going beyond the purely remedial context, the majority opinion in *Grutter* and the Powell position in *Bakke* present serious challenges to the capacity of the judiciary. When is the attainment of racial
diversity in education so slight a state interest as to be no longer compelling (*Grutter* contains language suggesting racial diversity might be
compelling only for law schools, because of their role in training government and civic leaders), when has sufficient racial diversity been
achieved so that the use of race must be phased out (*Grutter* seems to
create, in a judicial opinion, a legislative-like twenty-five-year duration
for the practice of using race), and how much of a plus factor becomes
a determinative factor (twenty points out of one hundred are too
many)—all are questions to which the opinions give no answer. A legislative solution would certainly offer more predictability, if the legislature cared to address each question in turn.

The inherent advantage of the legislative branch, to set rules clearly,
responsive to the present need, is nevertheless taxed in this context. Appeals to race occur in politics; and dangers of an appeal to race lurk
even in statutes with a benign purpose on their surface.

A possible solution would allow a policy-making political body to
make clear rules of general applicability, so long as the political body
had a First Amendment kind of protection in doing so and was insulated from the worst of racial politics. Alternatively, the entire enterprise of using race could be restricted to specific instances of remediation under a court's supervision.

The Fiesta Bowl: Cutting Off Federal Aid to a Recipient That Discriminates

Poor drafting by Congress created uncertainty as to what kind of discrimination by a recipient of federal funds was enough to trigger a cutoff of those funds. Overstepping its inherent advantages, the U.S.
Supreme Court attempted a Solomonic compromise: extending the
reach of the federal oversight but moderating the effect of its sanction.
Congress, in turn, missed the opportunity to make use of its own inherent advantages by simply rewriting the law. Instead, engaged in an
effort to chastise the Court, Congress literally reversed the Supreme
Court's opinion, construing the ambiguous words of the original statute rather than rewriting them. The result was a Draconian statute,

with a quick trigger and cataclysmic consequences, which became evident when the executive branch entered the dispute when the organizers of the 1991 Fiesta Bowl announced a scholarship for minority-race students at the competing schools.

It is an undoubted executive prerogative to choose whom to prosecute, or against whom to proceed civilly, but not every prerogative is wisely used. In threatening to terminate all federal funds to two colleges whose only failing was to accept students who in turn had accepted scholarships awarded to African Americans only, the federal Department of Education was applying the law, as newly amended by Congress, quite literally, but in a way virtually no one in Congress would have wished. Showing the advantage the executive has to move more quickly than either of the other branches, the Department of Education changed this policy in a matter of days. Further, in announcing guidelines for how it would prosecute such cases in the future, the executive branch effectively reversed both the U.S. Supreme Court and Congress. In the absence of a private right of action, prosecutorial discretion becomes the effective equivalent of suspending a statute, at least for the duration of a president's term.

Roe v. Wade

Perhaps the most contentious issue in modern American domestic discourse, the issue of abortion has also tested the boundaries of the inherent advantages of the several branches. The states begin our inquiry: they are the repository of all legitimate governmental powers not specifically given to the federal government. In exercise of those powers, some states had prohibited abortions, some had permitted them up until a particular point of a pregnancy. We can cast the issue as determining when human life begins. The Constitution does not state which branch of government makes such a decision; following the Tenth Amendment's language, therefore, it might seem it should be left to the states.

It is, however, the advantage and obligation of the federal judiciary to apply the U.S. Constitution even to laws of the states. In the abortion context, this role had two important ramifications. First, it fell to the Court to decide who gets to enjoy constitutional rights. In *Roe v. Wade*, the U.S. Supreme Court ruled that an unborn child or fetus was not a person for purposes of the U.S. Constitution. Second, the Court's role includes defining the contours of the constitutional right of privacy; the Court did so, so as to include a woman's right to terminate her pregnancy at least in the first trimester. Combining the two holdings, a state could not prevent a woman from exercising her constitutional right of privacy without a compelling reason, and saving the life of that which was not a person did not qualify.

Whether popular or not, the Court's unique role is to be the ultimate voice on constitutional rights. One can imagine the Court fulfilling that role in another way, however, in the *Roe v. Wade* context. The Court could have held that the Constitution's protections extend to unborn children or fetuses from the moment of conception. Hence, if a state wanted to prohibit abortion, it could do so. Further, a state hospital probably could not perform abortions, except to save the woman's life, since the state would be depriving the child of her or his life without due process of law. Either outcome appears consistent with the Court fulfilling its role.

In imposing trimesters, the *Roe* Court was roundly criticized for acting like a legislature.[6] Nineteen years later, the Court reformulated the trimester approach into an inquiry whether a woman's constitutionally protected right was being unduly burdened.[7] This approach demonstrates a much more judicial function, whereas *Roe* demonstrated more of a legislative one. Courts traditionally have had to assess whether neutral statutory schemes nevertheless unduly burdened constitutionally protected rights.[8]

The movement from *Roe* to *Planned Parenthood v. Casey*, however, was a difficult one for the Court to make and still claim consistency. In upholding the essential part of *Roe*, *Planned Parenthood* nevertheless reversed several cases decided in between, cases that had been decided more in keeping with *Roe*'s language of an almost absolute right in the first two trimesters. The Court was, quite obviously, experimenting with different phrases for the privacy right in question; and doing so did little to support its claim that all it was doing was finding and announcing constitutionally protected principle.

Could the other branches have done better? This is not an area where Congress or the executive appear to have institutional advantages, as compared with the Court. The whole issue arises because of the assertion of a federal constitutional claim, and that is for the Court to decide. Were that federal constitutional issue taken away, there is no doubt that both of the political branches would reflect a point of view on this issue and thus that they could adopt whatever was common between the president's and Congress's view. However, if there were no constitutional issue, it might be institutionally preferable to see the question revert to different states' solutions, rather than one answer for all, which Congress or the executive would give. If that happened, we would very likely see several different rules for abortion across the several states, just as we see different states' laws on marriage, divorce, and child custody. Our system of government allows, even encourages, that degree of difference between the several states.

But that degree of allowable difference does not permit a state to say freed slaves, or their descendants, are not citizens. Would we be content to say women have the right to end a pregnancy in some states but not in others? Would we be content to say an unborn child or fetus is a person in some states but not in others? Pro-life or pro-choice, there seems to be little room for the middle. The Court chose one side. The Court's critics, I believe, wish the Court had chosen the other side, not that the Court had never made a choice.[9]

The Burden of Proof in Civil Rights Cases

The crafting of the 1964 Civil Rights Act demonstrates advantages of the legislative branch. The 1964 Congress anticipated and provided, through compromise, for particular concerns that had been expressed about taking civil rights enforcement into the individual private employer context. The Court, however, six years later, adopted a broader application than the 1964 compromise. When the Court attempted to cut back on that ruling nineteen years later, Congress responded with a new law. The way in which the Court attempted to cut back purported to make use of judicial virtues: specifically, by setting burdens of proof rather than by trying to reinterpret phrases in the law.

Chapter 11 introduces the question of whether the setting of burdens of proof is a courtlike or legislative-like function. There is no doubt that it is an outcome-determining function.

In reaching this conclusion, Congress and the Supreme Court engaged in a dialogue. Had the Court never expanded the 1964 statute to allow proof in the absence of intent to discriminate, it's highly doubtful Congress would have enacted that rule on its own. Indeed, Congress chose not to do so in 1964. Once this kind of suit was permitted by the Court, however, it became impossible for a subsequent Court credibly to undo what the earlier Court had done. The response by Congress was to cut through the pretense that all that was being decided was the allocation of the burden of proof. Using its inherent advantage of writing a law specific to the problem at hand, Congress proceeded to codify how to make out a case of discrimination in employment in the absence of proof of intent. Congress had shied away from this attempt in 1964 but was emboldened to do so in 1991 because of the Court's intervening rulings.

Two Statutes—A Hundred Years Apart

In the immediate wake of the American Civil War, Congress dealt with the lingering effects of slavery. Many years later, Congress acted again, responding to the civil rights movement of the 1950s and 1960s. In between, the U.S. Supreme Court interpreted what Congress had done in such a way as to limit private enforcement of the rights guaranteed immediately after the end of slavery. Both Congress and the U.S. Supreme Court revived their interest in the area, but the Court was presented with its earlier decisions as obstacles. The Court attempted to interpret the words of the older statute in a more expansive way, hampered by its institutional need to appear to be consistent with the earlier interpretation and then, a few years later, tried to move back to the original, narrower view. The Court's approach showed it at a disadvantage. In attempting to reconcile new and old opinions, it inadvertently created a result that was not well suited to the modern era in which it was announced. Race and sex discrimination ended up being treated differently. The Court's efforts exposed its implausibility in asserting it was only interpreting congressional words and congressional intent.

Congress, by contrast, had no such impediment. It accepted the earlier decisions and proceeded to set up new statutory rights. The ensuing conflict was one that Congress, rather than the Court, had institutional advantages in resolving. Congress relied on its inherent advantage to address the specific problem at hand: the damages that victims of state deprivation of civil rights should receive. In separate statutes, Congress dealt with housing and employment discrimination by private actors.

Once again, there was a dialogue between Congress and the Court. The Court's reversal of its older, narrower reading of the statute provoked no change from Congress; the later Court's narrowing of interpretation, however, provoked a strong response. It is doubtful whether Congress, without the Court's recanting opinion, could have engendered the support to move from the status quo. In a manner that repeats itself often in these materials, we observe Congress reacting to the Court, a testimony to the active nature of the Court's modern role.

The executive figured in this example only in a small way. Through vetoing a first version of the bill and eventually signing a version only slightly different, the executive showed its inherent advantage to respond to changing circumstances of popular will.

The Second Amendment

The inherent advantage of the U.S. Supreme Court, to discern and define constitutional rights that must be upheld even against popular will, carries with it an obligation, too: that the Court actually take and decide cases presented to it that raise the issue of such constitutional rights. For the right to keep and bear arms, however, the Court has been content to remain silent for almost seventy years. Our constitutional scheme appears to have this as a flaw: barring an original jurisdiction case that presents an issue of personal constitutional privilege (and it is hard to see how such a case could be constructed), there is no way to force a ruling from the Supreme Court to uphold or to narrow a perceived personal constitutional right. One inference is that the Court is simply pleased with the lower courts' decisions. This assumption may have been valid while there was no split in the circuits; the widely varying bases on which the circuits have based their opinions, however, make it hard to infer what view it is in which the Court has acquiesced by silence.

The Court's understandable desire to avoid being taken into a highly controversial issue dividing the nation is a luxury it cannot forever indulge. While the Court does resist definitively ruling on the meaning of the Second Amendment, however, what is the role of the states and federal government? All officers of both state and federal government are obliged to take an oath to uphold the federal Constitution. It is an institutional disadvantage of the legislatures, state and federal, that adherence to that oath can lead to unpopular votes on bills, from time to time, with a resultant temptation to disregard the oath, or at least to say that it amounts to nothing more than an obligation to abide by the eventual, ultimate determination of a right by the branch with political insulation, the federal courts. How acceptable is that approach when the Court will not rule?

If Congress or the state legislatures were to undertake a serious consideration of their constitutional duty in this context, what guides should they take for the Second Amendment's meaning? Congress could take evidence on present-day needs for private ownership of firearms and on the present-day meaning of the word "militia." It could engage in a historical analysis, with an ability, much broader than that enjoyed by the courts, to summon experts and take live testimony on the question.

The role of the executive, in choosing to prosecute, is demonstrated in this context as well. The dismissal of a prosecution commenced by a previous administration was on appeal at the time the executive changed in 2001. Should the new executive have pursued that case for the purpose of creating a circuit split, possibly forcing the U.S. Supreme Court to take the case? Or is the inherent advantage of the executive branch also an obligation: that it choose whom to prosecute on the fundamental fairness of the facts of that case and not for some broader jurisprudential reasons? In *INS v. Chadha*, to be discussed below, the attorney general essentially created a case to challenge the constitutionality of the legislative veto. Is that an appropriate illustration of executive branch inherent advantage or a cruel jeopardizing of an individual's security in this country to win a point of institutional importance for the executive branch?

The inherent advantages of the states are also of importance in this topic. In that states are given the right to train militias and appoint their officers, and to "well regulate" those militias, the federal government should defer to the states' determination of whether and how their citizenry should be armed should service in the militia be required.[10] If a state explicitly chooses to have its militia drawn from among its citizens upon need, rather than create a National Guard, the state's choice should be honored, if there is any meaning at all to the Second Amendment. This might lead to a state preferring its citizens to possess their own weapons. Alternatively, another state may "well regulate" its militia by forming a National Guard and taking guns away from all others, unless the Second Amendment is read to grant an individual constitutional right. The trade-off thus entailed between safety from crime and accident and security against threat to person or state is one that the state governments can each develop more effectively than if there were one federal rule.

Methods of Solving Separation of Powers Issues

One approach to easing institutional friction between the executive and legislative branches is the legislative veto. Though held to be unconstitutional, it offered significant opportunity for both executive and legislative branches to utilize their inherent advantages.[11] Congress would set broad policy and allow the executive to tailor that policy to individual circumstances. Any particular instance could be called back by the same body capable of having prevented the grant of authority going to the executive in the first place. No one disputes that Congress can, constitutionally, pass statutes that deal with minutiae; it's just more efficient if Congress doesn't have to do so. The alternative of simply surrendering an entire area to executive discretion exists in theory, but what has happened since the demise of the legislative veto is an informal system of congressional oversight much less visible to the public and much less inclusive of all the members of Congress.

Another way to approach the fitting of general laws to difficult circumstances is to encourage in the courts a broader use of their powers of equity. This possibility also was cut back by Supreme Court opinion; and, I believe, the opportunity to benefit from an inherent judicial advantage was thereby lost. A fundamental reason we have judges with broad discretion, rather than ministerial magistrates applying legislatively set rules unwaveringly, is because we recognize broad rules don't always fit specific circumstances. One large but well-defined category for the exercise of this kind of discretion is the case where a new statutory regime impacts projects undertaken before the statute's effective date. Congress could establish an absolute rule of no retrospective application or an absolute rule of retrospective application; but an absolute rule loses the advantage of individual accommodation. I suggest the Court erred in denying this role to federal courts in the snail darter case; however, the Court's abnegation of this authority for itself led to a new statute creating an interagency, and intergovernmental, process for resolving such special cases.

Litigation by Legislators

Legislators will sometimes take matters of disagreement with the executive branch to the courts for resolution. I explore those cases and advocate that a broader willingness to entertain such challenges be adopted by the courts. At the very least, a case that otherwise fits the "case or controversy" requirement, is not moot, is ripe, and is not a political question should not be barred from adjudication simply because the plaintiff is a legislator. There should be greater, not lesser, use of the courts to resolve legitimate areas of disagreement between the two political branches, where the disagreements are not of a policy nature (should we go to war) but of a constitutional rights nature (what action by Congress is required before we go to war). The role of the Court to resolve such disputes is consistent with the Court's institutional advantages and is infinitely better than the alternative: stored-up resentment between the political branches or the escalation of disagreements that could have been resolved with no loss of face into "must-win" battles for supremacy going far beyond the constitutional issue of allocating power.

NOTES

1. *People v. Johnson*, 755 S.W.2d 92 (Tex. Crim. App., 1988).

2. *Bivens v. Six Unknown Named Agents of Federal Bureau of Narcotics*, 403 U.S. 388 (1971).

3. *Dickerson v. United States*, 530 U.S. 428 (2000).

4. However, it is fairer to see what the Court did in *Dickerson* as reaffirming a constitutional holding, that some prior warnings were needed to make custodial confessions admissible. Congress tried to say no warnings at all were needed. The post-*Miranda* Supreme Court decisions cited by Justice Scalia should be construed as saying *Miranda* warnings, per se, were not needed, but some warnings were.

5. *University of California Regents v. Bakke*, 438 U.S. 265 (1978); *Grutter v. Bollinger*, 2003 U.S. Lexis 4800; *Gratz v. Bollinger*, 2003 U.S. Lexis 4801.

6. J. Ely, "The Wages of Crying Wolf: A Comment on *Roe v. Wade*," 82 *Yale L.J.* 920 (1973).

7. *Planned Parenthood v. Casey*, 505 U.S. 833 (1992).

8. In free speech cases, for instance, a neutral regulatory regime that nevertheless impinges on expressive conduct can be upheld. See, e.g., *United States v. O'Brien*, 391 U.S. 367 (1968).

9. I believe most, not all, of the *Roe* Court's critics were not so much unhappy that the Court chose to take abortion to the constitutional level as they were that the Court failed to uphold the personhood of the unborn child or fetus.

10. U.S. Const., art. I, § 8.

11. *INS v. Chadha*, 462 U.S. 919 (1983).

PART ONE

Structural Features of the Separation of Powers

CHAPTER 2

Synopsis of the Advantages of the Separate Branches of Government

The Judicial Branch

The judicial branch can draw upon its experience with trials to develop rules of evidence and presumptions that yield orderly resolution of disputes. One of the most powerful of these rules is the burden of proof. Although it was developed by courts ostensibly to facilitate the most efficient methods of proof (principally by the rule that the party in the position most able to prove a salient point should have the burden of doing so), control of this rule can often determine the outcome in a case. In Chapter 11, I discuss one of the most powerful recent uses of the burden of proof, one that effectively closed off an entire class of civil rights cases. So powerful was this result that Congress took the unusual step of passing a new law in 1992, in response to the Supreme Court's decision, in order to reallocate the burden of proof in these cases.

Where an issue turns on a conflict of private claims, the judicial branch incorporates the best safeguards that each side will be fairly and fully heard. No legislative hearing can ever guarantee the procedural fairness of a court trial.

The judicial branch can accommodate a general rule to specific situations, so as to accomplish a result in any given case that accords with justice. The Supreme Court has both embraced and rejected this opportunity in different cases discussed in Chapter 14, focusing around the case of a fish (the snail darter) and a TVA dam. The judicial branch can propose statutory interpretations when the legislative branch has been ambiguous. Through "dialogue" with the legislative branch, necessary corrections of misinterpretations can be made and acceptable interpretations of ambiguous phrases that the legislature would not cure on its own can be adopted. This process is illustrated in the series of Court decisions and congressional reactions surrounding the right to sue for damages in two statutes passed a hundred years apart, discussed in Chapter 12. The two branches engaged in a conversation, a process, I contend, in which Congress has the institutional advantage by reason of its superior ability to craft language for multiple contingencies.

If it is accepted that a court will adapt a general statute to do justice in individual cases, however, the legislature might choose not to resolve difficult questions, simply relying on a court to make the difficult policy calls in the context of specific cases. This practice is discussed in Chapter 4. An instance in which Congress intentionally left a statute vague is drawn from the issue of retroactivity of the 1992 Civil Rights statute. This particular instance allowed a legislative compromise to be achieved, since both sides were able to point to the ambiguous language as a victory, although knowing full well that only one side could prevail when the matter eventually came before a court. I contend, nevertheless, that this is not good public policy, as the elected representatives should have been forced to decide the question.

The judicial branch has the strongest inherent advantage of discerning and describing constitutional rights of individuals. The political branches are under a great deal of pressure to disregard such rights, at least in many cases; key to the federal judicial branch's advantage here is the federal system of life tenure and no diminution of pay. Chapter 10 on *Roe v. Wade* deals directly with this process; so also does Chapter 7 on the exclusionary rule. In each area, the Supreme Court has been accused of "creating" new rights. However valid that criticism, there is no doubt that the Court has the duty of "discerning" constitutional rights. One way to assess whether the Court has gone too far, from discerning to creating constitutional rights, is to explore how an error by the Court can be corrected by the other branches or by the people directly in a constitutional amendment. This option is explicitly analyzed in Chapter 10, dealing with the constitutional right to privacy in the context of abortion.

The disadvantages of the judicial branch include the potential of overreliance on stare decisis, denying a just outcome to the parties in any particular case in service of the Court's institutional need to appear consistent. This problem is analyzed in Chapter 5. I provide some historical research, however, to suggest that very seldom has the Court actually practiced what it claimed—that is, ruling contrary to the expressed preference of the majority justices simply to stay consistent with an earlier interpretation. So, in practice, this disadvantage may not loom very large.

The judicial branch must rule by categories, in announcing a general principle that produces the result in a particular case. We will see in these materials many examples where the general principle then develops a life of its own, with unforeseen consequences. No clearer example can be presented than the circumstances surrounding the Fiesta Bowl in January 1991, discussed in Chapter 9. In completely unforeseen ways, doctrines announced by the Court in earlier cases and statutory responses from Congress converged to produce a result virtually no one had anticipated or actually desired.

In the constitutional area, one alternative to developing a general rule judicially is to make the change through a constitutional amendment, which can be as narrow as the immediate problem at hand, with no broader ramifications at all, if properly drafted. In Chapter 6, dealing with flag burning, I advance the position that a constitutional amendment specifically directed to this practice would run a lower risk of undermining First Amendment values than what Congress attempted, in literally creating a test case for the Supreme Court to reconsider a politically unpopular holding.

The judicial branch is hampered by the need to have a case arise, which is increasingly more of an obstacle as private rights of action are cut back (often by the Court itself). Hence, as a reliable engine for resolving a pending social issue, the Court is inferior to the legislative branch.

Contrariwise, the judicial branch is under no obligation to act. Hence, important social issues that require definitive, authoritative resolution, even of a constitutional issue, can linger for years. This problem is explored in Chapter 13, addressing the Second Amendment. Whether one is in favor of these rights or opposed to an expanded view of an individual's rights under the Second Amendment, it is my conclusion that the Supreme Court has been derelict in refusing to give modern interpretation to words almost two and a quarter centuries old—while not hesitating to do so in the context of the other provisions of the Bill of Rights. The failure of the Court to provide a ruling has kept both sides from attempting the one means of resolution that would be most appropriate to situations such as this: the drafting of a modern phrasing of either side's view of the issue in the form of a constitutional amendment.

The judicial branch is limited in what it can do to reconstruct legislative language when presented with partially invalid statutes or statutes that conflict. The result can be rules that would never have been adopted by the legislative branch on its own but which remain the law because of the lack of a majority in the legislative branch to affirm or to change them. This pattern is demonstrated in Chapters 11 and 12. The 1964 Civil Rights Act was a compromise on many dimensions; in subsequent cases, the Court broke some of those compromises, reaching a result that could not have been achieved at the time the law was passed. For many years, victims of race and victims of gender discrimination had different remedies as a result of this process, even though there was no evidence Congress intended such a result. The Fiesta Bowl instance in Chapter 9 also illustrates this process—laws intended to end discrimination by recipients of federal aid ended up being used to stop private philanthropy.

Lastly, the judicial branch is at a disadvantage in trying to ascertain facts not of the kind presented as evidence in trials. From time to time, the Court will cite publications of a social science nature; however, it has no means to order the production of studies or professional analysis of the studies of which it seeks to take judicial notice. This disadvantage becomes more apparent as the judicial branch bases its holdings on evidence beyond what the traditional adversary process develops. Chapter 7 most fully discusses this phenomenon. The context is the exclusionary rule. The Court expounds at length, over many years, on the likely deterrent effect of various rules of admissibility on police misconduct, on witnesses' willingness to perjure, and on the propensity of guilty defendants going free—each proposition the appropriate subject for social science research but wholly inappropriate to the means of proof available in the context of a specific criminal trial. Elements of this misanalysis occur as well in the affirmative action cases discussed in Chapter 8, where the Court finds the value of achieving racial diversity in law school classrooms compelling but dismisses it in (so far) every other context of governmental action.

The Legislative Branch

The legislative branch can order any kind of study it needs. While its hearing processes don't guarantee the rights of cross-examination and equal opportunity to rebut found in the judicial branch, a kind of rough equality exists from the composition of the legislature and its committees. The hearings before the Judiciary Committee on the flag-burning amendment, discussed in Chapter 6, show this process at work.

The legislative branch is the master of words. It can write the laws. It can amend them to deal with subsequent developments not originally foreseen. It has no need to be consistent over time or between laws; this, of course, is both an advantage and a disadvantage. We see this advantage to full effect in the 1992 Civil Rights Act discussed in Chapter 11. Only Congress could pull together different strands of civil rights jurisprudence extending for more than a century and produce a coherent rule going forward.

The legislative branch is the best branch at balancing interests. The intangible is its forte. How much money will be taken from crime deterrence to increase teachers' salaries is a question of everyday reality for legislators, for which the judicial branch is entirely unequipped and the executive branch substantially less equipped. Chapters 11 and 12 provide examples of this outcome. New rules to allow plaintiffs an easier chance of prevailing in civil rights actions were adopted by Congress, but with a sliding scale of damages depending on the size of the corporate defendant so as to take into account the competing interest of preserving employment. No court could have reached such a result. (One illustration of a court attempting it, nevertheless, is provided in Chapter 8 on affirmative action. Justice O'Connor ruled that affirmative action was permissible—but only for twenty-five years.)

The legislative branch can express the will of the people. Sometimes, a simple expression of belief is all that is required. The legislature errs when, to make a hortatory point, it enacts positive law. This conclusion stands out in the flag-burning discussion in Chapter 6. Criminal statutes were used to make patriotic statements, with an effect damaging to civil liberty.

The legislative branch can opine on how conflicts between constitutional rights should be resolved. It is not final in this enterprise, of course, but it can express its view, and the Court should pay it some respect. For instance, if a state legislature chooses to champion free exercise of religion over vindicating the ban on establishment of religion, in the area where more than one outcome would be constitutionally permissible, the legislature can and should be heard. The Supreme Court, however, has cut back on the ability of Congress to use the Civil War–era constitutional amendments to effect such a result, a restriction I believe is unwarranted. This issue is presented in Chapter 10, dealing with legislative approaches to abortion, and Chapter 8, dealing with the desire to advantage members of one race through government action.

The legislative branch can communicate with the judicial branch by compelling a case to be heard, assuming "case or controversy" requirements are met. The flag-burning statute discussed in Chapter 6 contained just such a provision.

The legislative branch has the final word about the meaning of statutes, provided no constitutional issue is involved. If the Supreme Court misinterprets a statute, Congress can correct it. The process is illustrated in detail in Chapters 9, 11, and 12, all dealing with civil rights.

The major disadvantage of the legislative branch is that, despite the oath requirement of the U.S. Constitution, analyzed in Chapter 3, legislators have strong incentives to ignore constitutional requirements that are not popular. The rush to pass a statute prohibiting flag burning illustrates this tendency; it is discussed in Chapter 6.

The legislature's ability to shift quickly can lead to inconsistency and uncertainty, a complaint often voiced in the tax area. However, the legislative branch can take that factor into account when it is deciding to make a change in the law; nothing compels it to make frequent changes.

The legislature tends to be nondeliberative. Problems of a complex nature are subjected to a process that lasts no more than two years. The founders' attempt at balancing this nature of the House by an appointed Senate of staggered six-year terms was substantially impeded by the direct election of senators. All the efforts at drafting an anti-flag-burning statute betrayed this weakness; none became permanent law.

The legislature cannot do justice in a particular case. The constitutional prohibition against ex post facto laws prevents this in the criminal sphere; in the civil area, the prohibition against takings without just compensation, or without due process of law, requires legislation by broad category. Some alleviation from this disability is provided in private bills. Attempts to accomplish individual oversight of broader congressional action are discussed in Chapter 14, with specific reference to the legislative veto.

The legislative branch is under no duty of consistency. Some state legislatures have a process in place to prevent inadvertent contradictions;[1] the U.S. Congress does not. The judicial branch, by contrast, operates under a process that fairly well guarantees all relevant precedent will be brought to the Court's attention. The congressional system has no such safeguard. The conflicting statutory provisions regarding damage actions in civil rights cases discussed in Chapter 12 came about as a result of this weakness.

The Executive Branch

The greatest advantage inherent in the executive branch is its flexibility. It can respond to a problem by instructing an agency to deal with it. It can order a rule to be promulgated, subject to the Administrative Procedures Act, much faster than it takes for a typical law to pass and, through enforcement policy statements or individual advice to particular individuals, can give guidance as to how a law will be enforced.[2] The Fiesta Bowl circumstances under President Bush in 1991 showed the flexibility of the executive branch at its best in this regard.

The executive branch, through its prosecutorial discretion in the criminal context and its choice of whether to enforce statutory obligations otherwise, can ameliorate the potential injustice that might come from the application of a harsh rule to specific conduct. The continuing consequences of the Fiesta Bowl circumstances under President Clinton demonstrated this attribute.

The executive branch is the only branch capable of carrying on diplomacy. It is vested with this unique authority so as to give confidence to our international interlocutors that a deal struck is a deal kept. Whether this should exclude legislators from insisting on their role in participating in the decision to go to war is extensively discussed in Chapter 15.

It is a potential vice of the executive branch that, where there is no private right of action, it can actually nullify the intent of the legislative branch by failing to bring enforcement actions in a particular area. The executive can also effectively veto a law, during the life of its administration, by not spending money appropriated for the purpose of the law. Courts have ordered the expenditure of funds to vindicate judicial judgments of a constitutional nature; they have not, however, finally resolved to overcome an executive impoundment of appropriated funds. I list this as a disadvantage, despite the fact that the executive branch may view it advantageously, since, like a decision not to enforce a law, it represents the assertion of a nullification power beyond the power to veto a law and hence, in my view, impermissibly intrudes upon the legislative branch. How the legislative branch is stymied by this practice is discussed in Chapter 15, dealing with the court-imposed barriers to the standing of individual legislators to bring a lawsuit against the executive.

The executive's power to present the other branches with a fait accompli is another problem. By its nature, the executive takes action. The other two branches must react. In the absence of a legislative majority to act one way or the other, therefore, it is the executive whose will prevails. Regarding the judicial branch, the same result obtains where the Court has followed a rule of abstention such as the political question doctrine. Once again, these issues are treated in Chapter 15.

The executive branch has the least "sunshine" of all the branches. Administrative agencies must comply with the Administrative Procedures Act, and, where a public advisory committee has been constituted, an executive department or agency must abide by the provisions of the Federal Advisory Committee Act.[3] There are state analogues as well. However, none of these precautions overcomes the fact that the great majority of decisions made by the executive branch are made without public hearing or public participation. This is inherent in the fact that the executive is one person, whereas the other two branches require the participation of more than one person. Since one person can act with no meetings of any kind, it is an inherent disadvantage that there is no structural way to compel public input or sunshine into the decisions reached by that one person.

The executive branch has no dissenting opinions and no minority party. Hence, the natural ameliorating influence of an institutional role of dissent is missing. The advantage is speed and resolve; the disadvantage is frequency and gravity of error. However, these disadvantages can be overcome by a willingness and ability to change, with no need to seek anyone else's approval to do so. The first decision in the Fiesta Bowl context illustrates this disadvantage: it appears that a policy decision of the greatest domestic consequence was implemented by a midlevel member of the executive branch—to the soon embarrassment of, and quick reversal by, the head of the executive branch.

The States

This work is one on separation of powers, not federalism. Nevertheless, we encounter some advantages traditionally ascribed to leaving matters at the state level and some disadvantages. The advantages are experimentation and the ability to tailor local solutions to local conditions. The disadvantages flow from the areas of constitutional right and bringing our nation closer together. It is no advantage to "experiment" with rights that the U.S. Constitution guarantees to all; however, that conclusion points out the importance of ascertaining those rights correctly and not in an overly broad manner. Once a matter is judged by the U.S. Supreme Court to be of federal constitutional right, the ability of states to work out possibly therapeutic approaches to the issue becomes circumscribed. Similarly, differences between states in some subjects can seriously impede the economic and social integration of our nation. These aspects of state versus federal authority are presented in the context of trying to interpret the Second Amendment's reference to states regulating their militia in Chapter 13 and each state interpreting when life begins in Chapter 10.

The Constitutional Amendment

A manner of dealing both with policy and with constitutional principle is afforded by the amendment process itself. Frequently overlooked in separation of powers discussions, this process can offer advantages over the judicial branch in the constitutional principle area. Since a court must rule by category, a holding in a matter of constitutional principle will often have consequences beyond the precise controversy presented in the case; and because the resolution is explained in constitutional terms, those unforeseen consequences will be difficult for the Court to overturn without damaging its perceived consistency. In such a setting, a constitutional amendment can be written as narrowly as a statute but have the status of constitutional principle. The process of seeking a constitutional amendment can also be a beneficial outlet for political resentment against constitutional holdings by the judicial branch. I offer this approach as potentially beneficial in the context of flag burning in Chapter 6, gun control in Chapter 13, and abortion in Chapter 10.

NOTES

1. The California legislature, for example, has an Office of Legislative Counsel, whose function, among other tasks, is to analyze every bill introduced for conflict with existing law. By the time the bill comes to the floor of the first house of the legislature, suggested language to "chapter out" these inadvertent contradictions is provided by the Legislative Counsel. Indeed, such language is present in the original draft of the bill, unless the legislative "author" explicitly asks that it be removed. This service is remarkable for its quality and public

benefit. It is made more possible in the case of the California legislature than in the case of the U.S. Congress by reason of the fact that there is a maximum limit on the number of bills that any member of the California legislature can introduce in any term, whereas there is no such limit in Congress.

2. 5 U.S.C. § 553.

3. 5 U.S.C. app. 2, §§ 6, 8.

CHAPTER 3

Rules of the Legislative Process

The Procedural Rules of the House of Representatives

The workings of the House of Representatives permit skillful manipulation of the rules of the House to govern substantive outcomes. Let us start with an example: the 2002 Campaign Finance Reform Act. This illustration demonstrates how the rules worked to delay a substantive outcome and how those rules were eventually overcome.

Example from the Campaign Finance Debate

On July 12, 2001, the U.S. House of Representatives defeated a motion establishing the procedural rules for the debate that was expected to take place regarding campaign finance reform.[1] The McCain-Feingold campaign finance reform measure had two main parts: the abolition of the unconstrained contributions going to political parties ("soft money") and a restriction on use of the airwaves in the time just before an election by political advertisements financed outside the strict candidate campaign contribution limits. In order for the bill to pass the Senate, the bill's authors had accepted an amendment that increased the size of individual contributions that could be made to specific candidates. Standing alone, that amendment appeared to be directly contrary to the spirit of the bill to limit the influence of money in politics; but as part of a compromise that entirely eliminated soft money, the amendment could be defended, at least by a candidate as well known as the typical incumbent U.S. senator is.[2] Members of the House, by contrast, are not well known, even within their district. Voting in favor of increasing the contribution limits to individual campaigns could be characterized by a political opponent as a vote against campaign finance reform, and it would take effort to communicate effectively to constituents that this was not so. That effort would be hampered by the fact that such an amendment would also attract the votes of those members of the House who were opposed to limits on campaign finance and, while intending to vote against the bill in chief, would be inclined to vote in favor of an amendment that made a bad bill, in their eyes, somewhat better. An effective campaign tool could be to link the "yes" vote of that amendment with the picture of a known opponent of campaign finance reform who also voted "yes."

To protect members in favor of limiting campaign finance from such a predicament, the House sponsors of McCain-Feingold proposed that all the changes necessary to make the House bill (called "Shays-Meehan" after its House sponsors) identical to the Senate bill be considered in a single en bloc amendment. It is normal to allow the authors of a bill being considered on the House floor to offer a series of "authors' amendments," en bloc, allowing the author to present his or her proposal as the author desires; but it is not universally so, particularly where a bill has been the subject of intricate debate and compromise in the committee. Shays-Meehan had not been considered by the relevant committee. Instead, the relevant committee, the House Administration Committee, had sent its own bill to the floor, allowing soft money to continue but imposing overall contribution limits on such money. The debate on the House floor was advertised as the showdown between McCain-Feingold and the campaign finance bill that the House leadership could accept. Procedurally, the Rules Committee of the House could have arranged for precisely that: by taking the McCain-Feingold bill directly to the House floor, as a Senate-originated bill that had passed the Senate.

Instead, the Rules Committee made the Shays-Meehan bill in order, along with the Administration Committee alternative. In the House, amendments to bills are most often limited, and this gives an advantage to those in control of the Rules Committee.[3] Composed of thirteen members, the party makeup of the Rules Committee is nine to four in favor of the majority party. It was thus under the Democrats, as well as under the Republicans, whatever the actual percentage of party members in the House itself. The Rules Committee permitted the Shays-

Meehan sponsors to make the amendments they needed but required that each amendment be voted on separately, rather than as part of a single en bloc amendment.[4] In that one requirement, the Rules Committee made it impossible, in the minds of the supporters of Shays-Meehan, to bring their bill into alignment with McCain-Feingold, because it meant that the increase in the limit on individual contributions would be voted on separately. It would stand out, alone, and any member voting for it would be subject to being tagged as in favor of expanding, not restricting, the role of money in the political system.

The Rules Committee could argue that they were doing no more than replicating what happened in the Senate. After all, the increase in the personal contribution limit had to be voted on separately there, apart from any other amendments. In reality, however, that kind of requirement was far more potentially controversial in the House, due to the relative obscurity of House members.

Rather than proceed under a rule with that consequence, the supporters of Shays-Meehan urged their colleagues to vote no on the rule, and it was defeated.[5] The House leadership was able to say that they had allowed consideration of campaign finance reform and that it was defeated by its own proponents, whose objections to the way of proceeding were related to their own political needs rather than the substance of the bill.[6] The supporters of Shays-Meehan could have gone ahead under the proposed rule, but if the bill passed the House without the Senate provision on lifting contribution limits, it would necessitate a conference committee before final passage. During the previous Congress, the Patients' Bill of Rights had died in a conference committee. Members of the conference committee are appointed by the leadership of each party, and there is no obligation that they finish their work before the end of the session. A conference committee, therefore, can be a "Bermuda Triangle"—bills fly in and are never heard of again. Individual members serving on a conference committee might be subject to discipline from their constituents for burying a popular bill; however, the leadership of both houses choose the members of conference committees, and, typically, they are chosen from among the most safe districts. For these reasons, a conference committee was seen as failure by supporters of Shays-Meehan.

Eventually, however, the supporters of Shays-Meehan were able to obtain 218 signatures on a discharge petition. A discharge petition brings a bill immediately to the floor of the House, bypassing all committees. Since the bill appears without a rule, the proceedings on debating such a bill are completely open: any amendment meeting the minimum test of germaneness can be brought up, which would surely have been disallowed by the Rules Committee. Since the House leadership might have issues it would rather not see brought to the House floor, and this is even more likely regarding amendments to a bill the leadership did not even wish to see on the House floor, the obtaining of 218 signatures on a discharge petition creates a threat of more than simply the necessity of facing the underlying bill. Accordingly, on those rare occasions when the necessary number of signatures has been reached, it has been traditional for the House leadership to bargain with a representative of those members of the same party as the leadership to define the rules for debate on the measure, without surrendering control of the House floor. In this rare instance, the dissident members of the majority have the upper hand in bargaining, and they can use that upper hand to craft the vote to be on a redraft of the bill that was the subject of the discharge petition (thus finessing the problem presented in Shays-Meehan of voting separately on amendments necessary to bring the bill into line with the Senate version). To make this work, the agreed-upon version, along with an agreement as to what limited amendments will be made in order, is then put into the form of a resolution from the Rules Committee, and that vote proceeds to the floor. If the rule passes (that is, if both sides keep their word), then the dissident members of the majority take their name off the discharge petition, cutting short that route to the House floor. That is what happened in the 2002 session, and Shays-Meehan passed the House in the form its authors intended. It was then approved, without amendment, in the Senate; a conference committee was bypassed, and the president signed the law.

This episode demonstrates a fundamental point about the congressional legislative process: that control of the rules often (but not always) is enough to control substantive outcomes. This tendency is abetted by the relative obscurity of House members, making it easier for an opponent to misconstrue a single vote in an election context, and by the apparent lack of interest on the part of the American electorate in anything procedural. An opponent can claim a vote on a rule actually determined the substantive outcome of an issue, but the incumbent can respond that it was purely a procedural vote. House members are vulnerable on any single substantive vote but not vulnerable on many, if any, procedural votes. The result, predictably, is the use of procedural votes by the House leadership to control outcomes.

What ultimately made campaign finance reform different was that the issue itself was not obscure; indeed, it became so much a subject of intense public scrutiny that enough members of the majority party joined the minority party in signing a discharge petition. It is unlikely that even that level of intense public attention would have been sufficient to generate those signatures had the rules not changed in 1993, making the signators to discharge petitions public. Prior to 1993, a member could (untruthfully) claim she or he had signed a discharge petition, and no one could disprove it. This tended to make the achievement of 218 signatures less likely.

Examples of Other Procedural Devices

Other practices in the House demonstrate the exceptional power of rules to control outcomes.

"King of the Hill"

Prior to 1995, a notorious practice was permitted in the House, by which various alternative budget resolutions were considered under a rule called "King of the Hill." The annual federal budget resolution must be approved before the individual appropriations subcommittees commence their work. The budget resolution provides the overall number in each category that binds the number of dollars each appropriations subcommittee is permitted to spend. The budget vote is a highly visible substantive vote.

The vote to apply the King of the Hill procedure, however, is quite abstruse. In adopting the procedure, the House would essentially guarantee the eventual outcome, while offering many political advantages to individual members. This is because the King of the Hill rule provided that the last of several budget alternatives to receive a majority vote would be the budget resolution, even if earlier alternatives had more votes. The rule then provided for the order in which budget alternatives were considered: invariably, the last two alternatives were the minority party's version, then the majority party's version. Earlier versions could include alternatives put forward by various caucuses within the House; for example, the Congressional Black Caucus often put forward its alternative, as did a group of budget-deficit hawks. Voting on those alternatives was essentially a free vote, since, even if they passed, they would not become law. Only the last alternative would. To the average voter, however, the claim that "I voted for the budget alternative to cut back spending far beyond what even my own party wanted" could be salient in a district of fiscally conservative voters; the claim of voting for the Black Caucus, or Women's Caucus, budget could be very helpful to an incumbent white male facing a black or a female opponent. Attractive as this mechanism was for many years, its notoriety eventually undermined the credibility of an incumbent relying upon it, and the King of the Hill rule was abolished after the Republicans became the majority party in the House in January 1995.

Substitute Amendments on Appropriations Bills

On appropriations bills, a motion to cut may be offered by any member of the House, but that motion may itself be amended, and the Speaker will give preference in recognition to a member of the Appropriations Committee. As a result, an effort to cut appropriations amounts can be effectively defeated by a substitute motion. Suppose a member of the House (not on the Appropriations Committee) offers an amendment to trim a particular appropriation by 10 percent. A member of the Appropriations Committee will, typically, then rise to offer a cut of 1, 2, or 5 percent as a substitute for the 10 percent cut. The way the second amendment reads, however, is simply that "in line 43 of page 256 of the bill, the number 100 shall be changed to 99." So, standing on its own, the amendment is a cut. Only in knowing the context would one realize that passage of such an amendment would prevent the other amendment from coming to a vote, the amendment that said, "In line 43 of page 256 of the bill, the number 100 shall be changed to 90." The natural inclination of many members of the House is to support a small percentage cut; some waste can be assumed in virtually any program. To vote the other way appears as though a member believes there is not even 1 percent (or 2 percent, etc.) waste in any given program. The curious point is that even the proponent of the 10 percent cut might be driven to vote for the 1 percent cut, lest he or she be open to the criticism next election that the incumbent would not even support a 1 percent cut. That kind of claim, of course, would not be believable were the incumbent's actual voting record, or history of making appropriations cuts, well known. For some members of Congress, such a record was well known; but for most, obscurity reigns, and the result is the smaller cut frequently prevails.

One possible route around this dilemma is to vote against the smaller cut but, if it passes, ask for a roll-call vote on the amendment as amended, on which the member could then vote aye. To obtain a roll-call vote, however, one must catch the eye of the Speaker or, more often, the person designated by the Speaker to preside. It is not uncommon for the Speaker or Speaker Pro Tempore to announce the result of the smaller-cut amendment and in the same breath, barely above the din on the House floor, to announce: "The vote now occurs on the amendment as amended, all those in favor say aye, those opposed say nay, the ayes appear to have it, the ayes have it, and the motion to reconsider is laid upon the table." That will leave those in favor of the greater cut with no recorded expression of their real sentiment. Indeed, their only recorded sentiment will be opposition to even a tiny cut.

The rules of the House do provide for a recorded vote when demanded by one-fifth of a quorum, which means forty-four members.[7] Should a particularly forceful member shout from the floor for a recorded vote with such volume that it would be embarrassing for the Speaker or Speaker Pro Tempore to ignore him or her, the forty-four-member rule will be easy to meet because there will be at least forty-four members still lingering on the floor after the vote just concluded (the one on the lesser percentage cut).[8] The Speaker or Speaker Pro Tempore, tipped to the likelihood of this occurring, will simply allow some time to elapse following the end of the recorded vote on the lesser cut and the motion by the member of the Appropriations Committee to approve the amendment as amended. Members will then have left the floor, and to obtain the necessary forty-four standing at the time of the request for a recorded vote, the member in favor of the greater cut will have to ask for a quorum call. That can be done. However, members do not take kindly to being summoned back from their offices, or their committees, to the House floor, simply to say "present." Members who call for a quorum risk that their irked colleagues will not stay on the floor, after voting "present" by their electronic voting card. As far as the record is concerned, the member was there since she or he voted "present." But when the member seeking the quorum call then asks for a recorded vote on the amendment as amended, she or he will find fewer than forty-four members standing (or even present). There is no record of who stays on the floor having voted "present" after a quorum call, and it is difficult to see how there could be. The recorded quorum call is the parliamentary manner of ascertaining who is present. Should it ever be relevant, a member could say she or he did, indeed, stand to request the recorded vote (whether she or he remained on the floor or not); but we are now at such a level of abstraction that no election can be expected to turn on this matter. To make an issue of it, an opponent would have to say something like, "You took part in an effort to prevent a deeper cut to an appropriation item by denying Congressman Jones a recorded vote on the amended version of his amendment, which amended version cut spending less than Congressman Jones intended, by your failing to stand when Congressman Jones asked for a recorded vote." The incumbent could easily reply, "The quorum vote proves I was there, and I did stand. (For all you know.) I vote to cut spending whenever I can. The 1 percent cut came up, so I voted yes. If the 10 percent cut had come up, I'd have voted for that, too."

In the face of such procedural advantages, the member offering the deeper cut runs the risk of going on record as opposed to a lesser cut and never being able, even in retrospect, to vote for any cut at all. By hypothesis, such a member would consider cutting spending important to her or his political persona; so it would be risky to oppose the substitute amendment.

Conclusion

In all these ways, the use of the rules can determine the substantive outcome desired by the party that controls the Rules Committee and that fills the Speaker's chair. The ability to make use of the rules in this manner is decided on the first day of a new session of the House, when the newly elected members vote for the Speaker and adopt the rules. Those are the two orders of business on the first day of a new session. The first day of the new session is the day of highest party solidarity. No substantive votes have yet been made to expose fissures within party groups. The set of rules includes committee assignments as well; and while not everyone can get her or his first choice, very few in the majority party are prepared to jeopardize their own committee assignments by voting down the rules. The minority party's set of rules most often mirror the majority party's, except with the former in control, so there is no improvement in the process by choosing that route and incurring the huge downside of political treason on the very first day. Further, even if one were to have an alternative set of rules ready to go, the Speaker's election comes first, and catching the Speaker's eye to offer such an alternative set of rules can be safely classified as having a probability of zero. Should the majority's rules be disapproved, it can be safely assumed the Speaker would immediately entertain a motion to adjourn for the day, rather than recognize the author of an iconoclastic set of rules. Game-set-match—until a Speaker is elected genuinely committed to altering a system under which he or she rose to prominence, a very unlikely possibility.

The Oath Requirement

The Senators and Representatives before mentioned, and the members of the several State Legislatures, and all executive and judicial Officers, both of the United States and of the several States, shall be bound by Oath or Affirmation, to support this Constitution.

U.S. Const., art. VI, cl. 3

Five Possible Meanings

Logically, one can propose at least five different interpretations of the oath requirement, with increasing levels of consequence for the individual obliged to take the oath.

Simplest is to interpret the oath requirement as a mere trapping of office; it is to be administered, then life goes on unchanged. It's just part of the celebration activities upon taking office and has no other purpose.

Second is to read the clause as requiring an affirmation of the sovereignty of the United States, with the attendant obligation, at least, not to rebel against that government.

Third is to require the person bound to observe the forms of the U.S. Constitution in carrying out the governmental functions to which that person is entitled by the office into which he or she is about to enter. Thus, it should constrain a U.S. senator from sending out an appointment of an ambassador.

Fourth, the oath requirement could be read to require that the taker of the oath not knowingly pass any law that the legislator believes to be unconstitutional. This interpretation takes the legislator as we find him or her; it does not impose a duty to inform oneself about how the Constitution might apply to any particular bill.

Lastly, one can read the oath requirement in its strongest possible terms, as requiring the taker to perform an independent analysis of the constitutionality of each bill on which he or she is called to vote.

The first interpretation is inconsistent with the fact that the requirement extends to state legislators, executives, and judges. The ceremonial function could have been limited to the federal Congress. There is no reason for a federal constitution to deal with ceremonies of the states.

The second interpretation leaves very little for the oath requirement to do, since there are laws against treason and provisions for impeachment, whether the offender has taken an oath or not.

Professor George Anastaplo appears to hold this second view, that the oath required little more than a promise not to deny the sovereignty of our government. "The oath required need include only the promise to support the Constitution. It is hardly likely that such an oath, required as it is of every National and State officer in the Country, presupposes that each such officer understands the Constitution, but rather only that he concedes it takes precedence over all other political arrangements and allegiances in the Country."[9] (It's ironic and a bit regrettable that Anastaplo sees no more to the duty incumbent upon taking an oath, in that in his own career, he sacrificed much for the principle of not having to take an oath.)

Such an oath requirement, for the sole purpose of clarifying to which country one owes allegiance, makes some sense for new citizens; and we do, indeed, require new citizens to take such an oath. But it seems totally unnecessary as a requirement for all judicial, executive, or legislative officers, federal or state, at least after the time of the American Revolution. (As of 1787, it might have been a minimum stopgap against Tories—or at least Tories who cared about giving their word falsely—sneaking into the new government or into the governments of the states.)

The third interpretation largely renders the clause empty, since the purpose of the Constitution is to prescribe forms of governmental action, and it adds nothing to that mandatory scheme to require an oath as well. Furthermore, the federal supremacy clause immediately precedes this oath clause of Article VI, and it explicitly binds the judges of state courts. Why go further than that to bind state legislators and executives, and all federal officers as well, since the final resolution of supremacy had already been dictated by the Constitution? The proximity of the supremacy clause to the oath clause suggests that the oath clause meant something other than simply that the forms of the U.S. Constitution were to be observed.

I have frequently heard a version of this third test, both in the House of Representatives and in the state senate of California. A legislator will frequently say that a particular matter "should be left for the courts to decide."[10] As long as Congress passes laws, the executive enforces them, and the judiciary applies them in specific disputes, the oath requirements of all three branches are met, according to this view.

There is a purpose, sometimes, in leaving a term of a statute ambiguous, where expectations differ about what the courts will eventually rule and when clarifying the term at the time of enactment will lose one or another critical part of a coalition. Familiarity with that reality has led legislators to apply the same thinking to a question of unconstitutionality as well, however; and that, I suggest, should be a totally different matter. A legislator is using a palliative: someone else (the Court) is looking after the constitutional issue, so I don't have to do so. But the legislator does have to do so—if the issue is whether the legislator is about to vote to violate the Constitution.

In the fourth and fifth interpretations, we move into an area imposing a more difficult burden upon members of Congress and state legislatures. Of the two interpretations, the fourth interpretation has the virtue of practicality, recognizing, as Anastaplo does, that it is a lot to require that legislators and executives make detailed study of the Constitution, as the fifth interpretation would.

Nor is the fourth interpretation devoid of effect, as the first three essentially are. If a legislator believes a bill to be unconstitutional, it would forbid him or her from voting yes. The easy out, "let's let the courts decide," would not be available. In Professor Donald Morgan's words, "Clearly the original oath [requirement] . . . was an effort to harness the force of conscience, even of religious conviction, to the maintenance of constitutional safeguards."[11]

An actual instance of such an attitude within my own experience dealt with an appropriations bill for the National Endowment for the Arts (NEA), to which an amendment was proposed to terminate grants to projects that denigrated a major religion. Upon pointing out the obvious First Amendment problem to the author, I was told by him, "We'll let the courts decide that."

The irony of this fourth view is that legislators better informed about the Constitution would be at a distinct political disadvantage. (Indeed, my "no" vote on the "major religions" NEA amendment was used against me by a conservative opponent in a subsequent campaign, even though I never voted for NEA funding itself.) A legislator who invests the time to consider the constitutionality of his or her act would be constrained, in a manner their colleagues are not, from doing what might be politically popular. There might even be an incentive to stay ignorant of a constitutional rule, to invest nothing in learning more of the

Constitution, salving one's conscience with the thought that the courts will, eventually, be the arbiters. No final harm will be done, the legislator may think, and the short-term political goal can be served.

Lastly, we can ask legislators to study the Constitution, at least to the same extent they study the subject matter of the legislation on which they are to vote. Expert witnesses are called upon to testify on the latter; they could also be called on as to the former. No one can fault a member of Congress for not being a physicist; nevertheless, all vote on appropriations that include different kinds of physics research based on their best study of what the nation's needs are. So it could also be regarding a question of unconstitutionality. Testimony of this kind was taken at the House Judiciary Committee hearings on the flag-burning law (discussed in Chapter 6); the tragedy is that academia did not speak with one clear voice.

Dean Paul Brest supports this fifth interpretation. "[L]egislators are obligated to determine, as best they can, the constitutionality of proposed legislation . . . [and] they should consider themselves bound by, or at least give great weight to, the Supreme Court's substantive constitutional holdings."[12] Allowing, indeed, requiring, deference to the Supreme Court's constitutional interpretations eases the practicality objection to this fifth interpretation of the legislator's oath. Independent research may not have to be very onerous, at least where there is a recent U.S. Supreme Court opinion on point. Brest derives this obligation directly from the oath clause. "[A]rticle VI requires that all legislators and officials 'be bound by Oath or Affirmation to support this Constitution.' . . . [T]he most obvious way for a legislator to support the constitution is to enact only legislation that is constitutional."[13]

Brest also bases his conclusion on the presumption of constitutionality accorded to acts of Congress by reviewing courts. "Finally, courts often accord a challenged law a 'presumption of constitutionality' based partly on the assumption that the legislature has previously passed upon the constitutional questions raised in litigation."[14]

I find this argument less persuasive. It is a good rule drawn from deference to a coequal branch, and efficient management of a system of checks and balances, for the Court not to strike down the work of Congress unless the statute in question admits of no other reasonable interpretation than the unconstitutional one. It is a fiction, however, to say that the Court follows this rule because it assumes Congress has, in fact, deliberated on the constitutionality of what it has done. It is a fiction because Congress seldom does so deliberate, at least in my nine years' experience.[15] When I would raise a constitutional issue with a colleague in Congress, the most common rejoinder was, "That's what we have courts for; our job is to make good policy and leave the fine legal points for the courts." I also believe it's a fiction that the Court actually accords any deference to whatever deliberations Congress has given to constitutionality. No brief that dealt with constitutional issues, for the year I served as a law clerk for Justice White, ever cited congressional debates as authority on constitutional issues. (Nevertheless, Justice White himself accorded a presumption of constitutionality to the fact that members of Congress, bound by oath to uphold the Constitution, had voted for particular legislation. This will be discussed below.)

The Intent of the Founders

The history of the constitutional convention does not offer much help in deciding which of the five possible interpretations is best. There is no recorded debate at all on the meaning of the oath requirement as to federal legislators. What debate did occur was entirely over the question of applying the oath requirement to state officials. The applicability to federal officers was added by delegate Gerry on July 23, 1787. The debate was reported as follows:

Resoln. 18. "requiring the Legis: Execut: & Judy. of the State to be bound by oath to support the articles of Union" taken into consideration. . . . Mr. Gerry moved to insert as an amendmt. that the oath of the Officers of the National Government also should extend to the support of the Natl. Govt. which was agreed to nem. con.

Mr. Wilson said he was never fond of oaths, considering them as a left handed security only. A good Govt. did not need them. and a bad one could not or ought not to be supported. He was afraid they might too much trammel the the [*sic*] Members of the Existing Govt in case future alterations should be necessary; and prove an obstacle to Resol: 17 just agd. to. [Resolution 17 provided for future amendments to the Constitution.] [Footnote omitted.]

Mr. Ghorum did not know that oaths would be of much use; but could see no inconsistency between them and the 17. Resol: or any regular amendt. of the Constitution. The oath could only require fidelity to the existing Constitution. A constitutional alteration of the Constitution, could never be regarded as a breach of the Constitution, or of any oath to support it.

Mr. Gerry thought with Mr. Ghorum there could be no shadow of inconsistency in the case. Nor could he see any other harm that could result from the Resolution. On the other side he thought one good effect would be produced by it. Hitherto the officer of < the two > [in original] Governments had considered them as distinct from, not as part of the-General System, & had in all cases of interference given a preference to the State Govts.

The proposed oaths will cure that error.—The Resoln. (18) was agreed to nem. con.[16]

A motion to strike the applicability of the oath requirement to state officials failed on a vote of four to seven.[17] The debate continued on why state officers should be obliged to take an oath to uphold the federal Constitution and whether such an obligation should be reciprocal, with federal officers swearing to uphold the constitutions of the several states.[18]

The *Federalist* offers scant insight into the purpose for the oath. Like the debates at the convention itself, the only references deal with the imposition of the obligation on state officials. Madison's view is simple and instrumentalist: the states were given explicit functions to perform on an ongoing basis under the U.S. Constitution; the oath would ensure they would be performed. (This would support the third interpretation of the clause: that the forms of government be observed.) In *Federalist* No. 44, Madison states,

It has been asked, why it was thought necessary, that the State magistracy should be bound to support the Federal Constitution, and unnecessary, that a like oath should be imposed on the officers of the United States in favor of the State Constitutions?

Several reasons might be assigned for the distinction. I content myself with one which is obvious and conclusive. The members of the Federal Government will have no agency in carrying the State Constitutions into effect. The members and officers of the State Governments, on the contrary, will have an essential agency in giving effect to the Federal Constitution. The election of the President and Senate, will depend in all cases, on the Legislatures of the several States. And the election of the House of Representatives, will equally depend on the same authority in the first instance; and will, probably, forever be conducted by the officers and according to the laws of the States.[19]

Hamilton also saw the grander federal purpose in the oath requirement, to make the systems of state government available to serve federal government objectives, when legitimate.

The plan reported by the Convention, by extending the authority of the federal head to the individual citizens of the several states, will enable the government to employ the ordinary magistracy of each in the execution of its laws. . . . It merits particular attention in this place, that the laws of the confederacy, as to the *enumerated* and *legitimate* objects of its jurisdiction, will become the SUPREME LAW of the land; to the observance of which, all officers legislative, executive and judicial in each State, will be bound by the sanctity of an oath. Thus the Legislatures, Courts and Magistrates of the respective members will be incorporated into the operations of the national government, *as far as its just and constitutional authority extends*; and will be rendered auxiliary to the enforcement of its laws. [Footnote omitted; emphasis in original.][20]

Consistent with this view, as the annotated Constitution observes, was the Judiciary Act of 1789, which gave diversity jurisdiction to state courts.[21]

Madison and Hamilton, therefore, each look at the oath requirement as a basis for federal supremacy. Neither deals with what effect on conduct by a federal legislator the oath requirement might have. As for a state official, Madison's and Hamilton's discussion is most consistent with the third interpretation, that proper forms be followed; their words cannot support any grander purpose.

Two pieces of collateral material reported by Farrand also suggest a less than profound purpose in the oath requirement.

An honourable member from Pennsylvania objected against that part of the sixth article which requires an oath to be taken by the persons there mentioned, in support of the constitution, observing (as he justly might from the conduct the convention was then pursuing) how little such oaths were regarded. I immediately joined in the objection, but declared my reason to be, that I thought it such a constitution as no friend of his country ought to bind himself to support.[22]

The part of the system which provides, that no religious test shall ever be required as a qualification to any office or public trust under the United States, was adopted by a great majority of the convention, and without much debate; however, there were some members so unfashionable as to think, that a belief of the existence of a Deity, and of a state of future rewards and punishments would be some security for the good conduct of our rules, and that, in a Christian country, it would be at least decent to hold out some distinction between the professors of Christianity and the downright infidelity of paganism.[23]

Court Opinions

There are few federal court decisions that help to resolve this question. The only reported cases at the Supreme Court level directly involving the oath clause are *Cummings v. Missouri*[24] and *Bond v. Floyd*.[25] The Court in *Cummings* struck down Missouri's immediate post–Civil War oath for state officers (and religious ministers) that they swear allegiance to the Constitution and swear that they had never taken up arms against it. The Court found this requirement, with its penalties, as an ex post facto law and a bill of attainder. The Court's inference is that Article VI, clause 3, does not give the state a right to impose such a requirement as incidental to the constitutional requirement that an oath be taken.

That inference became the holding a hundred years later in *Bond*, where the Court struck down the decision of Georgia's House of Representatives not to seat Julian Bond because, in their judgment, he could not honestly take the oath of allegiance to the U.S. Constitution in light of certain statements he had made about the Selective Service System and the war in Vietnam.

In neither opinion does the Court shed any light on the function of the oath requirement. This is not a surprise. It would be difficult to imagine how a court might enforce any interpretation it did find or how such an issue could be justiciably presented. Who would sue a state legislator for voting in favor of a statute he or she knew to be unconstitutional? For one obvious obstacle, the evidence would be lacking that this was, in fact, the legislator's subjective opinion; and even if there were evidence, we'd then reach questions of who would have standing and whether the issue was a political question.

One remaining source is to be found in *Marbury v. Madison*.[26] Professor Alan Dershowitz and former justice Arthur Goldberg made the following observation about *Marbury*:

Chief Justice Marshall gave as one of his premises for concluding that it was the office of the judiciary to declare what the law was, and, particularly, what laws were in contravention of the Constitution, that the judges were obliged to swear an oath to uphold the Constitution. Chief Justice Marshall's logic, as well as his own concluding words, extend the same obligation to all other officers sworn to uphold the Constitution.

"Why does a judge swear to discharge his duties agreeably to the constitution of the United States, if that constitution forms no rule for his government? if [*sic*] it is closed upon him, and cannot be inspected by him? If such be the real state of things, this is worse than solemn mockery. To prescribe, or to take this oath, becomes equally a crime. . . .

Thus the particular phraseology of the constitution of the United States confirms and strengthens the principle, supposed to be essential to all written constitutions, that a law repugnant to the constitution is void; and that courts, as well as other departments, are bound by that instrument. 5 U.S. (1 Cranch) 137 (1803)."[27]

Dershowitz and Goldberg develop this argument in the context of the death penalty. They contend that, when the courts have been silent, it is the duty of the executive and legislative branches to enforce the Constitution.[28] They refer to the U.S. Supreme Court's dicta in *Cooper v. Aaron*,[29] applying the oath clause as support for the obligation for state officials to be bound by the Supreme Court interpretations of the U.S. Constitution.

That, however, is the easy case. It follows directly from the supremacy clause. The obligation to rule when the courts have not ruled requires more. It cuts off from those who have taken an oath the possibility of leaving constitutional issues for eventual resolution by the courts, whenever "eventual" is. It requires the fourth or fifth interpretation of the oath clause.

Other U.S. Supreme Court justices have also referred to the oath requirement for members of Congress as binding them, at least, not to vote for bills they personally believe to be unconstitutional. In *Illinois v. Krull*,[30] the Court dealt with a statute that, on the basis of another recent ruling by the Court, was unconstitutional. The question was whether the defendant in the instant case should be given the benefit of the ruling. The basis of the ruling was to exclude evidence seized in violation of the Fourth Amendment; there was no doubt about the defendant's guilt. With the law now being defunct, there was no purpose in letting a guilty man go free. The instrumentalist purpose of an exclusionary rule, to create a disincentive for the violation of constitutional rights by police officers, was held not to apply to legislators. Justice Blackmun wrote for the majority,

> It is possible, perhaps, that there are some legislators who, for political purposes, are possessed with a zeal to enact a particular unconstitutionally restrictive statute, and who will not be deterred by the fact that a court might later declare the law unconstitutional. But we doubt whether a legislator possessed with such fervor, and with such disregard for his oath to support the Constitution, would be significantly deterred by the possibility that the exclusionary rule would preclude the introduction of evidence in a certain number of prosecutions.[31]

Accordingly, at least in dicta, the Court appeared to interpret the oath requirement as mandating a legislator not vote for a bill the legislator thought was unconstitutional.[32]

Justice White reached the same conclusion in his dissent in *INS v.*

Chadha,[33] which held unconstitutional the one-house veto device. "If the veto devices so flagrantly disregarded the requirements of Art. I as the Court today suggests, I find it incomprehensible that Congress, whose Members are bound by the oath to uphold the Constitution, would have placed these mechanisms in nearly 200 separate laws over a period of 50 years."[34]

Conclusion

One way of answering which interpretation of the oath requirement is correct is to ask what consequences would befall the legislator who violated the oath requirement, so understood. Violations of the first interpretation could be disciplined by their house of the legislature or Congress: members who did not take the oath would be barred from being seated. Violations of the second interpretation would be straightforward to prosecute as treason. Violations of the third interpretation could be set right by actions in federal court, to undo the effect of the presumed power. A concerned party could challenge the action of an ambassador the House purported to appoint or seek a court order against enforcement of a decree issued by a judge appointed by Congress.

Violations of the fourth or fifth interpretations, however, could not be addressed, in the very rare case they could be proven. The member of Congress himself or herself would have to give testimony that he or she voted or introduced a bill knowing it to be unconstitutional. Otherwise, proof of this necessary element of intent would be lacking. Virtually any bill realistically likely to be introduced or voted on would have some claim to constitutional plausibility. (A few I saw did stretch that gracious assumption, however: for example, an amendment offered in the Judiciary Committee to hold back pay from federal judges who were late in issuing opinions or the amendment on the floor of the House to cut off NEA funding for projects that "denigrated a major religion.")

Getting around the problem of proof, what would the remedy be? The only response I can contemplate would be that, possibly, the House or Senate could censure or even remove the member. It is a most unrealistic option. It would be inconceivable to punish a member whose view had been shared by the majority simply because of misgivings about his or her vote uttered by that member.

There is also the issue of comparative advantage. The courts possess the clear comparative advantage in interpreting and upholding those parts of the Constitution that are not popular.[35] It may be too much to expect officers in the political branches to resist the popular will. It would risk their jobs. By contrast, the federal judiciary is the most anti-democratic creation in the entire Constitution precisely in order to resist such pressure. If we were to assign tasks based on comparative advantage, which is the theme of this work, it would belong to the courts, not Congress, to apply the Constitution.

However, it is not too much to ask that they both do, and the president as well. (Practice for many years, however, has allowed the president to sign legislation while claiming to believe part of it to be unconstitutional.)[36] Urging each of the three branches to apply its own screen of constitutionality has the advantage of maximally protecting the Constitution from invasion or erosion. Relying solely on the Court runs the risk that the Court might let a constitutional violation "percolate" among the circuits, or in the states, for some years by denying certiorari. During those years of percolation, constitutional rights would have been violated with no redress. The Supreme Court waited thirteen years after striking down "separate but equal" to strike down anti-miscegenation laws, and it wasn't for lack of a case to consider.[37] It is, admittedly, quite unlikely that the legislators of the various states would have acted sooner to repeal their antimiscegenation laws, but is it wise to absolve them of any obligation to try? Also, it is possible that the Court will interpret the Constitution incorrectly. *Beauharnais v. Illinois*,[38] a vestige of the Communist Scare era in America, has still not been overturned; although, in light of *Cohen v. California*,[39] and other cases, it is highly unlikely that a state could put someone in jail today for distributing literature that criticizes a class of persons as a group. Is it so unlikely that Congress or the president might see a constitutional issue sooner than the court that we dispense with any effort to require them at least to look?

It is upon these considerations, rather than a compelling record of the history of the constitutional convention and surrounding materials, that a case for the strong interpretations of the oath requirement must be based. Recognizing the comparative advantage of the Court in the function of upholding constitutional principles, the fourth and fifth readings of the oath requirement nevertheless have superior advantage in creating incentives for all three branches to do so. This is true even if the only enforcement mechanism is the conscience of the person taking the oath.[40] If there is no outside enforcement possible, that should argue for the solemnity of the oath requirement, not its trivialization. The requirement should remain strong even among those with no faith in God. It is an appeal to a virtue we call integrity, found among believers and nonbelievers and not found, also, among believers and nonbelievers.

NOTES

1. 147 *Cong. Rec.* H3967-02, H3971 (2001) (vote on the resolution to provide a rule for the consideration of campaign finance legislation).

2. The higher visibility of a U.S. senator makes it more difficult for an opponent to convince the voters of a characteristic contrary to the senator's general persona. A representative, by contrast, is much more a clean slate, on which a well-financed opponent can write a compelling story based on only those votes the opponent chooses to emphasize.

3. The exception concerns appropriations bills. By tradition, any member of the House may amend any line of an appropriation bill containing a number, so as to increase or decrease an appropriation. Anything more than that, however, constitutes legislating on an appropriation bill, and it is not permitted without an explicit waiver. Such waivers are granted by the Rules Committee and then approved by the whole House when it adopts the rule for the consideration of the bill.

4. 144 *Cong. Rec.* H6790-02 (2001).

5. D. Rosenbaum, "Reporter's Notebook; For McCain and the House, a Day of Twists and Turmoil," *New York Times*, July 13, 2001 (describing Senator McCain's efforts to defeat the rule in the House).

6. H. Dewar and J. Eilperin, "Campaign Reform Bill Stalls; House GOP Leaders Shelve Measure after Losing Procedural Vote," *Washington Post*, July 13, 2001.

7. Thomas Jefferson, "A Manual of Parliamentary Practice: for Use by the Senate of the United States, Rule XX" (1812) (available at http://www.constitution.org/tj/tjmpp.htm).

8. If, however, the proponent of the lesser cut had not demanded a recorded vote on the substitute, then there would probably be very few members on the floor. The objecting member's recourse is then to note the absence of a quorum and demand a quorum call, which is discussed in the text.

9. G. Anastaplo, *The Constitution of 1787: A Commentary* 204 (1989).

10. Judge Abner Mikva, who served many terms as a member of the House, reports the same phenomenon. "Both houses contain members who cheerfully put off on the courts most if not all of the responsibility for squaring the statute with the Constitution." A. Mikva, "Leave It to the Courts," 38 *U. Chi. L. Rev.* 449, 497 (1971).

11. D. Morgan, *Congress and the Constitution* 48 (1966).

12. P. Brest, "The Conscientious Legislator's Guide to Constitutional Interpretation," 27 *Stan. L. Rev.* 585, 587 (1975).

13. Id.

14. Id. at 588.

15. Two notable exceptions were the debate over versions of campaign finance laws and the statute to ban flag burning.

16. 2 *The Records of the Federal Convention of 1787* 87–88 (M. Farrand, ed.) (1923).

17 1 Farrand, *The Records of the Federal Convention*, at 194.

18 2 Farrand, *The Records of the Federal Convention*, at 87.

19. *Federalist* No. 44 (Madison).

20. *Federalist* No. 27 (Hamilton).

21. The Constitution of the United States of America: Analysis and Interpretation, S. Doc. No. 99-16 at 939–42 (1987).

22. "Luther Martin's Reply to the Landholder" from Maryland Journal, March 21, 1788, in 3 Farrand, *The Records of the Federal Convention*, 286, 293.

23. "The Genuine Information, delivered to the Legislature of the State of Maryland, relative to the Proceedings of the General Convention, held at Philadelphia, in 1787, by Luther Martin, Esquire, Attorney-General of Maryland, and one of the Delegates in the said Convention" (delivered to the Maryland legislature, November 29, 1787), in 3 Farrand, *The Records of the Federal Convention*, 172, 227.

24. 71 U.S. (4 Wall.) 277 (1867).

25. 385 U.S. 116 (1966).

26. 5 U.S. (1 Cranch) 137 (1803).

27. A. Dershowitz and A. Goldberg, "Declaring the Death Penalty Unconstitutional," 83 *Harv. L. Rev.* 1773, 1807 (1970).

28. Dershowitz and Goldberg, "Declaring the Death Penalty Unconstitutional," 1806–18.

29. 358 U.S. 1, 18–19 (1958).

30. 480 U.S. 340 (1987).

31. Id. at 352, n. 8.

32. Ironically, the one justice on the Court who had been a legislator, Justice O'Connor, dissented. She thought it quite realistic that legislators might knowingly pass unconstitutional statutes, due to political pressure. However, if they did so, she explicitly stated, they would be breaching their oath. "Legislators by virtue of their political role are more often subjected to the political pressures that may threaten Fourth Amendment values than are judicial officers." 480 U.S. 340, 365–66 (O'Connor, J., dissenting). "While I heartily agree with the Court that legislators ordinarily do take seriously their oaths to uphold the Constitution and that it is proper to presume that legislative acts are constitutional . . . it cannot be said that there is no reason to fear that a particular legislature might yield to the temptation offered by the Court's good-faith exception." Id. at 366.

33. 462 U.S. 919, 967 (1983).

34. Id. at 976–77.

35. For this reason, Brest adopted his second obligation: that members of

Congress at least grant deference to Court interpretations of constitutionality, respecting "the judiciary" as the Constitution's "most skilled, disinterested, and articulate interpreter." Brest, "The Conscientious Legislator's Guide," 588.

36. In *INS v. Chadha*, 462 U.S. 919, 976, n. 13 (1983), the Court struck down the legislative veto, noting that eleven presidents, starting with Woodrow Wilson, had gone on record, often at bill-signing ceremonies, that the legislative-veto provision of a particular law they were signing was unconstitutional. Recently, President George W. Bush signed the McCain-Feingold Campaign Finance Reform bill while stating his "grave reservations" about its constitutionality. For the president, the question raised in this chapter is long settled. No one expects the president to veto a bill, otherwise desirable on policy grounds, simply because it is unconstitutional. For the president, at least, "leave it to the Courts" has become the settled rule. One notable exception was President Jackson's constitutionally based opposition to the Bank of the United States, but that was also in the context of his clear policy antipathy to creating such a bank.

37. See *Brown v. Board of Education*, 347 U.S. 483 (1954), and *Loving v. Virginia*, 388 U.S. 1 (1967).

38. 343 U.S. 520 (1952).

39. 403 U.S. 15 (1971).

40. As to whether it is the fourth or the fifth interpretation of the oath requirement that should be followed, either would constitute such a profound revitalization of this salubrious doctrine that I'd be happy even if the weaker, fourth version were adopted. It also has the marginal benefit of superior workability, especially where there is no clear U.S. Supreme Court opinion controlling. Even where there is, however, I would not oblige the legislator to follow it. The purpose is to create an independent check on unconstitutional action. I fear that, in those cases where the Supreme Court has erroneously ruled in favor of governmental authority and against individual rights, reference to the Supreme Court opinion would be too easy a means for the member of Congress to avoid taking the hard look required. This view puts me slightly at odds with Dean Brest, though we both favor a more vigorous interpretation of what the oath requirement demands of a legislator.

CHAPTER 4

Statutory Construction: The Courts Review the Work of the Legislature

LEGISLATIVE history has two different purposes in the interplay between the federal branches. First, it can demonstrate the intent of some legislators, when that becomes relevant. Some contexts where legislative intent is relevant include where the legislature can be shown to discriminate racially,[1] to be intending a religious rather than a secular goal,[2] to reveal religious bigotry,[3] to punish speech rather than action,[4] or to interfere impermissibly with the independence of the judiciary.[5] Dean John Hart Ely bases a considerable body of scholarly writing on an analysis of whether a legislature is intending to discriminate against a group incapable of defending itself within the legislative process.[6] And Dean Paul Brest has pointed out the importance of a legislator's consideration of his or her own motive in voting for legislation.[7]

There is an extensive political science literature dealing with the use of legislative history for the purpose of elucidating ambiguous phrases in a statute.[8] The claim of this literature, to use one example, is to provide rules for giving deference to the views of "the political actors who were pivotal in that their preferences had to be taken into account in order for a legislative agreement to be made" and for "identifying the actions and statements by a legislator and the president that convey meaningful signals about actual preferences."[9]

It is not my intent to attempt to add to the political science discussion here. My focus, instead, is on trying to draw meaning from the *actions* of the houses of Congress, not the *words* of any particular member or committee report. I offer this choice in order to provide something new but also, I admit, out of a strong disinclination to give any credence to what is said about a bill,[10] versus what was done in the bill's own words, in attempting to discern the meaning of the product of a collective body.[11] Discerning the intent of the "pivotal political actors" does not tell us anything about the intent of the 218th House member to vote yes on a measure; and I will not concede that the intent of the one is more constitutionally relevant than the intent of the other.

Far different from statements of individual legislators is the action of one of the two houses in considering and defeating an amendment. Courts have taken much meaning from that kind of episode to interpret congressional intent.[12] However, since the action of only one house is being cited, how, then, can this be taken as evidence of the will of Congress as a whole? The only logical reply, and it is sufficient, in my view, is that the *rejection* of an amendment is valid as an expression of negative will; that, at least, the substance of the amendment that was defeated should not be inferred positively into the bill that was passed.[13] Suppose an ambiguous phrase becomes law. Suppose, further, that one possible interpretation of that ambiguity is not accepted by the House or the Senate. Whatever else the phrase may mean, we can say the phrase does not have the meaning of the proposed interpretation that was rejected by a body whose consent was needed to make it law.[14] And that is all we can say, from the action of a single house.[15] It is a negative inference only. Two houses are necessary to determine what the law does say; but either of them[16] can go on record as to what an ambiguous phrase does *not* mean.[17]

The Court's application of this rule has a feedback effect on the legislative process. In *Runyon v. McCrary*, Justice Stewart, for a majority of the Court, reasoned on the basis of an amendment that had been rejected on the Senate floor. In a bit of overstatement, Justice Stewart contended, "There could hardly be a clearer indication of congressional agreement."[18] Aware of this, a knowledgeable member of Congress, contemplating an amendment to clarify an ambiguous phrase, might now hold off, lest Justice Stewart's line of thinking be applied to a losing vote. It is legitimate for a Court to take an inference from a defeated amendment.

Far different, however, is the case of taking meaning from no action. When a statute has been interpreted by the Court and Congress takes no corrective action, the Court has said that it takes guidance from the "acquiescence" of Congress to the interpretation of the statute.[19] This is erroneous reasoning. Properly speaking, the bill in question has already been passed.[20] The intent of the legislature passing it cannot logically be inferred from the inaction of subsequent legislatures. And subsequent legislatures did not act. From what source, therefore, can the inference arise?

Justice Scalia has called for the abolition of the "acquiescence" doctrine. "This assumption, which frequently haunts our opinions, should be put to rest."[21] He notes "it is impossible to assert with any degree of assurance that congressional failure to act represents (1) approval of the status quo, as opposed to (2) inability to agree upon how to alter the status quo, (3) unawareness of the status quo, (4) indifference to the status quo, or even (5) political cowardice."[22]

Professor Daniel Farber notes, and attempts to rebut, Justice Scalia's criticism of the acquiescence doctrine.[23] Farber recognizes Justice Scalia's (and Judge Easterbrook's)[24] point that many things can account for congressional inaction other than acquiescence. However, Farber puts forward a Bayesian rebuttal; that, since only interpretations that are fallacious will be overruled by a subsequent Congress, the fact that no overruling has taken place makes it more likely that an interpretation is correct.[25]

I disagree. If there were some kind of systematic process, then one might, indeed, be able to infer something from the failure of Congress to act in such a system. But there is no such process. Decisions of the Court are not served up like balls drawn from an urn, for consideration yes or no by Congress. Without such a system to ensure that the decisions are routinely considered, a Bayesian inference is inappropriate.

Further, the subsequent Congresses, in failing to reverse a court interpretation, are not attempting to judge the intent of the Congress that passed the law but, rather, their own policy preferences. Hence, even if we accepted the Bayesian argument, all we can infer is that a court interpretation left unreversed is more likely to express the views of the present Congress than one that was reversed. The intent of the Congress that passed the legislation in question, however, is unaffected by Farber's Bayesian inference. He needs one other assumption: that the subsequent Congress's views are correlated with the views of the enacting Congress and the president who signed the legislation. On points of ambiguity, and controversy, that is not a probabilistically likely statement. When Congress does nothing, Justice Scalia has the better side of this argument: any inference of acquiescence is treacherous.[26]

A stronger case for inferring acquiescence by Congress to the Court's interpretation of a statute is made when Congress subsequently re-enacts the statute and does not change the words.[27] The legislative history is now of the subsequent statute, not the original one. This is action, not inference from nonaction. The committee staffs are quite well aware of judicial interpretation of phrases, and the assumption becomes much more tenable that the drafters of the subsequent legislation intended the result of the Court's interpretation. The only caution I would offer is that the reenactment, to have this inference, should be of the very phrase that was interpreted, and it should be following a Supreme Court, not a lower court, ruling. A lower court's interpretation is not taken as definitive, and it would not be accurate to infer that it was accepted by those redrafting the legislation.

A middle case is presented where Congress does not reenact the specific provision but, rather, amends the statute to extend its reach, without saying anything about the provision that had been interpreted by the Supreme Court. For instance, in 1972 Congress amended the 1964 Civil Rights Act, extending the act's coverage to government employees. In 1970, the Court had handed down its interpretation of the 1964 act's words that intent to discriminate was not required for a plaintiff's prima facie case.[28] While the 1972 amendment did not discuss this, it is an acceptable use of the acquiescence doctrine to infer that, in extending Title VII's protections to government employees, they could bring a prima facie case without proving intent to discriminate. Having granted this, it would be absurd to require nongovernment employees to prove intent, since government employees did not have to do so. In that sense, the 1972 amendment could constitute evidence that, in passing the 1972 law, Congress was acquiescing to the Court's 1970 interpretation of the 1964 statute, even though the 1972 amendment did not actually constitute a repromulgation of the 1964 law.[29]

Another middle case involves single house action during consideration of an amendment to, or repromulgation of, an existing statute. Like the defeat of such an amendment on the Senate or House floor for the original bill itself, such action in connection with a bill that amends the original bill has value for legislative history, provided the bill to which the amendment was offered eventually passes. (If it doesn't, there's no legislative action from which to draw any inference.) That was the context of Justice Stewart's comment in *Runyon v. McCrary* that "there could hardly be a clearer indication of congressional agreement" with a proposition than the defeat of an amendment during Senate deliberation, though he carried the inference too far.[30]

Where the legislative "history" takes place subsequent to the passage of a statute and does not amend the statute, then the value of such evidence to the interpretation of the original statute becomes very small. Action or nonaction by another Congress with respect to such bills cannot be called indicative of the intent of the Congress that passed the law. It is not the same body.[31] The turnover rate in Congress has averaged 11 percent a session in recent years.[32] Any implication of congressional intent at the time the law was passed must diminish sharply with time. Even if all representatives were the same, however, the motivations and pressures felt by Congress and the president change with every moment. If a different president is in office, even were the composition of Congress to have remained largely the same, there is no assurance the bill would have passed in the same form. The president is an integral part of the legislative drafting process, through the threat of veto or through "horse-trading" on other matters; and those influences could have produced a very different bill at the later date.

Defenders of using this kind of "legislative history" know all this. Few, if any, contend that subsequent legislative action, inaction, or commentary tells us about the intent of the legislature that passed a bill. Citation to such authority, therefore, is not to tell us what was the intention of the enacting Congress but what the interpretation of a statute should be. The members of Congress, under this heading, are akin to judges writing opinions in cases generally on point but not controlling or to judges writing dicta in cases that do control. Their opinion is worthwhile to the extent it is the product of a thoughtful person, institutionally directed toward studying issues of this kind. While not characteristic of all members of Congress (or all judges), such a generalization fits well enough to make a legislator's comments valuable. It also explains why comments by legislators in later Congresses are considered in legislative history; and it is their commentary, rather than their failure to take action, that is entitled to consideration.[33] This view of legislative history preserves some role for what members of Congress say before, during, and after consideration of the legislation in question.

This role is similar to that which has been accorded by the courts to the interpretation of a statute by its administering agency.[34] It cannot be assumed that the agency had a hand in determining the drafter's intent (although they might have helped with the drafting). Rather, the agency's views matter because it has experience in working with the statute and in knowing which, among various alternative interpretations of a statute, will fit practical needs better. In Congress, the oversight committees have similar expertise. They observe the enforcement agencies year after year, members and staff often have long tenures, and they can be thoughtful commentators on what is going right and what is going wrong in the administration of a statute. Comment by members of such committees, no less than by executive branch administrators, should be useful in construing a statute. In no real sense, however, is it "legislative history," though such references are often swept up in that term.

The Use of Presumptions

In the dialogue between Congress and the Supreme Court, certain ground rules, set out clearly, can avoid many problems of statutory interpretation. For instance, the Court can announce certain default rules regarding whether a statute should be retroactive. Consider two possible rules: (1) if a statute is silent on retroactivity, it is assumed not to apply to any conduct that occurred before its effective date;[35] or (2) if a statute is silent on retroactivity, it is assumed to apply to every case still in court at the time of passage.[36] There is no strong reason to choose one of these rules over another;[37] but there is a tremendous reason to choose one of them and stick with it. Then Congress would know the consequence of its silence on retroactivity.[38] In 1994, the Court left open some possibility for retroactivity[39] but largely announced a rule of the first kind.[40] This replaced an earlier, much more difficult rule, that matters of policy would be applied retroactively, but matters predominantly of personal interest would be prospective only.[41] The new rule better serves the interest of division of labor between legislative and judicial branches. But Congress should have adopted it on its own. A generic statute, "Unless explicitly stated to the contrary, all new laws shall apply only to conduct taking place after the effective date of such law," or, "Unless explicitly stated to the contrary, all new laws shall apply to any cases not yet having reached final judgment," would have settled this issue for years to come.

Other default rules (sometimes called "clear statement rules")[42] have, in recent years, been adopted by the Supreme Court. The issue of severability, that is, whether the rest of a statute should be preserved when part has been held unconstitutional, is analyzed under a presumption in favor of severability in the absence of clear evidence of legislative intent to the contrary.[43] It is only a presumption, and it is possible for a court to deny severability even where there is a severability clause, though this has never occurred. An absolute rule, of course, would provide greater certainty: for example, no severability unless there is such a clause, but, if there is such a clause, then as much as logically can be severed will be allowed to be severed.[44]

Another example concerns whether a statutory rule carries with it the right of an individual to sue for relief when the rule is broken. A private right of action can be inferred unless a federal statute excludes it, or it can be excluded unless a federal statute explicitly includes it. The rule has switched from the first rule to the second, through U.S. Supreme Court opinions, during the latter half of the twentieth century.[45] Either rule is acceptable, of course; what is less so is for Congress to remain so supine in watching the rule change. There is nothing "courtlike" in deciding whether a private right of action should be inferred into a statute. Although the question appears to deal with litigation administrability, it really is a question of policy. Having created a statutory obligation, the legislature is the best branch of government to answer the next question of how it wishes to see that obligation enforced. Creating a private right of action prevents the executive from being able to control enforcement—a disadvantage, from time to time, such as in dealing with foreign nations whose actions are called into question in private suits.[46] On the other hand, private enforcement guarantees that there will perpetually be pressure to abide by the statute's policy, even if the attitude of the executive branch changes from administration to administration.

That decision, how much enforcement of an obligation we want and by whom, is quintessentially one of policy. It rests comfortably with Congress. A general statement of law, "Unless the statute explicitly states otherwise, standing to sue is hereby conferred to the maximum extent constitutionally possible, on any party injured in fact, by reason of breach of any duty imposed by federal law," therefore would have accomplished the same thing as the expansive Supreme Court standing rule. A different statute, "Unless the statute explicitly states otherwise, private parties shall lack standing to sue to enforce any duty imposed by federal statute," would have done the same from the other direction.

In each of these instances of the use of a presumption (retroactivity, severability, and a private right of action), the responsibility should be with Congress to express its will. The Court acts with presumptions only because Congress has not. Only where the constitutional guarantee against ex post facto criminal laws is applicable is there a primary role for the Court. Congress's willingness to let this power pass, how-ever, has led to an accretion of authority by the Court. As the Court has changed the rules from time to time, the Court's institutional failings have been exposed. A legislature can, and should, change policy from time to time; but if the Court is purportedly setting down what the leg-islature intends, there is no defensible basis to change that interpreta-tion as long as there is no newly discovered evidence of legislative in-tent. When the Court does make such a change, therefore, as it did regarding inferring a private right of action,[47] it exposes itself to fair criticism that it has stepped into the legislature's role.

What do we do with a statute passed during the time of one Supreme Court rule but interpreted after the Court has changed its rule? The safest assumption is that Congress knew it was legislating against a certain default rule, and that default rule should stay in effect for interpreting congressional intent of all statutes passed before the Court makes its new default rule clear. In *Alexander v. Sandoval*,[48] how-ever, the Court applied the opposite rule, denying a private right of ac-tion that would have been inferred at the time, 1964, that the statute was passed. Congress is master of the words of any statute. It is bound by no obligation of consistency over time or loyalty to precedent. Just like raising the jurisdictional limit for federal question or diversity ju-risdiction, Congress can say, we used to allow more suits than we are going to henceforward. On what premise, however, does the Court make that statement? It is not master of its own jurisdiction; Congress is.[49]

The thesis of this text is that each branch has inherent advantages: for each branch not to use its advantage and, worse, to allow another branch to encroach upon it dulls the mechanisms of governmental ac-tion. Eventually, the Court will rule on severability, retroactivity, a pri-vate right of action, or any other topic on which "default rules" have been created. From time to time, it will change its rules. Each of those issues, however, is policy, not judicial, in nature; and there is no guar-antee that the Court's substantive desire on the policy will mirror that of the people, whose will on a matter of policy ought to be paramount, barring an issue of constitutional significance.

NOTES

1. *Gomillion v. Lightfoot*, 364 U.S. 339, 344–45 (1960) (evaluating the intent of the legislature in drawing district lines). See also *City of Richmond v. J. A. Croson*

Co., 488 U.S. 469, 493 (1989) (racial pandering seen as potential intent in some affirmative action legislation).

2. *Lemon v. Kurtzman*, 403 U.S. 602, 612 (1971) (first prong of a three-pronged test is the "secular purpose" of the statute).

3. In *City of Boerne v. Flores*, 521 U.S. 507, 530 (1997), the Court said that a record of religious bigotry by a legislature might have created an adequate premise for Congress to act under section 5 of the Fourteenth Amendment to strike down facially neutral laws. In *Board of Trustees of University of Alabama v. Garrett*, 531 U.S. 356 (2001), the majority and dissent sparred over whether the record showed intentional discrimination against people with disabilities. The majority made much of the fact that there were no legislative findings that intentional discrimination against people with disabilities had been practiced by states and local legislatures; Justice Breyer, in dissent, cataloged many such instances able to be inferred from the congressional committee hearing record. According to the *Boerne* majority, in using the enforcement clause of the Civil War amendments, Congress has to select means congruent and proportional to the constitutional violations that are occurring. Part of the congruence analysis, apparently, is to determine if the legislature is directing its action to overcome a specific constitutional violation. Exactly how much of an inquiry, and how strong those findings must be, however, has been hotly debated since *Boerne*. We know, from the Court's dictum in *Boerne*, that the Voting Rights Act was based upon a record adequate to the purpose. 521 U.S. at 530.

4. *Texas v. Johnson*, 491 U.S. 397 (1989); *United States v. O'Brien*, 391 U.S. 367 (1968).

5. *Will v. United States*, 449 U.S. 200 (1980).

6. J. Ely, *Democracy and Distrust* (1980).

7. P. Brest, "The Conscientious Legislator's Guide to Constitutional Interpretation," 27 *Stan. L. Rev.* 585, 589 (1975).

8. See, e.g., McNollgast, "Positive Canons: the Role of Legislative Bargains in Statutory Interpretation," 80 *Georgetown L. J.* 705 (1992); McNollgast, "Legislative Intent: The Use of Positive Political Theory in Statutory Interpretation," 57 *Law and Contemporary Problems* 3 (1994); Posner, "Statutory Interpretation—in the Classroom and in the Courtroom," 50 *U. Chi. L. Rev.* 800 (1983); W. Eskridge, "Politics without Romance: Implications of Public Choice Theory for Statutory Interpretation," 74 *Va. L. Rev.* 275 (1988).

9. McNollgast, "Legislative Intent," 7.

10. Indeed, not even every part of a bill's text is legislation. A bill will often contain "whereas" clauses; even referring to these as evidence of legislative intent is potentially fallacious, since Congress does not codify the "whereas" clauses, and neither does any state legislature with which I am familiar.

11. Moving beyond the words actually passed in a statute, all that the exercise of researching legislative history can do is tell some legislator's intent or the intent of the staff working for a legislator. Newspaper articles of the time might be as useful.

It is treacherous to draw inferences beyond the one legislator speaking. Some legislator might express what she or he wishes a bill to accomplish, yet the bill remains silent on the point. That legislator's views might run completely contrary to the sentiments of those members who did not speak; indeed, the reason they remained silent might well have been that they counted the votes, knew the statute would not include the more explicit interpretation favored by the speaker, and found that outcome satisfactory. Hence, they tactically saw no purpose in speaking. They would prefer ambiguity in the statute following a failed attempt to clarify a phrase one way, as that sequence could be inferred as implicit approval of the opposite view.

More often, silence does not even have that kind of meaning. From personal observation and experience, the members of Congress most often speaking on the House floor are, except for committee chairs whose position requires their presenting a bill, those with the least influence in the legislative process. Indeed, they speak often on the House floor on a variety of subjects, in part because they lack alternative outlets for their desire to influence policy. I recall from the initiation week for new members of Congress the sage advice offered by Congressman Natcher, the member of Congress holding the record for the longest service without ever missing a floor vote. Natcher advised new members to be careful not to speak too much, lest one's colleagues infer we had nothing to say.

Lastly, the concept that other members of Congress even hear what their colleagues say about a bill is unlikely in the extreme. For members with hundreds of different bills to consider and whose presence in Washington comprises less than half of their work-year, silence on any given substantive issue will seldom reflect acquiescence to the statements of some colleague, which statements, even if made from the floor of the House or Senate, will not even be heard by them.

12. See, e.g., *City of Boerne v. Flores*, 521 U.S. at 547, n. 3; *J. Truett Payne v. General Motors*, 451 U.S. 557, 563 (1981). The same inference should be allowed when two versions of a bill are brought forward in the same Congress. If the second bill becomes law and the first is sufficiently narrow in scope, the defeat of the first can be used to interpret an ambiguity in the second. This was the approach taken by the Court in *City of Boerne v. Flores*, regarding the legislative history of the several versions of the Fourteenth Amendment. 521 U.S. at 520–21.

13. Although the U.S. Supreme Court has never seen the connection, in adopting this approach to legislative history, the Court is also saying something about the legislative veto, contrary to its holding in *INS v. Chadha*, 462 U.S. 919, 967 (1983), that such vetoes were unconstitutional because they did not express the will of the entire Congress. If every one-way valve through which legislation must pass (e.g., a conference committee or one of the houses) is capable of creating useful legislative history, is that not because the action of such lesser, included body was necessary for the act to pass? This was the essence of Justice White's dissent in *Chadha*, which argued that if a body's approval was necessary to pass a law, then that body could be entrusted with a veto on how the law was administered by the executive. 462 U.S. at 919 (White, J., dissenting).

14. Of course, the amendment might have been rejected as superfluous, rather than erroneous. However, that fact should be ascertainable by a minimally competent review of the tenor of the debate on the amendment. Where the debate does not make that clear, then I would reject any reliance upon the defeat of an amendment.

15. If both houses act, a potential logical conundrum could result. Suppose there are only two possible interpretations of an ambiguous word. The House debates and rejects an amendment giving the word one meaning. The Senate debates and rejects an amendment giving the word the second meaning. The bill becomes law with no amendment, and the ambiguous word stays intact. One would have to conclude that the particular phrase had no legal meaning at all, as one might with a clause that was unconstitutional, and see if the rest of the statute held up. I know of no such legislative episode actually occurring.

The common cases are where one house rejects an amendment and the other house never considers it, or where one house rejects an amendment and the other house adopts it and the conference committee rejects it. (Had the conference committee accepted it, it would be law.) In these cases, the inference should be allowed that the ambiguous phrase is not to have the meaning of the rejected amendment.

16. The president does not have a comparable power to make a negative inference felt. The president can say what he or she thinks the law does mean and sign it; but that's entitled to no more weight than comment by, say, a majority of the members of a single house during debate. When the president wants to say that he or she finds an interpretation of an ambiguous provision unacceptable, however, the president can express that only by vetoing a bill, and then it does not become law. By contrast, the House or Senate can show that sentiment by rejecting an amendment and then passing the law.

17. Note this rule would not apply to a House or Senate *committee's* consideration of an amendment. That is because no one committee's approval is necessary for a bill to come to the Senate or House floor. Even powerful committees can be bypassed by a discharge petition in the House or by a floor amendment in the Senate. It thus can be said of no House or Senate committee amendment what can be said of a floor amendment: that its failure expresses the will of a body whose assent was essential to passing a bill. There is one exception—the conference committee of both House and Senate members whose approval *is* essential when differing versions of a bill pass each house.

18. 427 U.S. 160, 174–75 (1976).

19. The Court has from time to time spoken as though that was their view of Congress: that Congress waits, across the plaza on Capitol Hill, for pronouncements on statutory interpretation from the Supreme Court and then sequentially considers whether to correct each one.

"The Court has emphasized that since 1922 baseball, with full and continuing congressional awareness, has been allowed to develop and to expand unhindered by federal legislative action. Remedial legislation has been introduced repeatedly in Congress but none has ever been enacted. The Court, accordingly, has concluded that Congress as yet has had no intention to subject baseball's reserve system to the reach of the antitrust statutes. This, obviously, has been deemed to be something other than mere congressional silence and passivity. . . . Congress, by its *positive inaction*, has allowed those decisions to stand for so long and, far beyond mere inference and implication, has clearly evinced a desire not to disapprove them legislatively." *Flood v. Kuhn*, 407 U.S. 258, 283–84 (1971) (emphasis added).

That's quite a statement based, literally, on nothing.

"[W]hen our earlier opinion gives a statutory provision concrete meaning, which Congress elects not to amend during the ensuing 3¹/₂ decades, our duty to respect Congress' work product is strikingly similar to the duty of other federal courts to respect our work product." *Rodriguez de Quijas v. Shearson/American Express, Inc.*, 490 U.S. 477, 486 (1989) (Stevens, J., dissenting).

How remarkable it is that the work of the Supreme Court in interpreting words Congress used has now become the "Congress' work product." Indeed, after passing the law initially, Congress did no "work" at all.

"Congress has not amended the statute to reject our construction, nor have any such amendments even been proposed, and we therefore may assume that our interpretation was correct." *Johnson v. Transportation Agency of Santa Clara County, California*, 480 U.S. 616, 628, n. 7 (1987).

"As the Court notes, the Solicitor General has filed a brief in this Court for the United States as *amicus curiae* urging us to overrule the Court's decision in Dr. Miles Medical Co. v. John D. Park & Sons Co., 220 U.S. 373 (1911). That decision has stood for 73 years, and Congress has certainly been aware of its existence throughout that time. Yet Congress has never enacted legislation to overrule the interpretation of the Sherman Act adopted in that case. Under these circumstances, I see no reason for us to depart from our longstanding interpretation of the Act." *Monsanto Co. v. Spray-Rite Service Corp.*, 465 U.S. 752, 769 (1984) (Brennan, J., concurring).

20. Had a subsequent Congress passed another law, one might raise the issue of whether that subsequent law implicitly amended the earlier law. That case will be considered below.

21. *Johnson v. Transportation Agency of Santa Clara County, California*, 670 (Scalia, J., dissenting).

22. Id.

23. D. Farber, "Statutory Interpretation, Legislative Inaction, and Civil Rights," 87 *Mich. L. Rev.* 2 (1988).

24. F. Easterbrook, "Stability and Reliability in Judicial Decisions," 73 *Cornell L. Rev.* 422, 428 (1988).

25. Farber, "Statutory Interpretation," 10.

26. Sometimes the Court will infer acquiescence from the fact that not a single bill was introduced to "correct" the Court's interpretation of a statute. "Furthermore, Congress not only passed no contrary legislation in the wake of Weber, but not one legislator even proposed a bill to do so." *Johnson v. Transportation Agency of Santa Clara County*, 629, n. 7.

The failure to introduce a bill tells us only about the intensity of a legislator's belief on a subject, not what that belief is. It could well be that the entire legislature disfavors the Court's recent interpretation of a statute and would vote that way if polled, but members have other matters that concern them more. That is especially true in those legislatures (like California's and unlike the federal Congress) that impose a maximum limit on the number of bills a legislator can introduce each session.

Even without such numerical limits, there can be costs associated with introducing a bill on a controversial subject. Indeed, it works the opposite way from what the Court assumed in *Johnson v. Transportation Agency of Santa Clara County*, quoted above. The more controversial the subject, the less likely bills will be introduced on it, unless there is a guarantee that a vote will be taken. Introducing a bill is the same as going on record yourself. It identifies a legislator on one side of a controversy, sure to alienate substantial numbers of voters. When the matter comes to a vote, the legislator can demonstrate that his or her position was reasonable, for it will be shared by a large number, if not a majority, of others. Until that vote, however, the legislator is on a limb. Since the fate of the overwhelming majority of bills in Congress is never to have a vote at all, introducing a bill on a controversial subject has a very adverse risk / reward ratio.

Further, the Court has occasionally taken exactly the opposite inference: that because many bills were introduced, but none has yet passed, it must be inferred that Congress acquiesced to the statutory interpretation that had been made. "Nonaction by Congress is not often a useful guide, but the nonaction here is significant. During the past 12 years there have been no fewer than 13 bills introduced to overturn the IRS interpretation of § 501(c)(3). Not one of these bills has emerged from any committee." *Bob Jones University v. United States*, 461 U.S. 574, 600 (1983). The Court has thus tried to have it both ways: if no bills are introduced, it infers agreement; if many bills are introduced, it infers agreement—just so long as no bill is passed.

27. See, e.g., *Alexander v. Sandoval*, 532 U.S. 275, 279, 300–301, 310 (2001) (Stevens, J., dissenting).

28. *Griggs v. Duke Power Co.*, 401 U.S. 424 (1970).

29. A very similar process of reasoning in legislative history is presented by the *"in pari materia"* doctrine. Two statutes might deal with the same general kind of topic. The Court might infer that the later Congress implicitly wished the two statutes to work together, if it did not repeal the earlier one. If the ambiguity occurs in the second statute, the words of the first statute can be an inference of legislative intent by the later Congress. If the ambiguity occurs in the first statute, the passage of the second can be an inference of legislative intent implicitly to amend the earlier statute *pro tanto* so as to clarify the ambiguity. Even without resorting to a quasi-fiction of legislative intent, it's simply a good rule for the Court to follow, consistent with respect for a coequal branch, that as much of what the Congress has passed be given as consistent a reading as possible.

The pro–affirmative action group of justices made such an inference in their opinion in *Bakke*. Title VI of the 1964 Civil Rights Act appeared to bar racial discrimination by any agency receiving federal funds, whether the discrimination hurt majority or minority race individuals. The pro–affirmative action group argued that the Court could refer to the fact that Congress, subsequent to 1964, passed affirmative action plans for federal set-asides in government contracts. Reading these subsequent acts together with the 1964 act argued for a pro–affirmative action interpretation of the 1964 act—assuming it was sufficiently ambiguous to invite resort to legislative history. See *Regents of the University of California v. Bakke*, 438 U.S. 265, 348 (1978) (opinion of Brennan, White, Marshall, and Blackmun, JJ.). Of course, this deals only with the statutory side of affirmative action; the issue of affirmative action's constitutionality is not affected by this argument.

30. See *Runyon v. McCrary*, 427 U.S. 160, 174–75 (1976). The context was as follows. In debate on the 1972 Civil Rights bill's extension of coverage of the 1964 act to government employees, Senator Hruska observed that the 1866 act had, in 1967, been interpreted by the Supreme Court to allow redress against private discrimination (*Jones v. Alfred H. Mayer Co.*, 392 U.S. 409 [1968]). This fact, of course, could not have been known by the Congress of 1964, since, as of 1964, the Court's interpretation of the 1866 statute precluded its application to private discrimination. Since the 1866 law had now been interpreted to reach the same subject matter as Title VII of the 1964 Civil Rights Act, discrimination by private parties, Senator Hruska proposed that Congress address this overlap now, by undoing the implication of the *Jones v. Alfred H. Mayer Co.* case and saying the Title VII remedies were exclusive. The House had added just such a provision in its version of the 1972 bill. Senator Hruska's amendment, however, was defeated on an equally divided Senate vote, and it was not added back in during conference. From this, Justice Stewart could, logically, infer that the 1972 statute should not be read to preclude relief under the 1866 statute. Taking one more step, one could infer that the 1964 statute could also be so read, since the 1972 statute was an amendment of the 1964 act. (This would have been absolutely clear had the 1972 statute repromulgated the entire 1964 act.) The step too far was to use this to infer anything about the 1866 statute, which was not under consideration by the Congress in 1972. Whether the 1866 law applied to private discrimination was a matter for the 1866 Congress to resolve, or any subsequent Congress that amended the 1866 law. The 1972 Congress did not amend the 1866 law.

Despite the weakness of this argument, it was repeated, this time in dissent, by Justice Brennan, thirteen years later, in *Patterson v. McLean Credit Union*, 491 U.S. 164, 200–204 (1989).

Inference from a failed amendment to a bill is relevant to understanding that bill when it does pass. One can say, "If construed as ordered by that amendment, that bill didn't have the consent of one of the houses, hence, with that understanding of the ambiguous phrase, that bill didn't pass. The bill that did pass, therefore, cannot have that meaning." By contrast, regarding statutory language that was already law, such as the 1866 Civil Rights Act, one can infer nothing. It is already law, without any reference to the amendment considered 106 years later.

31. See *Johnson v. Transportation Agency of Santa Clara*, 657 (Scalia, J., dissenting); and Farber, "Statutory Interpretation," 9.

32. Average of years: 2001, 9 percent (*Congressional Quarterly Weekly*, January 6, 2001, 43); 1999, 9 percent (*Congressional Quarterly Weekly*, January 9, 1999, 61); 1997, 7 percent (*Congressional Quarterly Weekly*, January 4, 1997, 25); and 1995, 20 percent (*Congressional Quarterly Weekly*, January 7, 1995, 47).

33. Dissenting in *Patterson* thirteen years later, Justice Brennan went back to the same legislative history relied upon by Justice Stewart in his majority in *Runyon*. Justice Brennan cited extensively from Senator Williams and Senator Hruska, pointing out that, while on opposite sides of the Hruska amendment, both recognized that existing law granted victims of race discrimination remedies not available to other employment discrimination victims. 491 U.S. at 202 (Brennan, J., dissenting). I have criticized, above, the attempt to consider this history definitive; however, it does have value of a different kind than the historical fact that the 1972 Senate rejected the Hruska amendment (which, I believe, should have no bearing on interpreting the meaning of the 1866 statute). It is commentary by two senators who were deeply involved in crafting public policy that became law and thus useful to a judge, part of whose charge is to interpret ambiguities in such a way as to make several different laws work together. This is the heart of the *in pari materia* doctrine, not that a later Congress can, without an explicit amendment, change a law passed by a former Congress but that the product of the two Congresses should, if possible, be construed to work together.

34. *Chevron, U.S.A. Inc. v. Natural Resources Defense Council, Inc.*, 467 U.S. 837 (1984).

35. *Bowen v. Georgetown University Hospital*, 488 U.S. 204 (1988). See also *Kaiser Aluminum & Chemical Corp. v. Bonjorno*, 494 U.S. 827 (1990).

36. *Bradley v. Richmond School Board*, 416 U.S. 696 (1974).

37. I do have a favorite, however, drawn from the nature of the legislative branch to make broad rules and the nature of the judicial branch to resolve individual cases. For a legislative change to apply to parties whose conduct occurred prior to the legislative change appears to be an attempt by the legislature to affect particular individuals. Were the legislature to attempt to *punish* particular individuals, the constitutional prohibition on ex post facto laws would prevent it. U.S. Const., art. I, § 9. If the noncriminal nature of the legislation keeps this clause from applying in its words, its spirit still has some force: that it should not be the business of the legislature to deal with specific cases. (For this reason, several states' constitutions require that all bills be of general applicability.) This sense, conveyed in the due process clause and the bill of attainder clause as well, was reflected in the majority opinion in *Landgraf v. USI Film Products*, 511 U.S. 244, 266 (1994). "[T]he presumption against retroactive application best preserves the distinction between courts and legislatures: the former usually act retrospectively, settling disputes between persons, the latter usually

act prospectively, setting the general rules for future conduct." See also *Simmons v. Lockhart*, 931 F.2d 1226, 1330 (8th Cir., 1991), quoted in *Hicks v. Brown Group*, 982 F.2d 295, 298 (8th Cir., 1992). Hence, as between the two rules, I would favor that no person be adjudged differently on the basis of a rule not known at the time of his or her action. However, short of a constitutional violation, Congress could decide differently. Indeed, one argument the other way is that, if the Court applies a presumption against retroactivity and, by hypothesis, the Congress has failed to address a pending case, then there are likely to be "orphans" left behind, whose treatment for no good reason is out of synchrony with the way people in general are treated.

38. Ambiguity, on the other hand, allows both sides to claim a potential victory on a contested point. In the 1991 Civil Rights Act, for example, the opponents argued the attorneys' fees provisions of the act were a boon for a class of civil rights plaintiffs' attorneys with cases pending in court who needed Congress to win their cases. The supporters, largely, wanted just such a result, but not as the main, or even minor, reason for supporting the bill. Nevertheless, they'd rather not give up the hope of retroactive application of the new attorneys' fees rules if they could. Leaving the matter ambiguous allowed both sides to have what they wanted, without foreclosing the other side in a way that clear language would have done. Justice Stevens catalogs this history in the context of the 1990 and 1991 versions of the Civil Rights Act, noting that the vetoed 1990 version was explicitly retroactive, while the 1991 version was silent. *Landgraf v. USI Film Products*, 263. "It is entirely possible—indeed, highly probable— that, because it was unable to resolve the retroactivity issue with the clarity of the 1990 legislation, Congress viewed the matter as an open issue to be resolved by the courts." Id. at 261.

See also *Hicks v. Brown Group, Inc.*, 297 ("[A] divided Congress intended 'to hand this controversial issue to the judiciary by passing a law that contained no general resolution of the retroactivity issue.' . . . Every other circuit to consider the question has agreed."). See also the discussion of retroactivity in the 1991 Civil Rights Act, C. Dale, "The Civil Rights Act of 1991: A Legal History and Analysis," Congressional Research Service, Report 92-85A, January 10, 1992.

While recognizing this ambiguity worked to advance the consideration of a particular bill, that is, in and of itself, not necessarily good. Indeed, it was a bit perverse, as it sent a legislative matter to the judicial branch for resolution, when the legislative branch lacked the will to resolve it.

39. "[T]here is no special reason to think that all the diverse provisions of the Act must be treated uniformly for such purposes. To the contrary, we understand the instruction that the provisions are to 'take effect upon enactment' to mean that courts should evaluate each provision of the Act in light of ordinary judicial principles concerning the application of new rules to pending cases and preenactment conduct." *Landgraf v. USI Film Products*, 280.

40. "The presumption against statutory retroactivity is founded upon sound considerations of general policy and practice, and accords with long held and widely shared expectations about the usual operation of legislation." *Landgraf v. USI Film Products*, 293; *Rivers v. Roadway Express Inc.*, 511 U.S. 298 (1994).

41. This approach came from an attempt to reconcile *Bowen v. Georgetown University Hospital*, 488 U.S. 204 (1988) with *Bradley v. School Board*, 416 U.S. 696 (1974), which *Bowen* did not specifically overrule. For one formulation of a single rule embracing both opinions, see Judge Heaney's dissent in *Hicks v. Brown Group, Inc.*, 301 (dissenting opinion).

42. See, e.g., *Gregory v. Ashcroft*, 501 U.S. 452 (1991) (absent a clear statement from Congress, the Court would not infer that the federal Age Discrimination in Employment Act applied to state government officials).

43. *Alaska Airlines v. Brock*, 480 U.S. 678, 684 (1987).

44. The latter half of that rule might encounter a serious constitutional challenge were the nondelegation doctrine ever to be revived. If Congress passes a statute, say, with ten quite different provisions, can it realistically be said that Congress would have intended all 3,628,800 permutations that could result from a court striking down one or more provisions of the statute, while keeping the others?

In the debate on campaign finance reform in 2000, an important amendment was proposed in the House by Representative Thomas that the provisions of the "McCain-Feingold" bill not be severable. Thomas's argument was that the will of Congress had been frustrated in *Buckley v. Valeo*, 424 U.S. 1 (1976), when the U.S. Supreme Court struck down expenditure limitations but upheld contribution limitations. Congress, Thomas argued, would never have approved limiting contributions to $1,000 per individual donor if there were no overall cap on expenditures, since the result was a huge commitment of time to fundraising from many individual donors. Either an expenditure cap or the ability to go to a few large donors would have obviated this burden on members of Congress and candidates for that office. Nevertheless, the 1974 campaign finance statute at issue in *Buckley* included a severability clause; see 424 U.S. at 180 (section 454 of Title 2). Thomas's argument would have to be that the 1974 Congress did not fully comprehend the enormity of what it was doing to have enacted the severability clause, in light of the possible permutations of some provisions being upheld and others being struck down.

45. In *Alexander v. Sandoval*, 288, the Court stated that *Cort v. Ash*, 422 U.S. 66, 78 (1975), reversed *J. I. Case v. Borak*, 377 U.S. 426 (1964), as to implying a private right of action. Actually, *Cort v. Ash* was careful to distinguish *Borak*, but the *Sandoval* Court was quite explicit in overruling *Borak*. Hence, the rule today, if not exactly in 1975, is against an implied private right of action. "In determining whether statutes create private rights of action . . . legal context matters only to the extent it clarifies text. We therefore begin (and find that we can end) our search for Congress's intent with the text and structure of Title VI." (Footnote omitted.)

46. See *In re Uranium Antitrust Litigation*, 617 F.2d 1248 (7th Cir., 1980), which discusses foreign sovereignties complaining about the pursuit of private litigation by Westinghouse complaining of an international uranium cartel. The foreign companies who were accused of having engaged in the cartel intimated that, if they were so engaged, it was with the understanding and approval of their governments. The Seventh Circuit observed that the U.S. State Depart-

ment, in letters sent to the court, supported the assertion of foreign sovereign immunity or foreign sovereign compulsion by the foreign defendants. Nevertheless, the case was allowed to proceed, with some embarrassment to the State Department, because the Sherman Antitrust Act created a private right of action.

47. In antitrust, the last three decades of the twentieth century were characterized by three major trends: an increasing reliance upon economics as a predicate for a successful claim (see, e.g., *U.S. v. General Dynamics Corp.*, 415 U.S. 486 [1974], and *Continental T.V. Inv. v. GTE Sylvania Inc.*, 433 U.S. 36 [1977]); restrictions on what the court would consider "antitrust harm" to be (a kind of denial of standing) (see, e.g., *Monsanto Co. v. Spray Rite Service Corp.*, 465 U.S. 752 [1984]; *Business Electronics Corp. v. Sharp Electronics Corp.*, 485 U.S. 717 [1988]; and *Matsushita Electric Industrial Co. v. Zenith Radio Corp.*, 475 U.S. 574 [1986]); and the expansion of court-made rules denying standing to plaintiffs who had previously been entitled to bring private antitrust lawsuits for damages (see, e.g., *Cargill Inc. v. Monfort*, 479 U.S. 104 [1986]; *Brunswick Corp. v. Pueblo Bowl-O-Mat, Inc.*, 429 U.S. 477 [1977]; and *Associated General Contractors of California, Inc. v. California State Council of Carpenters*, 459 U.S. 519 [1983]). As these three trends developed simultaneously, it is difficult to view the restrictions on standing as anything more judicial in nature than the other two trends. That is, all three reflect a desire to move substantive antitrust law. Though legislative efforts (to reverse *Monsanto* and *Sharp*) passed the House twice, Congress was unable to move the substantive law back to where it had been before the Court's rulings.

48. 531 U.S. 1049 (2001).

49. Except, of course, for original jurisdiction, which Congress cannot alter. U.S. Const., art. III, § 2.

CHAPTER 5

Stare Decisis: The Self-Imposed Constraint by the Judicial Branch Not Shared by the Other Branches

BY "STARE DECISIS," I mean the practice of the U.S. Supreme Court to adhere to previously announced doctrine in subsequent cases. At the level of the lower courts, there is a tremendous advantage in stability caused by adherence to precedent. That, however, is not stare decisis. It is simply adherence to the system of superior and inferior courts. Similarly, state courts following federal court decisions on matters of federal constitutional law is also very stabilizing, but it is not stare decisis. It is federalism. At its purest, stare decisis would compel a decision by the Supreme Court different from what the justices would have decided if the matter had first come up before them in the case at hand.

Recently, references to stare decisis in Supreme Court opinions appear to undermine the doctrine rather than support it.[1] In this chapter, I seek to explore whether it would be more appropriate to the judicial function to take this trend to its conclusion. If the Court were to put an end to reliance upon the doctrine, an important distinction traditionally perceived between the way the judicial branch differs from the executive and legislative branches would disappear. Each branch would be perceived to change its mind as circumstances changed. What harm would the Court suffer from being understood to act in that way? To answer that question, let us explore the arguments that have been raised in defense of stare decisis.

One of the most extensive discussions of the doctrine of stare decisis in recent Supreme Court jurisprudence occurred in *Planned Parenthood v. Casey*, a case that reaffirmed the holding of *Roe v. Wade* regarding the right of privacy in the context of abortion. In the majority opinion, Justice O'Connor held:

Because neither the factual underpinnings of Roe's central holding nor our understanding of it has changed . . . the Court could not pretend to be reexamining the prior law with any justification beyond a present doctrinal disposition to come out differently from the Court of 1973. To overrule prior law for no other reason than that would run counter to the view repeated in our cases, that a decision to overrule should rest on some special reason over and above the belief that a prior case was wrongly decided.[2]

Justice O'Connor then developed the thesis that the Court's ability to do its job rested on the popular perception that it acted on principle. There were two circumstances under which "the Court would almost certainly fail to receive the benefit of the doubt in overruling prior cases."[3] The first was when the overturning of opinions happened frequently. The second was where the issue was embroiled in public controversy.

On the first ground, Justice O'Connor posited that there was some numerical limit, and if "that limit should be exceeded, disturbance of prior rulings would be taken as evidence that justifiable reexamination of principle had given way to drives for particular results in the short term."[4]

This rule is not wise. It makes the adherence to precedent in one field of law turn on completely unrelated fields of law. If the Court has just overturned long-standing precedent in the field of taxation, for instance, it would then be more constrained to review the formulation for when states can make trucks change their mud flaps at the state line than if there had been no tax opinion that term of Court. A decently informed populace would, I think, be more alarmed at that kind of approach than it would at frequent overrulings of earlier precedent.

Furthermore, the expressed concern is overblown. Is the inference so shocking that a change in the Court brings changes in opinions? Who does not believe this? And what is wrong with that? That's healthy progress; and people vote for president, and senators, at least in part, on the basis of what kind of justice each will nominate and confirm.

Nor is there a misperception about close opinions. Citizens know five-to-four opinions don't have as much authority as opinions with a larger majority, even if that's not a legal rule. The Court's own striving for unanimous decisions in very important cases, *Brown v. Board of Education* or *U.S. v. Nixon*, for example, illustrates its own awareness of this perception.[5] President Nixon spoke of abiding by a "definitive ruling of the Supreme Court,"[6] sending what turned out, for him, to be a disastrous signal to the U.S. Supreme Court that he might not follow a closely decided case. When a five-to-four opinion is issued, legal and popular commentary notes that the ruling might not last. All that is transparent.

As a last refutation of this first special factor, consider again the quotation from Justice Stewart that the Court should be concerned about a "basic change in the law upon a ground no firmer than a change in our membership."[7] The frequency in change of Court membership leading to different outcomes, however, is not that high. We can estimate the probability of such an occurrence. The most concerned focus (especially in presidential campaigns) has been about the difference a single appointment to the Supreme Court might make. Obviously, that directs attention to five-to-four opinions. Yet the probability of any given five-to-four opinion changing within ten years, due to death or retirement, is under 25 percent.[8] (The probability of any other opinion changing, a six-to-three or a seven-to-two opinion, for instance, is less still, as it would involve more justices retiring, and in the right permutation.) The country's respect for the Court can probably withstand a one-in-four chance of a reversal of a five-to-four opinion within ten years. This is especially true if, as I suspect, the original issuance of the five-to-four opinion was greeted with public awareness of its more ephemeral nature.

Justice O'Connor's second special concern is also unconvincing: the more controversial the opinion, the more stare decisis should apply. She analogizes *Roe v. Wade* to *Brown v. Board of Education*, and she's probably right in regard to the controversy each generated. In such a charged environment, Justice O'Connor thought that a special duty of loyalty was owed by the Court to the people—especially to those not on the Court who, while disagreeing with the earlier outcome, nevertheless abided by it out of respect for the rule of law.[9]

Justice O'Connor is right to focus on the dilemma when public outcry puts pressure on the Court to change its opinion. Caving in to such pressure would, indeed, be devastating to the Court's place in our government. However, letting that feared perception overturn one's better judgment on what the law should be, and especially what the Constitution requires, is a greater harm. Some of the greatest failings in public policy have stemmed from people unwilling to change, lest someone say they caved in to pressure.[10] Sometimes you have to change and let your detractors have their cheap shot. Otherwise, you're letting their tactics succeed.[11]

Other justices have offered different reasons for stare decisis, but no more persuasive. Let us consider Justice Stevens's defense of the doctrine, developed in his concurrences in *Runyon v. McCrary*[12] and in *Johnson v. Transportation Agency of Santa Clara County*.[13] In *Runyon*, Justice Stevens begins with a remarkably candid statement, "For me the problem in these cases is whether to follow a line of authority which I firmly believe to have been incorrectly decided."[14] In *Transportation Agency*, he continues,

Thus, as was true in Runyon v. McCrary . . . , the only problem for me is whether to adhere to an authoritative construction of the Act that is at odds with my understanding of the actual intent of the authors of the legislation. I conclude without hesitation that I must answer that question in the affirmative, just as I did in Runyon. . . . Bakke and Weber have been decided and are now an important part of the fabric of our law. This consideration is sufficiently compelling for me to adhere to the basic construction of this legislation that the Court adopted in Bakke and Weber. There is an undoubted public interest in "stability and orderly development of the law."[15]

In neither case, however, was Justice Stevens's vote necessary to make a majority. I do not mean he was insincere. I only point out that neither case tests the real proposition of stare decisis; namely, that a justice would adhere to an earlier opinion she or he believed to be wrong simply because of stare decisis. Justice Stevens had the luxury of not being the deciding vote.[16]

I have been struck by how often such statements about stare decisis are found in opinions that are not necessary to comprise a majority. Accordingly, I undertook a search of how often the doctrine of stare decisis was actually determinative: that is, where the outcome would have been different except for a justice's adherence to an earlier opinion that he or she still believed to be wrong. The results of that research appear as an appendix to this chapter; for this main text, I simply report my conclusion there that the cases of stare decisis, when it really counts, constitute almost a null set. Stare decisis might not be so much a flawed a doctrine as it is an irrelevant doctrine, due to the paucity of instances when it actually mattered.

Passing the question of whether Justice Stevens actually based a decision on stare decisis, let us turn to the reasons he gives for the doctrine in *Runyon*. The first reason is the expected one, to foster "stability and orderly development of the law."[17] The second is much more thought-provoking. Citing Justice Cardozo, Justice Stevens said:

[W]hen a rule, after it has been duly tested by experience, has been found to be inconsistent with the sense of justice or with the social welfare, there should be less hesitation in frank avowal and full abandonment. . . . If judges have woefully misinterpreted the Mores of their day, or if the Mores of their day are no longer those of ours, they ought not to tie, in helpless submission, the hands of their successors.[18]

Though the Cardozo quote was in favor of departing from stare decisis, Stevens uses it to support stare decisis. "In this case, those admonitions favor adherence to, rather than departure from, precedent. For even if *Jones* did not accurately reflect the sentiments of the Reconstruction Congress, it surely accords with the prevailing sense of justice today."[19] Justice Stevens appears to be saying, "If a prior opinion happened, by coincidence, to predict today's mores correctly, then adhere to it. If the prior opinion didn't, then ignore it." So stated, this is not a defense of stare decisis. It is simply an imprecation for the Court to decide cases in compliance with contemporary mores.[20]

Exploring the intricacies of the doctrine of stare decisis leads us to further grounds for questioning it. Traditionally, the distinction is made between statutory and constitutional stare decisis.[21] However, the Civil Rights cases show how unrealistic that distinction is. The mantra is that Congress can always change a judicial construction, but it can't change a constitutional one; hence, the Court ought to abide by stare decisis more in the statutory arena, since there is a coequal branch able to correct it if it's wrong. The failure of Congress to act is supposed to mean something.

The truth, however, is that Congress will often lack a majority for either position on a controversial issue. The Court will act, and that action will set the terms of later debate. That was the case in *Griggs v. Duke Power*, regarding disparate impact. It was the case in *Runyon* and *Jones*, regarding private rights of action. It is also the case regarding the retroactivity of the 1992 Civil Rights Act, which issue was intentionally left ambiguous.[22] The Court finally acted where Congress couldn't.

Judge Easterbrook ably notes these difficulties with the traditional assumption about stare decisis in statutory rather than constitutional cases.[23] He embraces an iconoclastic alternative: apply stare decisis even more when a constitutional interpretation is involved.[24] He regrets the fact that "none of the sitting Justices feels bound by precedent in the way the second Justice Harlan did. Today's Justices cast their votes just as if prior cases did not exist."[25] The upshot is that constitutional misinterpretations would require constitutional amendments, a consequence Judge Easterbrook explicitly embraces.[26]

In Chapter 10, dealing with the right of privacy in the context of abortion, I describe the institutional advantages of a constitutional amendment over a Supreme Court discovery of a fundamental right. The one major disadvantage, however, remains. The Court exists to hear cases. While the Court has occasionally been unwilling to fulfill that duty,[27] and the certiorari docket is discretionary, the constitutional issues will, by and large, get resolution. There is no such guarantee for a constitutional amendment. Two-thirds of each house and three-quarters of the states are very hard to obtain. The default is not neutral; under Judge Easterbrook's rule, the default is to the oldest Supreme Court decision on point. (Indeed, over time, the Supreme Court's constitutional decision-making would be reduced to a series of citations of earlier opinions and the words "stare decisis.")[28]

I share Judge Easterbrook's preference for a greater use of the constitutional amendment process, but I do not share his willingness to freeze the process of Supreme Court decision-making in the constitutional field. Good and bad opinions should continue to issue over time, reflecting the current justices' best judgment. Given the low likelihood of obtaining constitutional amendments, however much I or Judge Easterbrook would encourage them, I would rather have as a default a Supreme Court opinion ignoring stare decisis than an ever-more ancient Supreme Court opinion giving undue preeminence to the first justice to decide an issue, just because he or she was first.

We are left, I believe, with many serious disadvantages of adhering to stare decisis. It is a doctrine that has been much criticized.[29] Its one great advantage, purportedly, is predictability. However, the doctrine of stare decisis is not necessary to obtain the virtue of predictability in law. The system of common law does this.

The system of common law affects all aspects of our judicial process. Most obviously where the law is judge-made because there is no text; next most likely when a court is interpreting very general language, as in many constitutional cases; and even when specific language in a statute is being interpreted and applied, it is always advantageous for an American court to research what previous courts have said when presented with a case similar to the one before it. The ability to craft a decision seemingly in keeping with the previous set of decisions enhances a court's reputation for applying, as opposed to making, the law. In a close case, the preference for the virtues reflected in the common law tradition undoubtedly counsel against a change in judicial rule, an abrupt change all the more so. Wisdom and humility are often found together: a court that recognizes a close question might defer to prior decisions by respected justices for that reason alone. All these approaches would lend predictability to the system without embracing the doctrine of stare decisis.

Indeed, at its heart, the doctrine of stare decisis seems likely to undermine respect for the law, where a losing litigant is quite literally told his or her case was meritorious, but a dead hand from the past controlled the outcome nonetheless. Respect for the law has equally been jeopardized by the contortions in which the Court has engaged to avoid applying stare decisis when it clearly applied, just because the Court didn't like the outcome. I conclude this chapter with three recent, embarrassing, examples.

Relying on the fact that we have created several exceptions to Miranda's warnings requirement and that we have repeatedly referred to the Miranda warnings as "prophylactic," . . . and "not themselves right protected by the Constitution," the Court of Appeals concluded that the protections announced in Miranda are not constitutionally required. . . . We disagree with the Court of Appeals' conclusion, although we concede that there is language in some of our opinions that supports the view taken by that court.[30]

This rule conforms with the usual method for allocating persuasion and production burdens in the federal courts, . . . and more specifically, it conforms to the rule in disparate-treatment cases that the plaintiff bears the burden of disproving an employers' assertion that the adverse employment action or practice was based solely on a legitimate neutral consideration. . . . We acknowledge that some of our earlier decisions can be read as suggesting otherwise. . . . But to the extent that those cases speak of an employer's "burden of proof" with respect to a legitimate business justification defense, . . . they should have been understood to mean an employer's production—but not persuasion—burden.[31]

We first wish to dispel the notion that the Law School's argument has been foreclosed, either expressly or implicitly, by our affirmative-action cases decided since *Bakke*. It is true that some language in those opinions might be read to suggest that remedying past discrimination is the only permissible justification for race-based governmental action. See, e.g., Richmond v. J. A. Croson Co., supra, at 493 (plurality opinion).[32]

Perhaps it was a lack of confidence in their own rectitude that prevented the Court, in these three and many other cases, from saying forthrightly, "That was our decision. We were wrong. Accordingly, to-day, we change. We don't like to do this often, but it's better than sticking with a wrong decision."[33] Instead, we observe tortured distinctions with earlier cases that would never have been embraced by their authors. Since change is inevitable, the virtue of clarity may help the cause of predictability as much as the virtue of consistency does.

Appendix: Does Stare Decisis Matter?

From its first reversal in 1810[34] up until 1998, the U.S. Supreme Court has failed to follow stare decisis and explicitly reversed earlier precedent 216 times.[35] With that record, the question occurred to me whether there was anything to the doctrine of stare decisis. The Court had shown no hesitation to overrule its earlier precedent, whether statutory (see, famously, *Boys Market v. Clerks Union*, 398 U.S. 235 [1970]) or constitutional (see, famously, *Brown v. Board of Education*, 347 U.S. 483 [1954]). Was stare decisis at least a brake on the Court's inclination to set right an earlier error? Or was it merely an empty doctrine, added as makeweight to opinions that would have come out the same without such a doctrine?

My search was for the case where the alignment of justices was such that the switch of those relying on stare decisis would have caused a different outcome and where the use of the doctrine appeared to be contrary to how the justice would have ruled on a clean slate, by the justice's own words. I chose 1940 to March 2003 as a rough approximation of what might be called the modern era.

I searched for opinions relying on stare decisis either in a majority, plurality, or concurrence, where the margin was sufficiently close that those justices explicitly relying on stare decisis, calculated on the other side, would have caused a different outcome. Almost all candidates were five-to-four opinions. This is because when the majority was higher than five, I could not be sure that the other justices would have switched to the minority side were it not for stare decisis. Virtually all opinions relying on stare decisis include other grounds as well; even if I might infer that stare decisis was determinative for the opinion writer, I could not be sure it was so for the silently concurring justices.

Lastly, by relying on computer-assisted research, I recognize that I would not have picked up a case that relied on stare decisis unless it actually used the words "stare decisis." It is possible, though not likely, that an opinion would have been based on the principle without actually citing it. The result of this research turned up only one case in the legislative context[36] and one case in the constitutional context.[37]

Granting that the criteria were very strict, I do still offer the observation that, over a sixty-two-year period, the citation to stare decisis was overwhelmingly in the context where it made no difference. Indeed, it was so in every case I turned up but the two.

There are many examples of discussion of stare decisis without reliance upon it. I attempt here to deal with the major instances where stare decisis appeared to be the basis but turned out not to be. It is possible, of course, that I have missed some such instance or that my judgment of the obviousness of a makeweight is not shared by another reviewer. However, here are the "near misses" since 1940.

The pair of cases discussed in Chapter 12 is most illustrative. In *Runyon v. McCrary*, the Court extended the right to sue to redress discrimination by a private party from the context of real estate to the context of other contracts.[38] *Jones v. Alfred H. Mayer Co.*[39] had established the former right, interpreting 42 U.S.C. section 1982 to cover real estate contracts. *Runyon* interpreted 42 U.S.C. section 1981. Hence, consistency between related statutory provisions was the Court's rationale; stare decisis based on *Jones* was not. Indeed, Justice White offers a powerful dissent in *Runyon* based on the different legislative origins of the two sections[40] and advising that one could uphold both the pro-plaintiff result in *Jones* and his own view denying the plaintiff relief in *Runyon*. So, the majority's expressed reliance on stare decisis was actually inappropriate.[41] Justice Powell's concurring statement also sounds like stare decisis reasoning,[42] but he does not invoke the doctrine; as is appropriate, since it was not the holding of *Jones v. Alfred H. Mayer* that was controlling, it was only a sense of symmetry between the two sections of title 42 of the U.S. Code.

Thirteen years later, in *Patterson v. McLean Credit Union*,[43] the Court entertained argument on whether to reverse *Runyon*, then ruled that it would not. Here, the majority did rely on stare decisis, in a five-to-four opinion, but the holding as to which stare decisis was awarded was shared by the dissent. Hence, since nine justices held that *Runyon* would not be overruled, this case fails the test. That is, we cannot say that, if Justice Kennedy had been willing to overrule *Runyon*, contrary to his opinion for the majority, the four justices in the minority would have agreed with him. Indeed, they said they would not. They favored *Runyon* and only regretted that, in upholding *Runyon* in form, the majority limited it in application.[44] Once again, there is broad language on stare decisis in the majority opinion;[45] it's just not controlling.

As noted in the main body of this chapter, *Planned Parenthood v. Casey*[46] contains the strongest recent colloquy between justices on stare decisis: Justice O'Connor for the majority of five and Justice Scalia for the four dissenters. However, this case does not qualify since nowhere in her opinion does Justice O'Connor state her belief that, had she to rule on *Roe v. Wade*,[47] she would have ruled with the dissent. The entire powerful discussion on stare decisis, therefore, and the equally forceful rebuttal from the dissent deal with a makeweight.

Similarly, in *Lee v. Weisman*,[48] Justice Souter, writing for three justices within the majority in a five-to-four decision, refers to stare decisis, but he makes it clear that the rule advanced was not one he disagreed with anyway.[49]

The one remaining case during this period that appears to rely determinatively on stare decisis equally falls short. In *Guardians Association v. Civil Service Commission of City of New York*,[50] Justice O'Connor opined, in joining the majority in this five-to-four case, that she might have ruled that Title VI did not require proof of intent to discriminate[51] were the issue not foreclosed by *Bakke*.[52] However, that was not the issue on which *Guardians* was decided. Rather, it was decided on whether regulations implementing Title VI could allow a plaintiff to prevail without proving intent. On the question to which Justice O'Connor gave stare decisis effect, there were seven justices on record, in *Guardians* itself, that *Bakke* was correctly decided, as Justice Powell noted in his own concurrence in *Guardians*.[53]

Several other opinions, in majority or concurrence, make reference to stare decisis; but in all of these, there were enough votes by those justices who wrote separately, or who silently joined an opinion that did not rely exclusively on stare decisis, to have formed a majority not based on the doctrine.[54]

When a Supreme Court justice cites stare decisis as the basis for his or her opinion, I do not question the sincerity of a single instance.[55] Nevertheless, I was struck by the fact that, however often or strongly[56] a Supreme Court justice might cite stare decisis, the doctrine can seldom be shown to make a difference—only two cases in more than forty years and only one of them constitutional. More valuable than any additional criticism of stare decisis may be the simple observation that stare decisis, in practical effect, hardly exists.

NOTES

1. See, e.g., *Ring v. Arizona*, 536 U.S. 576, 607–8 (2002), overturning *Walton v. Arizona*, 494 U.S. 639 (1990) ("'Although "the doctrine of *stare decisis* is of fundamental importance to the rule of law[,]" . . . our precedents are not sacrosanct.' *Patterson v. McLean Credit Union*, 491 U.S. 164, 172 [1989] [quoting *Welch v. Texas Dept. of Highways and Public Transp.*, 483 U.S. 468, 494 (1987)]. 'We have overruled prior decisions where the necessity and propriety of doing so has been established.' 491 U.S., at 172. We are satisfied that this is such a case. . . . Accordingly, we overrule *Walton*.").

See also *Arkansas v. Sullivan*, 532 U.S. 769 (2001) (concurring opinion of Justice Ginsburg, joined by Justices Stevens, O'Connor, and Breyer). See *Vasquez v. Hillery*, 474 U.S. 254, 266 (1986) (observing that Court has departed from stare decisis when necessary "to bring its opinions into agreement with experience and with facts newly ascertained") (quoting *Burnet v. Coronado Oil & Gas Co.*, 285 U.S. 393, 412 [1932] [Brandeis, J., dissenting]).

2. See, e.g., *Mitchell v. W. T. Grant*, 416 U.S. 600, 636 (Stewart, J., dissenting) ("A basic change in the law upon a ground no firmer than a change in our membership invites the popular misconception that this institution is little different from the two political branches of the Government. No misconception could do more lasting injury to this Court and to the system of law which it is our abiding mission to serve."), cited in *Planned Parenthood v. Casey*, 505 U.S. 833, 864 (1992).

3. 505 U.S. at 866.

4. Id.

5. G. Gunther and K. Sullivan, *Constitutional Law* 678–79 (1997).

6. B. Woodward and C. Bernstein, *The Final Days* 279 (1976).

7. See note 2.

8. The probability of any given justice retiring in any given year may be estimated by dividing the number of justices who have retired or died in office, 101, by the number of years of the Court's operation, 212, or, 47.64 percent. That means the probability of no retirements in any given year is 52.36 percent. Over ten years, the probability that one or more justices will retire is 99.85 percent. (That's 1 minus the probability that none retires in each of ten years, or 1 minus the quantity 0.5236 raised to the tenth power, which equals 1 minus 0.0015, which equals 99.85 percent.) If a justice retires, to change a decision, the retiring justice must have been in the majority, and the replacement justice must be of the opposite view. That single probability is the probability of any given justice being in the majority of a five-to-four opinion ($5/9$), multiplied by the probability that a randomly chosen replacement justice will be of a different opinion. The only number we can use to estimate the latter is $4/9$—drawn from the assumption that the five-to-four decision in question reflected the split on the issue among all justice candidates as well (assuming, as we must by hypothesis, that none would decide on the basis of stare decisis). Hence, the probability of changing a five-to-four opinion by the substitution of a single justice is $5/9$ times

$4/9$, or 0.2469. That, multiplied by the entire likelihood of one or more justices retiring in a ten-year period (99.85 percent), yields 0.2465.

9. 505 U.S. at 869.

10. In the Vietnam War, Ho Chi Minh resisted going to the peace table lest it appear the American bombing worked; Lyndon Johnson resisted going to the peace table lest it appear he caved in to U.S. domestic demonstrations. The delay of both men cost thousands of lives.

11. Justice Scalia had other, cogent criticisms of this algorithm of stare decisis algebra. "The first difficulty with this principle lies in its assumption that cases which are 'intensely divisive' can be readily distinguished from those that are not. The question of whether a particular issue is 'intensively divisive' enough to qualify for special protection is entirely subjective and dependent upon the individual assumptions of the members of this Court. In addition, because the Court's duty is to ignore public opinion and criticism on issues that come before it, its members are in perhaps the worst position to judge whether a decision divides the Nation deeply enough to justify such uncommon protection." 112 S.Ct. at 2863 (Scalia, J., dissenting).

12. 427 U.S. 160 (1976).

13. 480 U.S. 616 (1987).

14. 427 U.S. at 189 (Stevens, J., concurring).

15. 480 U.S. at 640 (citations omitted).

16. Furthermore, in *Transportation Agency*, at least, it is clear that Justice Stevens would now uphold affirmative action against a challenge under the 1964 Civil Rights Act, even apart from stare decisis. In the paragraph immediately following his citation to stare decisis, and quite independent of his reasoning about stare decisis, Justice Stevens finds that "the logic of antidiscrimination legislation requires that judicial constructions of Title VII leave 'breathing room' for employer initiatives to benefit members of minority groups." 480 U.S. at 645. There is no shame in changing one's mind; I think it is clear that Justice Stevens has changed his mind since his opinion opposing affirmative action in *Bakke*. This fact, rather than stare decisis deference to an opinion he still considers wrong, was the foundation on which Justice Stevens's concurrence in *Transportation Agency* was actually based, in my view.

17. 427 U.S. at 190 (Stevens, J., concurring).

18. Id. at 191 (Stevens, J., concurring) (citation omitted).

19. Id.

20. Furthermore, the enterprise of determining contemporary mores is not a judicial function. Imprecise as legislative history may be, searching historical records of the time a piece of legislation is enacted comports with the judicial role much more than to try to sound out what the prevailing public sense might be at the time of the argument. The legislative branch, not the judicial, institutionally is equipped to speak to the mores of the present, if only because legislators are elected, and the Congress is replenished every two years.

21. "[C]onsiderations of stare decisis weigh heavily in the area of statutory construction, where Congress is free to change this Court's interpretation of its

legislation" *Illinois Brick Co. v. Illinois*, 431 U.S. 720, 736 (1977), cited in *Burlington Industries Inc. v. Ellerth*, 524 U.S. 742, 763 (1998). Cf. Brandeis, J., dissenting in *Burnet v. Coronado Oil & Gas Co.*, 285 U.S. 393, 410 (1932) ("The reasons why this Court should refuse to follow an earlier constitutional decision which it deems erroneous are particularly strong where the question presented is one of applying, as distinguished from what may accurately be called interpreting, the Constitution.").

22. C. Dale, "The Civil Rights Act of 1991: A Legal History and Analysis," Congressional Research Service, Report 92-85A, January 10, 1992, at CRS-14. The issue was eventually resolved by the U.S. Supreme Court in a pair of cases decided two years after the act's passage, *Landgraf v. USI Film Products*, 511 U.S. 244 (1994), and *Rivers v. Roadway Express Inc.*, 511 U.S. 298 (1994).

23. F. Easterbrook, "Stability and Reliability in Judicial Decisions," 73 *Cornell L. Rev.* 422, 427 (1988). "Today's Congress may leave in place an interpretation of a law simply because today's coalitions are different. The failure of a different body to act hardly shows that the interpretation of what an earlier one did is 'right.' "

24. Id. at 429.

25. Id. A good example is the flag-burning case. Given the Court's decision in *Texas v. Johnson*, the majority in *U.S. v. Eichman*, 496 U.S. 310 (1990), might simply have cited its opinion of one year before. More important, the dissenters might have joined the majority, on very clear stare decisis grounds, if any of the four dissenters really embraced the principle of stare decisis.

26. Easterbrook, "Stability and Reliability," 430.

27. See Chapter 13 on the Second Amendment.

28. Such opinions would soon qualify their authors for Judge Easterbrook's "Most Insignificant Justice" award, 50 *U. Chi. L. Rev.* 481 (1983), given that one of the criteria for selecting the winner was the paucity of verbiage in a justice's constitutional opinions.

29. See, e.g., H. Monaghan, "Stare Decisis and Constitutional Adjudication," 88 *Columbia L. Rev.* 723, 741–43 (1988) (collecting citations to scholarly criticism). Monaghan himself finds a useful role for the doctrine as an agenda-limiting tool for the U.S. Supreme Court. Id. at 748ff.

30. *Dickerson v. United States*, 530 U.S. 428, 439 (2000). Justice Scalia, in dissent, went through those instances of "language," demonstrating that they were holdings, not dicta. Id. at 445.

31. *Ward's Cove Packing Company v. Atonio*, 490 U.S. 642, 659–60 (1989).

32. *Grutter v. Bollinger*, 2003 U.S. Lexis 4800 at 36–37. The disavowal would have been a bit more credible had the author of the quoted passage, Justice O'Connor, not also been the author of the cited contradictory message in *Croson*. Essentially, Justice O'Connor is saying, "Please ignore what I said in *Croson*. It was only a plurality opinion, after all."

33. The closest I have seen the Court come to just such a statement in recent times was in *Lawrence v. Texas*, 2003 U.S. Lexis 5013, where Justice Kennedy, for the Court, reversed *Bowers v. Hardwick*, 478 U.S. 186 (1986), holding: "The ra-

tionale of *Bowers* does not withstand careful analysis. . . . *Bowers* was not correct when it was decided, and it is not correct today. It ought not to remain binding precedent. *Bowers v. Hardwick* should be and now is overruled." Id. at 35–36.

34. *Hudson v. Guestier*, 10 U.S. (6 Cranch) 281, 285 (1810), reversing *Rose v. Himley*, 8 U.S. (4 Cranch) 241 (1808).

35. S. Doc. No. 106–8, at 127 (1998), supplementing The Constitution of the United States of America, Analysis and Interpretation, Annotations of Cases Decided by the Supreme Court of the United States to June 29, 1992, S. Doc. No. 103–6 at 2245 (1992).

36. The one statutory case is *Flood v. Kuhn*, 407 U.S. 258 (1972). The majority opinion, for five justices, was written by Justice Blackmun. The issue was baseball's antitrust exemption. The prior opinion, to which stare decisis honor was paid, was *Toolson v. New York Yankees*, 346 U.S. 356 (1953). Discussing *Toolson*, Justice Blackmun held, "It is an aberration that has been with us now for half a century, one heretofore deemed fully entitled to the benefit of stare decisis, and one that has survived the Court's expanding concept of interstate commerce." 407 U.S. at 282.

Other reasons were suggested for the continued exemption for baseball—its uniqueness in American life and the effect of retroactive application of a new rule. 407 U.S. at 283. But it is clear the Court would not have had a problem with those factors had it been ruling *ab initio*. Chief Justice Burger's concurrence, which was necessary to make five votes, while not using the words "stare decisis," was clearly based upon it. "I have grave reservations as to the correctness of Toolson v. New York Yankees, 346 U.S. 356 (1953) . . . but the least undesirable course now is to let the matter rest with Congress." 407 U.S. at 285–86.

37. The one constitutional case is *Scott v. Illinois*, 440 U.S. 367 (1979). The majority held there was no constitutional right to counsel where a defendant was not actually imprisoned. The dissent argued the right to counsel attached to the fact that the defendant could have been sentenced to prison, whether or not the defendant actually was. The majority relied upon *Argersinger v. Hamlin*, 407 U.S. 25 (1972), apparently with approval. Hence, this would not have qualified, were it not for Justice Powell's concurrence, necessary to constitute the fifth vote, in which he stated, "Despite my continuing reservations about the Argersinger rule, it was approved by the Court in the 1972 opinion and four Justices have reaffirmed it today. It is important that this Court provide clear guidance to the hundreds of courts across the country that confront this problem daily. Accordingly . . . [I concur]. I do so, however, with the hope that in due time a majority will reason that a more flexible rule is consistent with due process and will better serve the cause of justice." 440 U.S. at 374–75 (Powell, J., concurring). Had Justice Powell chosen to disregard *Argersinger*, as did the four dissenting justices, the case would have been decided differently.

Justice Powell, writing for the Court in *City of Akron v. Akron Center for Reproductive Health, Inc.*, 462 U.S. 416, 420 (1983), observed that "stare decisis . . . [was] never entirely persuasive on a constitutional question." Nevertheless, he made it so in *Scott*.

38. 427 U.S. 160 (1976).

39. 392 U.S. 409 (1968).

40. 427 U.S. at 192 (White, J., dissenting).

41. "In these circumstances there is no basis for deviating from the well-settled principle of *stare decisis* applicable to this court's construction of federal statutes." 427 U.S. at 174.

42. "If the slate were clean, I might be inclined to agree with Mr. Justice White that section 1981 was not intended to restrict private contractual choices. Much of the review of the history and purpose of this statute set forth in his dissenting opinion is quite persuasive. It seems to me, however, that it comes too late." 427 U.S. at 186.

43. 491 U.S. 164 (1989).

44. Id. at 189.

45. "[T]he burden borne by the party advocating the abandonment of an established precedent is greater where the Court is asked to overrule a point of statutory construction." 491 U.S. at 172.

46. 505 U.S. 833 (1992).

47. 410 U.S. 113 (1973).

48. 505 U.S. 577 (1992).

49. The question was whether the establishment clause prohibited favoring religion as such or merely the promotion of one religion over another. The former was dictated by precedent, and Justice Souter stated, "Such is settled law. Here, as elsewhere, we should stick to it absent some compelling reason to discard it. . . . While a case has been made for this [latter] position, it is not so convincing as to warrant reconsideration of our settled law; indeed, I find in the history of the Clause's textual development a more powerful argument supporting the Court's jurisprudence following *Everson* [the former position]." 505 U.S. at 621–22. "Our aspiration to religious liberty, embodied in the First Amendment, permits no other standard." 505 U.S. at 627.

50. 463 U.S. 582 (1983).

51. Id. at 612 (O'Connor, J., concurring).

52. 438 U.S. 265 (1978).

53. 463 U.S. at 608, n. 1.

54. See, e.g., the following opinions where a concurrence relied on stare decisis, but the majority had five votes not counting the justice who quoted the doctrine: *Mathews v. United States*, 485 U.S. 58, 67 (1988) (the Brennan, J., concurrence "bows to stare decisis," but on a collateral point, namely, the need for the entrapment defense to demonstrate lack of predisposition by the defendant. The majority held the entrapment defense was impermissibly truncated by the trial court, which had insisted the defendant admit culpability but for the defense); *Johnson v. Transportation Agency of Santa Clara County, California*, 480 U.S. 616, 642 (1987) (Justice Stevens, in concurrence, discussed in text above); *Michigan v. Jackson*, 475 U.S. 625, 637 (1986) (Burger, C.J., concurs in extending *Edwards v. Arizona*, 451 U.S. 477 [1981] to a case where a request for an attorney was at arraignment, deferring to stare decisis but admitting doubt about *Ed-*

wards; a majority of five, however, applied *Edwards* without question); *Orozco v. Texas*, 394 U.S. 324, 327–28 (1969) (concurrence by Justice Harlan, who dissented in *Miranda v. Arizona*, 384 U.S. 436 [1966], and in *Mathis v. United States*, 391 U.S. 1 [1968], which extended *Miranda* beyond the station house, now feels compelled to follow *Miranda* as settled law; but majority opinion for five justices applies "our well-considered holding in [*Miranda*]."); and *J.E.M. Ag Supply, Inc. v. Pioneer Hi-Bred International, Inc.*, 534 U.S. 124, 147 (2001) (Justice Scalia relied on stare decisis in his concurrence but gave no indication he would not otherwise have reached that conclusion; and there were five other votes in the majority opinion that did not cite stare decisis).

55. The second Justice Harlan was distinguished particularly by his willingness to cite the doctrine, "when it hurt," that is, when he had ruled with the minority in the very case to which he would later give stare decisis. H. Bourguignon, "The Second Mr. Justice Harlan: His Principles of Judicial Decision Making," 1979 *S. Ct. Rev.* 251, 277 (1979).

56. As noted in the section on statutory construction, chapter 4, note 19, *supra*, Justice Stevens has made for stare decisis, in the statutory context, a role as strong as the duty of lower courts to follow Supreme Court precedent. "[W]hen our earlier opinion gives a statutory provision concrete meaning, which Congress elects not to amend during the ensuing 3$^{1}/_{2}$ decades, our duty to respect Congress' work product is strikingly similar to the duty of other federal courts to respect our work product." *Rodriguez de Quijas v. Shearson/American Express, Inc.*, 490 U.S. 477, 486 (1989) (Stevens, J., dissenting). See also *Shearson/American Express v. McMahon*, 482 U.S. 220, 268 (1987) (Stevens, J., concurring in part and dissenting in part) ("If a statute is to be amended after it has been authoritatively construed by this Court, that task should almost always be performed by Congress."), and *Guardians Association v. Civil Service Commission of New York City*, 463 U.S. 582, 641 (1983) (Stevens, J., dissenting).

PART TWO

Case Illustrations of the Separation of Powers

CHAPTER 6

The Proper Roles of Government:
The Case of Obnoxious Speech

A PROTESTOR at the Republican National Convention held in Dallas, Texas, in the summer of 1984 set fire to an American flag. The protestor could have been arrested for breach of the peace. I don't say convicted; I just say arrested. The flag burning could have been stopped by the police at the moment it occurred and the flag burner taken into custody.

Instead, the police did not intervene. The district attorney, however, prosecuted the protestor under the Texas law punishing one who "intentionally or knowingly desecrates (1) a public monument; (2) a place of worship or burial; or (3) a state or national flag."[1]

The decision not to interrupt the flag burning was made by an officer of the executive branch. So also was the decision to prosecute the protester under the desecration statute, rather than for breach of the peace, or not at all.

The passage of the statute by the Texas legislature was part of a pattern of state laws following the Uniform Flag Act of 1917, associated with the patriotic fervor of America's entry into World War I. Forty-eight states passed similar legislation.[2] The passage of this law is an example of legislative action.

The U.S. Supreme Court struck down Texas's law. This is an example of action by the judicial branch.

The U.S. Congress responded to the Supreme Court's decision with a new federal statute, taking up an invitation implicit in the Court's opinion about how a law might be crafted to survive constitutional challenge. Congress also contemplated an amendment to the U.S. Constitution. Within a year, that statute was to be struck down and the amendment dead, as a practical matter. In these two steps, we also have examples of legislative action.

A serious flaw inhered in each of these steps.

In the facts of the case, as the Supreme Court majority emphasized, there was, in fact, no breach of the peace at the time of the flag burning. That was relevant, because Texas based part of its defense of the statute on the fact that a breach of the peace is often associated with flag burning; hence, it was permissible, and not content related, for the legislature to ban the general category of activity that led to such breaches of the peace. The Court held this was an impermissible generalization, especially because expressive conduct was restricted as a result of it.

There were, in fact, no hearings, no taking of surveys, no analysis of statistical evidence by the legislature when it passed this statute to prove that public flag burning led to breaches of the peace in a high proportion of cases. (I infer this from the fact that the Texas attorney general produced no such evidence at trial, or on appeal, and the constitutionality of the statute was challenged at each stage.)

Evidently, the action by the Texas legislature was not about breach of the peace. Nor was the action by the Dallas district attorney. The latter can be shown by a thought experiment: Suppose the police had intervened, and the Dallas district attorney had then chosen not to prosecute. The police could have arrested the protester and put out the fire, extinguishing his protest. There would be no court case, unless the protester brought one. If the protester did (say that he sued the sheriff's police for violating his federal constitutional rights under 42 U.S.C. sec. 1983), the law enforcement agents would in great likelihood have prevailed. To rule against the police would require criticizing a decision to stop someone from setting fire to something, with kerosene, in a place with a lot of people. That would have been the end of a rather simple episode, if that were all that was involved.

The decision to prosecute under the flag-burning statute was intended to make a statement. The legislature's passage of the statute similarly had nothing to do with public order. Each, rather, was itself expressive conduct. Each was a statement about patriotism.

The legislature's statement was from an earlier time, a statement that America should pull together as one as it entered World War I. A resolution of the Texas legislature, rather than the creation of Class A misdemeanor, would have sufficed. The legislature, therefore, overstepped. It certainly is legitimate for a legislature to pass resolutions expressing patriotic goals. That freedom ends, however, when it chooses a means that inhibits another's expression. That is what the Supreme Court eventually held. Had the legislature stuck to its area of comparative advantage, it would have done one of two things: (1) pass a patriotic resolution to which all could vote yes, or (2) ascertain seriously whether breaches of the peace, or wildfires, or other civil harms, did occur with such frequency upon flag burning that public safety required banning the practice. Either would have fit within the legislature's relevant area of expertise: to express popular will and to ascertain facts upon which to base legislation conducive to public order.

The prosecutor also overstepped. His choice of statute for prosecution—indeed, his decision to prosecute—was to make a political statement. The defendant protested President Reagan's policies in Dallas. Dallas was Reagan country. The prosecution intended to make that statement. That, of course, is beyond the comparative advantage of the executive. The district attorney was free to make any public statement he wished. And he was free to prosecute any breaches of the peace for which he had evidence.[3] (It's hard to believe he could not have mustered sufficient evidence for a breach of the peace conviction for stealing an American flag from a flagpole outside a federal building, accepting said stolen property, dousing it with kerosene in public, and setting it on fire with at least a hundred people in immediate proximity.)[4] Such a prosecution would have been within the executive's discretion. Using a prosecution as a public statement of support for a president, a policy, or a national symbol is not. The awesome, one-sided power to haul an individual out of private life and before a court to stand trial at risk of his or her freedom and finances must not be used to make a political statement.

The Court also overstepped. Flag burning is expressive conduct. The Court's precedents were apposite, that a clear and present danger of imminent physical harm was necessary to prevent expressive conduct. The Texas statute allowed prosecution without proof of those elements. Furthermore, the statute had an antiexpressive word in it, "desecrate," defined by the Texas penal code to mean "deface, damage, or otherwise physically mistreat in a way that the actor knows will seriously offend one or more persons likely to observe or discover his action."[5]

The overstep was the majority opinion's gratuitous concession, "The Texas law is thus not aimed at protecting the physical integrity of the flag in all circumstances, but is designed instead to protect it only against impairments that would cause serious offense to others. [Court's footnote:] Cf. Smith v. Goguen, 415 U.S. at 590–91 (Blackmun,

J., dissenting) (emphasizing that lower court appeared to have construed state statute so as to protect physical integrity of the flag in all circumstances); id., at 597–98 (Rehnquist, J., dissenting) (same)."[6]

It was a five-to-four opinion, written by a master at obtaining fifth votes, Justice Brennan. Perhaps this statement was the price of obtaining Justice Blackmun's vote to make five. Justice Stevens filed a separate dissent, and Justice Blackmun may have been tempted to join it instead. The footnote citing Justice Blackmun's opinion in *Smith v. Goguen* for the "physical integrity" exception suggests that may have been the case.

However, this statement was gratuitous. Given the Court's holding that flag burning was expressive conduct, preserving the flag's physical integrity "in all circumstances" would have meant preventing expressive conduct "in all circumstances." Justice Brennan could not have believed that such a simple change would result in a constitutional statute. We know this because Congress presented exactly that kind of language in *United States v. Eichman*,[7] and the Court struck it down ten days short of one year after *Texas v. Johnson*. And Justice Blackmun joined the majority.

Perhaps Justice Blackmun simply changed his mind. It is not unheard of, or wrong, to do so. However, it could also be that Justice Brennan put something into *Texas v. Johnson* as a gesture to Justice Blackmun that was not necessary to get his vote. If so, the "gesture" was overstepping. The Court rules by formula. It purports to be deciding the case before it by application of a formula more general than the facts contained in that case. It thereby attempts to establish a veneer of consistency, of predictability of future outcomes. Providing more than one rationale for a judgment cuts against that predictability, since the other branches, let alone the citizenry, have no idea which rationale was essential to the outcome. The better practice would have been a plurality opinion holding on the ground of expressive conduct and, if it had to be, a separate concurrence by Justice Blackmun. If Justice Blackmun did not author that separate concurrence but merely joined the now less complex majority opinion, then we would have been spared the exercise in Congress that ensued. If Justice Blackmun did author that separate concurrence, then the exercise that ensued would not have been in vain.[8]

Did Congress overstep?

Presented with the Court's opinion in *Texas v. Johnson*, the chair of the Veterans' Affairs Committee (a Democrat) held a public appearance with the president of the United States (a Republican) at the Iwo Jima Memorial to introduce a constitutional amendment to empower the Congress to outlaw flag desecration.

That, I submit, was entirely appropriate—from the perspective of separation of powers and the utilization by each branch of the powers possessed by that branch. Whether it made America better or worse to have a specific constitutional amendment modifying the First Amendment is not what I am arguing; all I am claiming is that to attempt a constitutional amendment was precisely the role of Congress. If two-thirds of each chamber agreed, the draft would go to the states for three-quarters of them to approve.

Whether wise or foolish to use in this context, this is the specified process by which the legislative branch should deal with a constitutional interpretation by the judicial branch with which it disagrees. It had been done before.[9] And, from the point of view of those most concerned about exceptions to the First Amendment, a narrow exception crafted in a new amendment might be less dangerous than the creation of a new category of a judicially created exception, should the Court have taken the bait on "physical integrity."[10]

Professor Frank Michelman makes this case strongly, suggesting that there was good reason to prefer a narrowly drawn constitutional amendment to an invitation to the Court to uphold a statute, with the attendant stretching of First Amendment principle necessary to that result. He also makes clear he would prefer neither.[11]

The proposed constitutional amendment, however, was not the only congressional reaction. Responsive to Justice Brennan's gratuitous statement, a statute was also drafted, and this was passed instead of the constitutional amendment.

Was this a legitimate exercise of legislative authority?

In a simple way, the answer is easily yes. The Supreme Court had said one kind of law was unconstitutional ("flag desecration"), but another kind might be constitutional ("to preserve the flag's physical integrity in all circumstances"). So those members of Congress desiring the policy outcome, to prevent flag burning, tried the other kind. They even put an expedited review provision into their statute[12] to ensure that the Supreme Court would have to hear an appeal of the first prosecution under that statute and ordered the Court to "advance on the docket and expedite to the greatest extent possible a hearing in such a case."[13]

Those members of Congress who believed it was constitutional to ban flag burning were entitled to take the Supreme Court's invitation to find a way to implement their policy view, which was also permitted by their view of the Constitution. But not all members were of that stripe. Some believed that it was unconstitutional to ban flag burning but that a statute would take the heat off for a constitutional amendment. It would take some time for the statute to make its way up to the Supreme Court (as things turned out, less than one year), and, during that time, the public outcry for a constitutional amendment may have simmered down (as things turned out, it did).

Are such members of Congress to be admired or condemned? My point of view is that of this text—an inquiry into the responsible use of inherent assets of the members of each branch of government. By hypothesis, these members of Congress each voted to pass a statute he or she believed to be unconstitutional.[14] Each was willing to see an individual summoned before the justice system, and tried criminally, at risk of loss of wealth and freedom, for conduct they did not believe should be punished or even punishable.

My own view is to condemn such members of Congress. The only constitutionally cognizable act of a member of Congress is to vote. No amount of speaking about the vote changes its effect or its significance as a constitutional act. They acted to harm at least one individual they believed to be blameless. And they acted hoping the legal consequence of their action would be overturned. They were cynical.

Those who defend them claim they were acting in the spirit of the First Amendment and that their actions did, indeed, prevent a constitutional amendment from happening. This conclusion confuses outcomes with process. The Constitution is a process document. It is not unconstitutional to amend the Constitution. It might be ill advised, but it is not unconstitutional. However, to pass a law outlawing a form of free speech is unconstitutional. So, it has to be admitted that these members acted unconstitutionally, by their own lights, for some higher purpose. That the higher purpose took its origin from another part of the Constitution, the unamended First Amendment, does not make it any more defensible than other higher purposes that have been advanced from time to time by those who break the law.

Each group of members of Congress had experts willing to testify for them. Former D.C. Circuit judge and solicitor general Robert Bork gave testimony that *Texas v. Johnson* was wrongly decided.[15] Of course, he is entitled to that view, though it appears to contradict several of his statements before his Supreme Court rejection.[16] Four justices dissented in

Texas v. Johnson; their view was respectable and may well have been shared by many members of Congress. Had Judge Bork become Justice Bork, the decision might have been different.[17]

Laurence Tribe gave ambiguous testimony, that several statutory routes existed to get a flag-burning statute upheld under existing Supreme Court case law.[18] He clearly urged the statutory route. Nowhere, however, in his testimony did he say that he believed that such a statute would be constitutional. Yet his testimony was intended to be relied upon by members of Congress who pursued the statutory route of "physical integrity." If we believe Tribe thought such statutes would be unconstitutional, yet he failed to say so and offered instead comfort to those advocating the existence of a statutory route, we would judge him along with those members of Congress I labeled above as cynical and deserving of blame.[19]

Former solicitor general Charles Fried changed his testimony the day he presented it. Summoned for the purpose of stating that *Texas v. Johnson* could be "corrected" by statute and giving assurances that that is what he would say, Fried confessed that he had been troubled ever since giving those assurances, that the decision was, actually, correct, and that no statutory route around it existed. Points for candor, and for upsetting anticipated expectations in a congressional hearing, are surely due.[20]

Eight years later, Congress held further hearings on a possible constitutional amendment to ban flag desecration. Among the witnesses at that time was Richard Parker, who testified that *Texas v. Johnson* was correct but that our nation would be better with a constitutional amendment to prohibit flag desecration.[21] He was intellectually consistent and honest. His view, however, represented one of the smallest of all possible permutations: that the Supreme Court acted correctly *and* should be reversed by constitutional amendment. No matter how few members of Congress were of the same mind as he,[22] from the point of view of the natural attributes of each branch of government, the fundamental topic of this text, Parker's analysis was flawless.

The flag-burning episode came to a close in *U.S. v. Eichman*, the Supreme Court's reversal of the federal anti-flag-burning statute passed in the wake of *Texas v. Johnson*. The Court alignment was the same. The majority, again written by Justice Brennan, gives this treatment to the "physical integrity" exception that Justice Brennan had been willing to entertain (but not adopt) only a year earlier. "The Government's interest in protecting the 'physical integrity' of a privately owned flag rests upon a perceived need to preserve the flag's status as a symbol of our Nation and certain national ideals. But the mere destruction or disfigurement of a particular physical manifestation of the symbol, without more, does not diminish or otherwise affect the symbol itself in any way."[23] So went, in a sentence, the polemic that a statute concerned with preserving the physical integrity of the flag in all circumstances might be constitutional. It couldn't be, since there was no purpose, let alone one that would override a citizen's expressive interest, in preserving individual flags from being burned. The symbol lived, no matter what happened to any individual manifestation of it. Good enough; but Justice Brennan might have said that a year earlier.

In the foregoing incident, each branch of government at some point overreached: it went beyond its own inherent functional advantages. The state prosecutor did this in choosing the statute under which to prosecute. The Texas legislature did this in enacting a criminal law to cover a fact situation that would, in virtually every case, already be covered by law, in order to do what they should have done by resolution. Some, but not all, members of Congress did in voting for a statute, believing it to be unconstitutional and hoping it would be reversed. And the Supreme Court did, at least in *Johnson*,[24] by intimating the existence of an avenue for possible future legislation that defied the Court's fundamental holding (that flag burning was expressive conduct) and was, in any event, slammed shut a year later. If the Court had not issued that insincere invitation, it would have been clear at the time of *Texas v. Johnson* that it was a constitutional amendment or nothing. And if that led to a constitutional amendment, that, at least, would have been a constitutional result.[25]

There is one remaining actor to be considered in this analysis: the private sector. The case of the Nazis marching in Skokie, Illinois, presents a question that still remains open regarding the extent to which governmental decision-making in the field of expressive speech can be privatized.

On May Day 1974, some members of the National Socialist Party of America (the Nazis) planned a march in Skokie, home to several thousand Holocaust survivors. The village obtained an injunction against the march, which was stayed by the U.S. Supreme Court. The U.S. Court of Appeals for the Seventh Circuit eventually struck down the village's attempt to prevent the Nazis from marching. The Circuit panel held the march, banners, and arm bands were expression protected under the First Amendment.[26]

A significant reason for the court's decision was that, before the march began but after the Nazis had applied for a permit, Skokie passed a new ordinance requiring permits for all parades of more than fifty persons and requiring applicants to obtain insurance adequate to cover substantial sums of property and personal damage.[27] Suppose the permit and insurance requirements had been passed long in advance of the Nazis' planned march, so as to remove the factor conceded by the village that their intent was to repress Nazi marches?[28] Is this a way to solve the problems associated with demonstrations for unpopular causes? Could we apply the same technique to the flag burners?

In advance of any particular application, and following hearings on the kind of damage that demonstrations of various kinds have caused,[29] a city like Dallas or Skokie might adopt a requirement that any demonstration of more than a few people be preceded by the posting of a bond or the taking out of casualty insurance, against risk of damage to city property. It could well be that no bonding agency or private insurer would want to do business with the Nazis. It could well be that no bonding agency or private insurer would want to write a policy that covered risks attendant upon flag burning.[30] In this way, the city would be able to shift the antiexpressive component of its approach to private parties.

In his separate opinion, Judge Sprecher stated he would uphold a neutral insurance requirement; however, he was not clear about how it would work for a party that could not find any such private insurance. Judge Sprecher left open the possibility that, "if all else failed the requirement could then be waived if necessary to avoid constitutional infirmity."[31]

This is an instance where legislative motive would control the outcome of judicial review. Passed as they were in the wake of the Nazis' request, and with the admitted purpose of stopping the Nazis from marching, the Skokie village ordinances stood no chance of surviving First Amendment challenge.

In a different setting, however, lacking such clear antiexpressive intent, I believe a state actor could effectively relegate to private parties certain functions it could not itself constitutionally perform. The insurance company could deny the Nazis a permit simply because they were Nazis, barring any "common carrier" obligation imposed by state law to take all similarly situated customers. Discrimination by an insurer on the basis of the message of the applicant is constitutional. The majority in *Collins v. Smith* left this open.[32]

In analyzing the various advantages inherent in the several branches of government, this discussion of private insurance warns us not to ignore the inherent advantages of nongovernmental actors as well and to be alert to the opportunities for making use of them, where the motives of the governmental actors are not suspect.[33] This is not to say that a good or a bad policy outcome would be reached in any given case. It is only to recognize that a popularly willed outcome, prohibited by First Amendment considerations from being effectuated by the government, could nevertheless be effectuated by leaving the matter to the private market.[34]

NOTES

1. Texas Penal Code Ann. sec. 42.09 (1989), cited in *Texas v. Johnson*, 491 U.S. 397, n. 1. (1989).

2. *Texas v. Johnson*, 397, n. 1 (Rehnquist, C.J., dissenting, with White and O'Connor, J.J.).

3. The majority noted: "The State's emphasis on the protestors' disorderly actions prior to arriving at City Hall is not only somewhat surprising given that no charges were brought on the basis of this conduct but it also fails to show that a disturbance of the peace was a likely reaction to Johnson's conduct." 491 U.S. at 408.

4. 491 U.S. at 400. The district attorney chose not to prosecute the individual who stole the flag from public property. All this shows rather dramatically that it was the utilization of the flag desecration statute, rather than the punishment for and hence future deterrence of breaches of the peace, that was on the prosecutor's mind.

5. Texas Penal Code Ann. sec. 42.09(b), cited in *Texas v. Johnson*, 397, n. 1.

6. 491 U.S. at 411, n. 6.

7. 496 U.S. 310 (1990).

8. Justice Blackmun could still change his mind a year later. But I suggest he would have been less likely to do so, having put his name on a separate opinion setting forth a test that Congress then explicitly met. Simply by concurring in Justice Brennan's multiply based opinion, Justice Blackmun preserved his maximum freedom to jump either way in the next case. That, however, was not a service to those who look to the Court for predictability.

Whether, as a policy matter, one should welcome a nonvain act of Congress in this area, effectuating an exception to the First Amendment's protection of expressive conduct in order to ban flag burning, is not my point here. My point is that a coequal branch set out on a fruitless journey because the judicial branch was sloppy in exercising its function.

9. The Fourteenth Amendment overturned *Dred Scott*. Other examples include the Eleventh Amendment (overturning holding that state sovereign immunity did not protect states from suits in federal court by citizens of other

states), the Sixteenth Amendment (overturning holding that Congress lacked authority to impose an income tax, given the constitutional prohibition on federal direct taxes except in proportion to the census), the Twenty-fourth Amendment (overturning holding that a poll tax did not violate the Fifteenth Amendment's ban on denying the right to vote on the basis of race), and the Twenty-sixth Amendment (overturning holding that Congress could not lower the age of voting in state elections, even those held at same time as federal elections).

10. Over the years, the Supreme Court has created many exceptions to the rather clear admonition "Congress shall make no law . . . abridging the freedom of speech," such as for slander, obscenity, fighting words, group libel, words creating a clear and present danger of physical harm, and expressive conduct in the presence of the need to run a selective service system. Admittedly, each of these exceptions may have been met with disapproval by advocates of absolute free speech; and it is entirely consistent to fight for no exception in the case of flag burning at all, whether by constitutional amendment or by Supreme Court opinion. If, however, one were to grant that an exception was inevitable, then it would be better to accomplish the exception by a constitutional amendment written specifically to the practice of flag burning, rather than to do so the way the Supreme Court would. That is because the judicial function, unlike the legislative one, has to deal with broader categories, which, having been discerned, are then applied to the facts of the case before them. What broader category would be found, of which flag burning would be but one instance? The question invites an answer that, obviously, creates a broader exception than just flag burning. Perhaps "sacred symbols of our country" would be read to have been inviolate, within the intent of the framers of the First Amendment.

Drafting a new constitutional amendment is a legislative, not a judicial, function. The Court was being invited to draft a new "amendment" to the First Amendment. Had it done so, it would have been at an institutional disadvantage, compared with the legislative branch. In *Eichman*, of course, the Court declined the invitation to do so.

11. F. Michelman, "Address: Saving Old Glory: On Constitutional Iconography," 42 *Stan. L. Rev.* 1337, 1340, 1359 (1990).

12. See 496 U.S. at 313 n. 2.

13. It seems to me presumptuous for the first branch to give orders to the third branch about how to handle the docket of cases before it; but the Congress can make "regulations" for the Supreme Court's appellate jurisdiction, Article III, section 2, clause 2, and the Court did not fight it in *Eichman*. Should a *Pentagon Papers*, *U.S. v. Nixon*, or *Bush v. Gore* have been pending before the Court at the time, however, Congress might have felt a bit foolish in ordering the Court to put all else aside and consider flag burning a second time.

14. To consider whether this violates the members' oath of office, see Chapter 3; and P. Brest, "The Conscientious Legislator's Guide to Constitutional Interpretation," 27 *Stan. L. Rev.* 585, 585–89 (1975).

15. Statutory and Constitutional Responses to the Supreme Court Decision

in *Texas v. Johnson*: Hearings Before the Subcomm. on Civil and Constitutional Rights of the House Comm. on the Judiciary, 101st Cong., 199 (July 19, 1989) (statement of R. Bork).

16. See J. Ely, "Another Such Victory: Constitutional Theory and Practice in a World Where Courts Are No Different from Legislatures," 77 *Va. L. Rev.* 833, 875, n. 138 (1991).

17. Justice Kennedy filled the vacancy for which Judge Bork was originally nominated, and Kennedy voted with the majority.

18. See Statutory and Constitutional Responses to the Supreme Court Decision in *Texas v. Johnson*, 99, 101ff. (July 18, 1989) (statement of L. Tribe).

19. Contemporaneous criticism of Tribe's testimony noted how it contradicted the second edition of his own treatise on constitutional law published only one year earlier. See, e.g., S. Taylor, "Smarm-Splattered Banner," *Legal Times*, July 17, 1989, at 13. See also R. Taylor III, "Casenote: The Protection of Flag Burning as Symbolic Speech and the Congressional Attempt to Overturn the Decision: *Texas v. Johnson*, 109 *S.Ct.* 2533 (1989)," 58 *U. Cin. L. Rev.* 1477, 1506. Both authors opined that Tribe was advancing the statutory alternative merely to take wind out of the sails of the constitutional amendment effort. Burt Neuborne of N.Y.U. Law School also made a contemporaneous criticism of Tribe's "searching for a way to head off a proposed constitutional amendment." B. Neuborne, Letter to the Editor, *New York Times*, July 19, 1989.

20. Statutory and Constitutional Responses to the Supreme Court Decision in *Texas v. Johnson* 219ff. (July 19, 1989) (statement of C. Fried).

21. Amending the Constitution to Protect the Flag, Hearings Before the Subcomm. on the Constitution of the House Comm. on the Judiciary, 105th Cong., 1st sess., 100 (April 30, 1997) (statement of R. Parker).

22. I know of at least one.

23. 496 U.S. at 315–16.

24. This flaw was not entirely removed in *Eichman*. The Court noted that the language Congress used "confirms Congress' interest in the communicative impact of flag destruction." 496 U.S. at 317. The Court left open the possibility, however remote, that a statute that simply made "burning the flag" illegal might be constitutional, since shorn of the words "defile, deface, mutilate" and shorn of the exception allowing for burning a flag in respect when it is soiled, the Congress might have eliminated all antiexpressive phrases from the law.

I sincerely doubt, however, that would happen upon review of such a statute. Rather, the fact that flag burning is offensive because it is expressive would be used to conclude that a law to ban flag burning was a law to ban expression. A general law against burning things in a public place would do for any nonexpressive purposes.

25. The demand for a constitutional amendment, so popular at the time of *Texas v. Johnson*, had so died down by the time of *U.S. v. Eichman* that not even a hearing was held on it in Congress. The delay was only one year, much shorter than the time the great majority of amendments have taken to be ratified by the states; so it may well be that had the constitutional process for an

amendment been followed, the same eventual outcome would have resulted due to diminished popular enthusiasm. It could also be that, whereas the appetite of Congress for a constitutional amendment had diminished, the state legislatures would still have supported one. It is dangerous to infer much from inaction by Congress.

26. *Collin v. Smith*, 578 F.2d 1197 (7th Cir., 1978).

27. Id. at 1199.

28. Id. at n. 3.

29. Substantial evidence of recent racial strife was cited by the Supreme Court in upholding Illinois's statute barring "group libel" in *Beauharnais v. Illinois*, 343 U.S. 250, 258–61 (1952). The Court cites extensive findings—though it's not clear that the legislature made these findings. Rather, it appears that the Court, in taking judicial notice of them, concluded the legislature could have made such findings. Modern Supreme Court practice has required the legislature actually to make the findings, as opposed to allowing a Court simply to determine that it might have (see, e.g., *U.S. v. Lopez*, 514 U.S. 549 [1995]). That change is good from the point of view of the inherent advantages of the branches, since legislatures summon witnesses and commission research that, with rare exceptions, is subject to public comment, minority input in the legislative process, and rebuttal, whereas the sources of information judges research to make social science–type findings are not open to adversarial challenge. Trial evidence is, but not the kind of general evidence cited in *Beauharnais* about race relations in America's large cities.

30. The example works simplest with the Nazis—insurers might simply refuse to deal with them, and thus the Nazis would get no permits. Regarding flag burning, the mechanism would be a bit more complex but still could be made to work. The city ordinance could require a casualty package that covered all major risks; the insurance company could require a higher premium, or the posting of a bond, if the applicant engaged in flag burning. Or the insurer might offer a policy that explicitly did not cover damage incident on flag burning. The city would then refuse the permit if the applicant could only offer such an incomplete package. If the demonstrator pledged to the insurance company not to engage in flag burning and then did so, the contract could be set up so that the insured forfeited some deposit, as liquidated damages.

31. 578 F.2d at 1202, n. 9 (Sprecher, J., concurring in part and dissenting in part).

32. "On the other hand, we do not need to determine now that no insurance requirement could be imposed in any circumstances, which would be a close question, in our view. . . . Accordingly, we accept the Village's concession that the insurance requirement cannot be applied here." 578 F.2d at 1208.

33. It is not unusual to strike down and uphold identical laws where the only difference is the conceded intent of the state in passing the laws. *Washington v. Davis*, 426 U.S. 229 (1976), and *Gomillion v. Lightfoot*, 364 U.S. 339 (1960). See also Brest, "The Conscientious Legislator's Guide," 589–94.

34. Insurers who turned down Nazis' business would be leaving a source of

business to their competitors. If this were a large piece of business, so as to affect economies of scale in the industry, the firm refusing it would be driven out by a firm that accepted it. Gary Becker has shown that this is not the case, however, where the "taste" is shared by consumers. Indeed, I would suspect that the insurers who did business with the Nazis would be the target of a major consumer boycott, rather than enjoy economies of scale from a larger operation. G. Becker, *The Economics of Discrimination* (1971).

CHAPTER 7

The Exclusionary Rule: When Is a Matter Constitutional, When Is It Only Policy?

THE STRONGEST comparative advantage of the judicial branch is to identify constitutional rights enjoyed by those not popular with the political branches and to vindicate those rights against other, nonconstitutional interests. A stark contrast between the branches' approaches to constitutional rights versus interests is to be found in the criminal law area. Legislators will often say, "What about the victims' rights?"[1] The answer is that, with few exceptions,[2] the Constitution protects individuals from government, not from other people. A legislature and executive will, and ought to, be acting to advance the general interest, including preventing people from hurting each other; indeed, that is what consumes most of their energy. Each of these matters can be called an interest. Superior to an interest, however, is a constitutional right. It is the duty of each branch of government to protect such rights. When the Court announces a new area for the identification and protection of criminals' rights, however, the pressure from the political branches to undo that definition is instantaneous and strong.

In the case of the exclusionary rule, the U.S. Supreme Court gave in to that pressure and, over the course of a quarter century, went from its unique role of identifying constitutional rights to a role indistinguishable from that of the legislature, the role of weighing interests. By the end of the twentieth century, the Court had surrendered its comparative advantage, almost entirely.[3] It is a progression that illustrates the distinction between identifying rights and weighing interests and the Court's relative incompetence in the latter task.

When in *Mapp v. Ohio*[4] Justice Clark announced the exclusionary rule for state courts, with regard to evidence seized in violation of the Fourth Amendment, he was using an inherently courtlike function. *Mapp* built on *Weeks v. United States*,[5] which had required an exclusionary rule for federal courts. The *Weeks* decision demonstrated federal court authority at its greatest, as it drew not only upon U.S. constitutional authority but also upon the authority of the Supreme Court to manage the business of the lower federal courts. The extension of *Weeks* to *Mapp* had to be under federal constitutional grounds alone, as there is no structural role for the U.S. Supreme Court to administer the operation of state courts. The *Mapp* opinion held that *Weeks* was constitutionally based, and hence its principle applied directly to state courts.

Thus, in the year 1914, in the *Weeks* case, this Court "for the first time" held that "in a federal prosecution the Fourth Amendment barred the use of evidence secured through an illegal search and seizure." . . . This Court has ever since required of federal law officers a strict adherence to that command which this Court has held to be a clear, specific, and constitutionally required—even if judicially implied—deterrent safeguard without insistence upon which the Fourth Amendment would have been reduced to a "form of words."[6]

As to whether a "constitutionally required" rule might somehow not apply to the states, the *Mapp* Court decided

to close the only courtroom door remaining open to evidence secured by official lawlessness in flagrant abuse of that basic right, reserved to all persons as a specific guarantee against that very same unlawful conduct. We hold that all evidence obtained by searches and seizures in violation of the Constitution is, by that same authority, inadmissible in a state court.[7]

The reasoning of *Mapp* was that, if evidence seized in violation of the Fourth Amendment could nevertheless be used in state court, it would be "tantamount to coerced testimony."[8] Hence, just as a coerced confession could not be used in evidence without violating the Fifth Amendment, so also for evidence seized in violation of the Fourth Amendment. The court held, "[I]t was logically and constitutionally necessary that the exclusion doctrine—an essential part of the right to privacy—be also insisted upon as an essential ingredient of the right newly recognized."[9]

This did not have to be. For almost a hundred years, the Fourteenth Amendment had not been read to incorporate this requirement upon state courts. However, in reaching the conclusion that the exclusion of illegally seized evidence was not compatible with the Fourteenth Amendment, incorporating the Fourth Amendment, Justice Clark made two respectable points. First, he observed that the Fifth Amendment barred coerced testimony from being used in trial; indeed, the Fifth Amendment speaks about "any criminal case." Hence, using predictable tools of construction, Justice Clark held that the founders would have intended the same result for evidence seized in violation of the Fourth Amendment, the immediately proximate guarantee in the Bill of Rights. Second, he reasoned that the right guaranteed by the Fourth Amendment was essentially a "right to privacy," which would be violated anew by the introduction of personal material, no less than it had by the original invasion of the home or other place being searched. Arguments, of course, could be made the other way: that the very specificity of the Fifth Amendment to trials meant the Fourth Amendment should not be so construed and that the Fourth Amendment speaks only of searches and seizures, not introduction at trial, so that the constitutional violation was over once the search was done. Justice Clark ruled that to credit such arguments "is to grant the right but in reality to withhold its privilege and enjoyment."[10]

So far, this analysis could be described as traditionally judicial—the identification and delineation of a constitutional right. However, the *Mapp* Court introduced one additional element, that of deterrence. "Only last year the Court itself recognized that the purpose of the exclusionary rule 'is to deter—to compel respect for the constitutional guaranty in the only effectively available way—by removing the incentive to disregard it.'"[11] This is not a judicial function. The distinction is vital for what was to follow.

To identify a constitutional right, and to define its boundaries, is courtlike. The U.S. Supreme Court can perform this task well or ill, but it is the Court's to perform.

To determine what rule of policy will best deter constitutional violations is legislature-like. The deterrence of constitutional violations is an interest. So also is the deterrence of the harm individuals do to each other, like automobile accidents. How shall the legislature of a state spend the people's money? There is no federal constitutional basis for compelling that expenditure for deterrence of harms caused by the government rather than harms caused by fellow citizens or by the forces of nature.

Remedying past wrongs by the government is a different matter; there, federal courts have ordered legislatures to spend money.[12] That is a courtlike function, in ordering relief for a violation proved to have occurred. Looking forward, however, to constitutional violations that might occur is no more the duty of the courts than it is the legislature.

A thought experiment might illustrate this point. With $100 to spend, a state legislator is presented with three choices: (1) make public school buildings safer against fire hazard; (2) repave the roads so that fewer accidents occur; (3) train police officers about arrest and search practices so as better to comport with the Fourth and Fifth Amendments. It is the legislator's business to allocate the $100, and no court would overturn her or his decision to skip category three entirely. Imagine the difficulty of fashioning an order upon a legislature otherwise: how much of scarce resources, considering the competing needs of the people of the state, is constitutionally required to be spent on category three? The question in entirely intractable for a court. It is, however, the grist of the legislator's job. Weighing interests demonstrates a legislative advantage; identifying constitutional rights demonstrates a judicial advantage.[13]

The superfluous reference to deterrence, in *Elkins v. United States*[14] and in *Mapp*, allowed the Court in subsequent exclusionary cases to engage in what was essentially legislative decision-making. Eventually, in *Arizona v. Evans*,[15] this led to the evisceration of the claim that the exclusionary rule was constitutionally compelled. If it were not constitutionally compelled, however, then the U.S. Supreme Court had no authority to apply the exclusionary rule to state court proceedings. *Mapp* would have been wrongly decided; so also *Escobedo v. Illinois* and *Miranda v. Arizona*.[16] It would have been better simply to reverse those decisions. Instead, the Court went through thirty-four years of reasoning that was, at its heart, legislative. It demonstrated its inherent comparative disadvantages at legislative reasoning in doing so. When Congress recognized that the Court was engaged in legislative reasoning, it offered its own correction of the path the Court had taken. That should have been allowed to prevail: a legislative function should, presumptively, be for the legislature to perform. However, presented so starkly with the truth of what it had been doing, the Court sought to reassert the constitutional premises for its action—the one trump it has—at least insofar as the Fifth Amendment was concerned. In this attempt, the Court was severely handicapped by its pronouncements, and by the nature of what it was doing, over the previous thirty-four years.

Even before *Mapp*, exceptions had been allowed to the exclusionary rule in federal court, the only place it had constitutionally been held to apply. In *Walder v. United States*,[17] evidence seized in violation of the Fourth Amendment was allowed to impeach the defendant on a collateral issue. If it were against the Fourth Amendment to use evidence seized in violation of the Fourth Amendment, however, there should not have been an exception. That's what it means to be a constitutional principle. The countervailing interest that held sway with the *Walder* Court was to prevent a criminal from giving false testimony. It should not have mattered. The application of the exclusionary rule leads, on some occasions, to criminals going free, a much worse outcome than criminals testifying falsely with the hopes of going free. Society surely does have an interest in not having criminals go free. But the interest is subordinate to the constitutional principle, if it's truly a constitutional principle.

If it comes to weighing interest against interest, however, the Court has no institutional advantage. It was drawn into thinking so, however, by reason of its supervisory authority over federal courts. Whether or not any member of the Court had actually ever been a trial judge,[18] in the exclusionary rule cases from *Mapp* to *Evans*, the Court speaks in detail about what causes people to testify truthfully and what will deter them from testifying at all. Where does the Court derive its knowledge of these matters? How can it go about expanding its knowledge, before ruling? It has only the weakest possible means of doing so: permitting the submission of briefs from amici curiae and asking for additional briefing on points of law (not fact) from the litigants. By contrast, even on such trial-related issues as who is likely to commit perjury and what criminal defense attorneys are likely to do, the legislature has infinitely greater capacity of doing research. It can conduct hearings, order studies by its own investigative arm (the General Accounting Office in the U.S. Congress, the Legislative Analyst's office or State Library in the California legislature), and interrogate the authors of other studies. Whereas there is no guarantee of balance, and no legislator is likely to take the criminal's side, there is at least a spectrum of public opinion represented in the composition of the legislature, and the minority, as well as the majority, has the right to call witnesses and to cross-examine. If the enterprise of determining the nonconstitutional boundaries of the exclusionary rule was permitted to the legislature, it would have the means of doing a better job than the courts. Nevertheless, the courts went ahead, using, for the most part,[19] a legislative, rather than a judicial, means of proceeding.

In a line of cases following *Mapp*,[20] the Court set out to predict the impact of creating an exception to the exclusionary rule in the case before it and, as it saw the task it was performing, to weigh that impact against the benefit of continuing the rule without the proposed exception. As each case turned out, however, there really was no weighing. All the factors pointed in favor of the exception, or, in one case, all the factors pointed against it. This had to be: the Court had no means of making a decision in a real weighing context. Suppose an exception to the exclusionary rule would induce a 10 percent increase in the number of violations of Fourth Amendment rights by police in America but that same exception would increase convictions of guilty defendants by 15 percent. No Court can make that trade-off.[21] The Court was disingenuous to purport to do so. And it made errors.

In *Harris v. New York*[22] the Court permitted an exception to the exclusionary rule to impeach a defendant taking the witness stand on a fundamental point, not a collateral one as had been allowed in *Walder*. The impeaching testimony had been obtained in violation of *Miranda*. Chief Justice Burger ruled that

the impeachment process here undoubtedly provided valuable aid to the jury in assessing petitioner's credibility, and the benefits of this process should not be lost, in our view, because of the speculative possibility that impermissible police conduct will be encouraged thereby. Assuming that the exclusionary rule has a deterrent effect on proscribed police conduct, sufficient deterrence flows when the evidence in question is made unavailable to the prosecution in its case in chief.[23]

How does Chief Justice Burger know what amount of deterrence is "sufficient"? Sufficient to deter 95 percent of all constitutional violations? Assuming the answer is known precisely, say, 92.73 percent, we next need to ask how much value is "valuable aid to the jury" in allowing the un-*Miranda*-ized testimony to be heard. And why does Chief Justice Burger assume that the earlier un-*Miranda*-ized testimony was truthful? The entire point of *Miranda* was that custodial testimony, without a warning, is inherently untrustworthy.

The purported balance was a sham. What Chief Justice Burger could have said, which would not have been a sham and would have been courtlike, is "today, the Court reverses *Miranda*." Less fundamentally, he could have said that the defendant waived his right against the introduction of non-*Miranda*-ized testimony by taking the witness stand. Waiver analysis is quite courtlike; it is the Court's business to define constitutional rights but also to determine when they have been waived. A third alternative, of course, would have been to reiterate that the exclusionary rule is constitutionally compelled and to reverse the conviction. That was the view of Justice Brennan in dissent.[24]

Walder and *Harris v. New York* took their places alongside other exceptions to the exclusionary rule, for habeas corpus proceedings,[25] for grand jury testimony,[26] for civil proceedings,[27] and for testimony against co-conspirators.[28] With so many exceptions, any police officer informed of the law would realize there was virtually always some potential to make use of illegally seized material, or un-*Miranda*-ized testimony, in some way. So, if presented with a proposed new exception, the Court's "balance" became quite easy. Granting a new exception would allow testimony (presumably of value if truthful); denying a new exception wouldn't deter police—since they already had so many other exceptions, they already had all the incentive they needed to gather evidence illegally. The existence of previous exceptions made any new exception a sure thing. This outcome was unavoidable once the first exception was allowed. And that is how the Court ruled in every subsequent case but one.[29]

Along the way, further to bolster the exception being considered, the Court adopted the approach that the exclusionary rule was to deter police, not judges,[30] not magistrates,[31] not court employees,[32] not state legislators.[33] As a result, no exclusionary rule was applied to their errors. This distinction, between police and all others, does not flow from the Constitution. Judges, magistrates, court employees, and legislators are as much state actors as police. Each is capable of ministerial and discretionary conduct. Each can violate a citizen's rights. To exempt them all from possible deterrence of constitutional violations is another flaw of the Court's escapade into legislative decision-making, aptly noted by Justice Stevens in dissent, "The Amendment is a constraint on the power of the sovereign, not merely on some of its agents."[34]

Other errors include confusing the marginal with the average in assessing statistical evidence; the assumption in assessing the social value of increased convictions that a suspect is guilty; and the assumption in deciding the social value of an exception to the exclusionary rule that the excluded testimony or evidence is truthful.[35] In his *U.S. v. Leon* dissent, Justice Brennan complained, "A doctrine that is explained as if it were an empirical proposition but for which there is only limited empirical support is both inherently unstable and an easy mark for critics. The extent of this Court's fidelity to Fourth Amendment requirements, however, should not turn on such statistical uncertainties. I share the view, expressed by Justice Stewart for the Court in *Faretta v. California*, that 'personal liberties are not rooted in the law of averages.' 422 U.S. at

834."[36] That statement identifies well the difference between the court-like and the legislative function in this area.

Justice Brennan, knowing better, nevertheless engaged in the sham balancing in the one case from this era that went the other way, *James v. Illinois*.[37] With no more support than his colleagues had shown for their generalizations, Justice Brennan wrote, for the Court in *James*, "much, if not most of the time, police officers confront opportunities to obtain evidence illegally after they have already legally obtained (or know that they have other means of legally obtaining) sufficient evidence to sustain a prima facie case."[38] If we could accept that as a universal fact (which is how it is stated), then the exclusionary rule would never have an exception. The "balance" would be perpetually tipped the other way: there would be no gain from admitting the evidence, since the police could have obtained sufficient evidence otherwise. Note that, like the majorities that upheld exceptions to the exclusionary rule, Justice Brennan, writing for a Court that, for once, denied an exception, purports to balance. There really is nothing to balance, however, since all factors point against an exception.[39] The benefit to society from having the evidence admitted is zero because the police can get it another way. Furthermore, Justice Brennan assumed the testimony (against which the illegally obtained evidence would be used for rebuttal) was inherently trustworthy testimony.[40] Regarding the last point in the balance, whether an exception to the exclusionary rule would induce more police misconduct, Justice Brennan found such inducement to be large in the *James* fact situation, even given the previous exceptions, because the category of cases at issue in *James* (to impeach witnesses other than the defendant) is so large.[41] With all factors pointing the same way, the conclusion was easily reached against an exception to the exclusionary rule.

What *James* illustrates is that the facially neutral "balance" approach is entirely corruptible, can be manipulated to reach either outcome, and should, at bottom, never have been engaged in by the Court anyway since it is not a judicial function.[42]

An additional element in the exclusionary rule cases to which reference is occasionally made is the desire to preserve the courts' integrity. It's unsavory for a court to admit some evidence that was gained in violation of an individual's constitutional rights, and the Supreme Court stated that this feeling of unease is closely related to the degree to which keeping the evidence out would deter future misconduct.[43] The latter connection has some resonance and was picked up again in *New York v. Harris*,[44] decided the same day as *James*. If allowing the evidence into court would cause the court a sense of unease, it is probably because of the court's suspicion or awareness that law enforcement officers conspired to invade an individual's rights, as opposed to having done their best to abide by the law. Hence, deterrence and sense of judicial integrity are related.

Nevertheless, this ephemeral concept should not be allowed to supplant a simple analysis of whether the use of illegally obtained evidence is itself a constitutional violation. It is not a question of the courts' integrity, just a question of what the personal right guaranteed by the Constitution means, that should control. The Fifth Amendment says evidence can't come in; the Fourth Amendment doesn't, explicitly, say that—so, what should the right answer be? Focusing on "integrity of the courts" asks the wrong question.

Asking whether to admit evidence in a particular case seems to draw upon an inherent advantage of the judicial branch; namely, that the judicial branch will know best how to preserve its own integrity. A court would decide to exclude evidence when to admit that evidence would cast contempt upon the court.[45] However, such a rule provides no basis for the U.S. Supreme Court to overturn the actions of state courts. It is not constitutionally derived. And it introduces a second trial into the midst of the first: to determine how egregious the police action really was, considering all the circumstances. To do that analysis properly, a judge might have to bring the officers onto the witness stand in the midst of the case-in-chief. Whether that kind of intrusion is helpful to the conduct of a trial is a matter that should be left to state courts to resolve for themselves; it's hardly a U.S. constitutional issue.

Judicial integrity, thus, is not a successful rubric to convert the essentially legislative function of weighing interests into a judicial function. An exclusionary rule is either constitutionally compelled or it is the business of the legislature.

In 1995, in *Arizona v. Evans*, the Court disavowed the exclusionary rule's constitutional origin in the Fourth Amendment context. The majority did not provide guidance as to why it had ever been applied to the states, if it had no U.S. constitutional origin. The majority did not say why *Mapp* was wrong or attempt to take back the words used so clearly there. The majority in *Evans* simply would not have signed on to the majority in *Mapp*. "We have recognized, however, that the Fourth

Amendment contains no provision expressly precluding the use of evidence obtained in violation of its commands. . . . [T]he use of the fruits of a past unlawful search or seizure 'works no new Fourth Amendment wrong,' [citations omitted]."[46] All that is left is "a judicially created remedy designed to safeguard against future violations of Fourth Amendment rights through the rule's general deterrent effect."[47]

If that's all the exclusionary rule has become, then the Court has no business enforcing it. It is a purely legislative function.

Similarly, Congress should be free to overrule the exclusionary rule. Several attempts have been made, but, as yet, no reversal of the exclusionary rule has passed Congress. This is an illustration of a principle explored below in the chapters on civil rights: a right created by the Courts, that would never have passed Congress, nevertheless stays because Congress also lacks the majority to repeal it. The congressional attempts that have happened so far have been limited to creating a statutory good faith exception for warrantless searches, to go along with the exception recognized in *Leon* for good faith searches with a deficient warrant.[48] Several states have adopted precisely this kind of exception.[49]

Congress did, however, pass a law reversing *Miranda v. Arizona,*[50] and the U.S. Supreme Court's reaction to that law, in *Dickerson v. United States,*[51] tells us that severing a rule from its constitutional premises does not, necessarily, invite Congress to enter the field. Under the Fifth Amendment, once a confession is deemed to be coerced, its exclusion from use in the criminal trial of the person who made it is automatic. So, the exclusionary rule kind of question arises earlier, as to whether a confession is conclusively presumed to be coerced if not made in accordance with *Miranda*. Many confessions not given with *Miranda* warnings have nevertheless been admitted, starting with the exception in *Harris v. New York* to impeach the defendant's own testimony. Hence, it was impossible for the Court, in reviewing a criminal conviction based on a voluntary but non-*Miranda*-ized confession, to ignore the fact that the lower court had good grounds to suspect *Miranda* was not constitutionally compelled and thus could be altered by Congress.

This case therefore turns on whether the Miranda Court announced a constitutional rule or merely exercised its supervisory authority to regulate evidence in the absence of congressional direction. . . . Relying on the fact that we have created several exceptions to Miranda's warnings requirement and that we have repeatedly referred to the Miranda warnings as "prophylactic," . . . and "not themselves rights protected by the Constitution," the Court of Appeals concluded that the protections announced in Miranda are not constitutionally required.[52]

Nevertheless, the Court pointed to the fact that *Miranda* had been applied to the states to show that it was, indeed, constitutionally compelled. No attempt was made to square this with *Evans's* repudiation of the exclusionary rule's constitutional base. The exceptions to *Miranda*, the Court explained, were natural modifications to a general rule that developed in a common law way as the courts gained experience with the rule. By itself, this is quite an acceptable example of the judicial branch mechanism and advantage: to proceed through experience to refinements of a general rule of common law or constitutional law. What is less acceptable, as Justice Scalia's dissent points out, is to be disingenuous about earlier rulings that had quite clearly stated *Miranda* was not constitutionally compelled.[53]

Today, the exclusionary rule is still part of Fourth Amendment law but not constitutionally compelled. How it can apply to the states, therefore, remains a mystery. The *Miranda* holding, that a custodial confession is conclusively coerced unless warnings are given, is constitutionally compelled. However, evidence derived from an un-*Miranda*-ized confession might not have to be excluded.[54]

This is a poor state of affairs. The virtue of the judiciary is to rule by accretion, attempting to the maximum extent possible to reconcile new rulings with old, so as to achieve the reality, and convey the impression, of consistency. Such consistency is the check against arbitrary use of power. Legislative decisions, by contrast, are permitted to change overnight and sometimes do: the ballot box serves as the check to control the exercise of legislative power other than in the public interest.

The Court is master of finding and defining constitutional rights. The Court must move by category, announcing a rule that fits the case before it but seemingly of general applicability lest it be thought to be deciding a matter out of favoritism to one of the parties pleading the case. Congress is master of words: it can propose a solution to any problem, so long as it doesn't violate the Constitution, after taking evidence on the question; and it can compose words that fit the exact problem and no other.

Into that scheme of what should be, however, there will occasionally be found the need for the Court to correct itself. It is not such a difficult task for Congress to correct itself; but, for the Court, it is. This, I believe, is really what happened over three decades in the area of the exclusionary rule.

In *Mapp*, after forty-seven years of a federal-only exclusionary rule, the Court decided in favor of an exclusionary rule for state courts as well. It rested its opinion on its interpretation of the Fourth Amendment. For a government agency, whether court or police officer, to take or to use evidence seized in violation of the Fourth Amendment was wrong. Similarly, in *Miranda* the Court ruled on the meaning of "compelled" in the Fifth Amendment. It held that, absent an advance warning, any testimony given in custody was compelled.

Each ruling proved to have unforeseen and undesirable outcomes. The Court attempted to adjust to these circumstances by carving out exceptions to the exclusionary rule and to its specific application in *Miranda*. Instead, the Court could have done so in terms of the constitutional premise that it had set out in *Mapp* and in *Miranda*; it would have been courtlike to define what constitutional rights are.

One such formulation might have been: There is a constitutional right against coerced testimony. Custodial confessions without warnings are inherently coercive. But this right can be waived by the defendant taking the witness stand or putting on a defense witness to say something contrary to the statement made in custody without warnings, in much the same way an evidentiary privilege can be waived. Barring such a waiver, the use, by any agency of government, of evidence obtained in violation of the Constitution, whether Fourth or Fifth Amendment, is illegal. Under this approach, *Miranda* was rightly decided. The confession was presumptively coerced, and there was no waiver.

The outcome in *New York v. Harris* would also have been the same. *New York v. Harris* used an attenuation analysis. There is a right not to have your home invaded by police without a warrant or your consent. However, not everything that chronologically follows thereafter causally flows from that in a legal sense. It is courtlike to decide causality questions of this nature.

Some cases would have to be decided differently. The exclusionary rule would have been applied in *Evans*, *Krull*, and *Leon*. It would have been subject to the waiver exception in *James*, as it was in *Harris v. New York* and *Walder*.

Adhering to the constitutional origin of the exclusionary rule, the Court could, with experience, nevertheless refine its statement of what the right is. That is the common law rule, and it is appropriately courtlike to do so in constitutional law as well. The key that preserved the Court's inherent right to act, and its inherent advantages, is that it is keeping to what the Constitution compels. When Congress tries to undo what the Court holds the Constitution compels, it is the act of Congress that must fall. *Dickerson v. United States* was rightly decided under this approach.[55]

An alternative path would have been for the Court to reverse *Mapp* and *Miranda* soon after they were decided. Then every subsequent case would have come out the way it did, with the exception of *James* and *Dickerson*. Whether or not that is good constitutional law, it would have been honest adherence to the Court's functional responsibilities and advantages.

The Court, however, did not follow either path. Instead, it departed quickly from the only premise that gave legitimacy to its having entered these topics in the first place: that the Constitution compelled it to do so. It set about claiming to do what a legislature does: to weigh interests against each other, without any of the legislature's inherent advantages—notably, commissioning studies and drafting a solution adapted to the exact problem at hand.

In reality, it did not even do this. The "weighing" process was rigged from the start, to denigrate the constitutional right,[56] with the Court often saying it was doing so because there was no constitutional grounding for the right.

In the *Miranda* context, Congress called the Court on what it had been doing. Congress said to the Court, since you're doing a legislative act, we should be able to do it as well or better. The Court resented the intrusion. It returned to the one unassailable defense it had: that it was defining constitutional rights. This, however, was a defense poorly chosen to explain all the exceptions to the *Miranda* rule that the Court had fostered over thirty-four years. It had been acting as a legislature, not a court, and its credibility suffered in attempting to reclaim its original courtlike posture while preserving all the legislative-like exceptions it had created to *Miranda*. Should the same challenge arise from Congress in the context of the Fourth Amendment exclusionary rule, the Court should yield—or reassert its constitutional role by repudiating the exceptions it created to the exclusionary rule over the last forty years it has been acting as a legislature.

NOTES

1. One of the provisions of a recent bill entitled the "Victims' Bill of Rights" compelled a trial judge to permit victims of a crime to be present for all testimony in court, despite the potential for affecting their own testimony. S.J. Res. 3, 106th Cong. (1999). The courtlike function of the trial judge is to determine in each case whether there is danger to the integrity of further testimony by permitting potential future witnesses to be present in court; in this legislation, Congress would take away the exercise of that judicial function. However, the right to a fair trial is a constitutional one; the victim's right to see the trial, however important socially, is an interest, not a constitutional right.

2. The Thirteenth Amendment, for one instance, prohibits slavery, whether or not there is any governmental involvement.

3. See *Arizona v. Evans*, 514 U.S. 1 (1995). But cf. *Dickerson v. U.S.*, 530 U.S. 428, 429 (2000), calling *Miranda* a constitutional rule.

4. 367 U.S. 643 (1961).

5. 232 U.S. 383 (1914).

6. 367 U.S. at 648.

7. Id. at 655.

8. Id. at 657.

9. Id. at 656.

10. Id.

11. Id. citing *Elkins v. United States*, 364 U.S. 206, 217 (1960).

12. See, e.g., *Hadley v. Junior College District of Metropolitan Kansas City*, 397 U.S. 50 (1970); *Missouri v. Jenkins*, 515 U.S. 70 (1995); *Kadrmas v. Dickinson Public Schools*, 487 U.S. 450 (1988); and *Green v. New Kent County School Board*, 391 U.S. 430 (1968).

13. Legislatures may also engage in identifying constitutional rights; the Court, however, has the final word. See *City of Boerne v. Flores*, 521 U.S. 507 (1997).

14. 364 U.S. 206, 217 (1960).

15. 514 U.S. 1 (1995).

16. *Escobedo v. Illinois* 375 U.S. 902 (1963); *Miranda v. Arizona*, 384 U.S. 436 (1966).

17. 347 U.S. 62 (1954).

18. Only Justices Souter and O'Connor have been.

19. *New York v. Harris*, 495 U.S. 14 (1990), illustrates "attenuation analysis," a courtlike function that doesn't seek to weigh the value of deterring constitutional violations against other interests but limits itself to determining in a causal sense, with which courts have long dealt, whether the link between the constitutional violation and the introduction of evidence was too attenuated.

20. *Harris v. New York*, 401 U.S. 222 (1971); *U.S. v. Leon*, 468 U.S. 897 (1984); *Illinois v. Krull*, 480 U.S. 340 (1987); *James v. Illinois*, 493 U.S. 307 (1990); and *Arizona v. Evans*, 514 U.S. 1 (1995), are most illustrative.

21. Can a legislature? Yes; but will it? It would be wrong to assume it wouldn't,

that zeal for crime fighting would overcome all civil libertarian instincts among legislators and the people who elect them. A constitutional amendment to repeal the Fourth Amendment would not pass; it might not get a single vote. It is the height of presumption, in any event, to say that a court must make the decision of balancing between interests because the legislature cannot be trusted to do so.

It is entirely courtlike, however, to say that this is what the Fourth or Fifth Amendment means, and no general interest in crime control can overcome it. That is not a weighing process but a process of delineation of what a right is.

22. 401 U.S. 222 (1971).

23. Id. at 225.

24. Id. at 226. Justice Brennan tried to distinguish *Walder*, drawing on the difference between collateral impeachment and impeachment on a matter of the case-in-chief; however, his stronger argument is simply that the Constitution compels an exclusionary rule. "[I]t is monstrous that courts should aid or abet the law-breaking police officer." Id. at 232. This approach is courtlike: Justice Brennan is defining the nature of the right guaranteed, finding that the right against self-incrimination is guaranteed against any action by government—whether police officer or court.

25. *Stone v. Powell*, 428 U.S. 465 (1976).

26. *United States v. Calandra*, 414 U.S. 338 (1974).

27. *United States v. Janis*, 428 U.S. 433 (1976).

28. *Alderman v. United States*, 392 U.S. 919 (1968).

29. *James v. Illinois*, 493 U.S. 307 (1990).

30. The harmless error rule reflects the judgment that there is no valuable deterrent purpose to cause trial judges to be more careful by reversing them. *Arizona v. Fulminante* 499 U.S. 279 (1991).

31. *United States v. Leon*, 468 U.S. 897 (1984).

32. *Arizona v. Evans*, 514 U.S. 1 (1995).

33. *Illinois v. Krull*. The only former state legislator on the U.S. Supreme Court, Justice O'Connor, dissented, noting that, without an exclusionary rule that applied to searches conducted in accordance with a facially legal state law, legislators would continue to pass statutes authorizing unconstitutional searches. Would such a legislator be deterred by an exclusionary rule? It's possible. One situation would be if a campaign opponent plays up the civil liberties infringement, the legislator will have no offsetting criminal conviction to "compensate" for it.

The majority in *Krull* thought that an unlikely scenario.

It is possible, perhaps, that there are some legislators who, for political purposes, are possessed with a zeal to enact a particular unconstitutionally restrictive statute, and who will not be deterred by the fact that a court might later declare the law unconstitutional. But we doubt whether a legislator possessed with such fervor, and with such disregard for his oath to support the Constitution, would be significantly deterred by the possibility that the exclusionary rule would preclude the introduction of evidence in a certain number of prosecutions. Moreover, and of equal importance, just as we were not willing to assume in Leon that the possibility of magistrates' acting as "rubber stamps for police" was a problem of major proportions, . . . we are not willing to assume now that there exists a significant problem of legislators who perform their legislative duties with indifference to the constitutionality of the statutes they enact. If future empirical evidence ever should undermine that assumption, our conclusions may be revised accordingly. 480 U.S. at 352, n. 8.

This appeal to empirical evidence is remarkable. How can we imagine a court would come by such evidence? Would a trial judge, on a motion to suppress, invite both parties to submit live expert witnesses on the question whether legislators care or don't care about abiding by the Constitution? If not, would a judge canvass the available political science literature seeking for a study of this difficult subject? Finding such a study, should the judge then rely upon it or offer it to the parties for possible rebuttal? The practical difficulties of this suggestion point up that the court will, in truth, never have evidence causing it to rethink this assumption; and that's as it should be, since this is not evidence of the kind suited to fact-finding in the judicial sphere. The Court has not retreated from its reliance on social science literature, but a recent case has shown some change, for the better, in how it does so. In the affirmative action area, discussed in Chapter 8, dueling interpretations of the social science literature were available concerning the effects of minority participation upon classroom discussion. Compare *Grutter v. Bollinger*, 2003 U.S. Lexis 4800 at 37, 40, 41 (referring to the law school's own conclusions, the views of amici curiae, and the district court's findings) with 2003 U.S. Lexis 4800 at 128 (Thomas, J., dissenting, referring to additional social science literature). The majority finessed an outright comparison of competing social science literature by adopting a presumption in favor of the law school's findings. Id. at 38. Although such deference to a state agency is unprecedented in a case raising an equal protection challenge to a state's explicit use of race, the device is courtlike, unlike the intractable effort by a court to survey social science literature on its own as was done in the exclusionary rule cases discussed here. There is simply no process established in our judicial system to ensure that such a survey of social science literature is complete or even adversarial in the minimum sense that cross-examination of a live witness would guarantee.

34. *Arizona v. Evans*, 18 (Stevens, J., dissenting).

35. *United States v. Leon*, 907, n. 6, is particularly egregious on all these points.

Researchers have only recently begun to study extensively the effects of the exclusionary rule on the disposition of felony arrests. One study suggests that the rule results in the nonprosecution or nonconviction of between 0.6% and 2.35% of individuals arrested for felonies. Davies, A Hard Look at What We Know (and Still Need to Learn) About the "Costs" of the Exclusionary Rule: The NIJ Study and Other Studies of "Lost" Arrests, 1983 A. B. F. Res. J. 611, 621. The estimates are higher for particular crimes the prosecution of which depends heavily on physical evidence. Thus, the cumulative loss due to nonprosecution or nonconviction of individuals arrested on felony drug charges is probably in the range of 2.8% to 7.1%. Id., at 680. Davies' analysis of California data suggests that screening by police and prosecutors results in the release because of illegal searches or seizures of as many as 1.4% of all felony arrestees, id. at 650, that 0.9% of felony arrestees are released, because of illegal searches or seizures, at the preliminary hearing or after trial, id. at 653, and that roughly 0.05% of all felony arrestees benefit from reversals on appeal because of illegal searches. Id., at 654. See also K. Brosi, A Cross-City Comparison of Felony Case Processing 16, 18–19 (1979); U.S. General Accounting Office, Report of the Comptroller General of the United States, Impact of the Exclusionary Rule on Federal Criminal Prosecutions 10–11, 14 (1979); F. Feeney, F. Dill, & A. Weir, Arrests Without Convictions: How Often They Occur and Why 203–206 (National Institute of Justice 1983); National Institute of Justice, *The Effects of the Exclusionary Rule: A Study in California* 1–2 (1982); Nardulli, The Societal Cost of the Exclusionary Rule: An Empirical Assessment, 1983 A. B. F. Res. J. 585, 600. The exclusionary rule also has been found to affect the plea-bargaining process. S. Schlesinger, Exclusionary Injustice: The Problem of Illegally Obtained Evidence 63 (1977). But see Davies, supra, at 668–669; Nardulli, supra, at 604–606.

Many of these researchers have concluded that the impact of the exclusionary rule is insubstantial, but the small percentages with which they deal mask a large absolute number of felons who are released because the cases against them were based in part on illegal searches or seizures. "[A]ny rule of evidence that denies the jury access to clearly probative and reliable evidence must bear a heavy burden of justification, and must be carefully limited to the circumstances in which it will pay its way by deterring official unlawlessness." *Illinois v. Gates*, 462 U.S., at 257–258 (WHITE, J., concurring in judgment). Because we find that the rule can have no substantial deterrent effect in the sorts of situations under consideration in this case, see *infra*, at 916–921, we conclude that it cannot pay its way in those situations.

Suppose Justice White was right—that the exclusionary rule results in, say, 1,000 arrestees going free. That conclusion is based on an *average*. However, the question in *Leon* was whether there should be a new exception to the exclusionary rule. That calls for a *marginal* statistic. If the new exception would result in 900 of the 1,000 no longer going free, presumably Justice White would favor it more than if it would only prevent 10 from going free. Yet none of his statistics speak to that question. Further, we should only count an arrestee not going free as a good thing if we know the arrestee was guilty or if we know the newly permitted evidence was reliable. We know neither a priori.

36. 468 U.S. at 943 (Brennan, J. dissenting).

37. 493 U.S. 307 (1990).

38. Id. at 318–19. There is no citation of any authority for this; but I would criticize it if there were—for the gathering of the kind of evidence to sustain

such a conclusion is the legislature's responsibility and comparative advantage.

39. The balance had to be "cooked," because of its inherent intractability. Suppose, for example, that it were shown that nine out of ten times the police could get adequate information otherwise; would that be enough to render an exclusionary rule always preferable? What consideration should be taken of police resources? Other evidence might have been available, but at what cost in hours, money, and police officers' safety?

40. Justice Brennan uses another remarkable generalization: that witnesses' testimony is likely to be more truthful than defendants (an arguable proposition), and from that he concludes witnesses' testimony is so inherently truthful that the truth-finding process would not be advanced by impeachment evidence. 493 U.S. at 316.

41. 493 U.S. at 316–18. This is also an empirical conclusion, with no support, either as to the predilections of police to engage in illegal searches or as to the number of times illegally obtained evidence is useful in impeaching nondefendant witnesses.

42. Justice Brennan continued to protest that the exclusionary rule was constitutionally compelled; he might have justified his lapse into "balancing" in *James* as necessary to round up a majority. However, he should have offered his own constitutionally based view in a concurrence in that case and allowed another member of the majority to write the opinion that purported to do the balancing. The danger of the way he proceeded was that it gave legitimacy to a function that Justice Brennan himself considered inappropriate for the Court to have undertaken.

43. *United States v. Leon*, 911, n. 7 ("'Where there is a close causal connection between the illegal seizure and the confession, not only is exclusion of the evidence more likely to deter similar police misconduct in the future, but use of the evidence is more likely to compromise the integrity of the courts.' Dunaway v. New York, 442 U.S., at 217–18 [citation omitted].")

44. *New York v. Harris* traced through the line of causation between a *Miranda*-ized confession that was introduced at trial and the fact that the defendant was arrested at home by officers who lacked a warrant (thus violating *Payton v. New York*, 445 U.S. 573 [1980]) but had probable cause. Instead of balancing the risk that allowing the confession would create an inducement for future *Payton* violations against the gain from having the confession before the jury (a balance to which the answer could have been predicted to be yes), Justice White much more simply asked about the causal link between the police officers' error and the testimony. Since there was probable cause, the police officers would have arrested Harris anyway, once he left his home. His confession was *Miranda*-ized. No one alleged it was coerced. The evidence sought to be excluded, therefore, did not really flow from the constitutional violation of entering his home.

Obviously, this kind of reasoning won't be available in many cases; but it was available here, and it was an improvement that the Court followed this approach. It is a courtlike analysis, drawing on rules of causality and attenuation familiar to tort law. It does not purport to balance one interest against another, which is the legislature's job, but to connect outcomes to acts of legal consequence, a quintessentially judicial function.

45. Under Eighth Amendment jurisprudence, a court might similarly take a judicial integrity approach, outlawing those punishments the imposition of which would bring contempt upon the judiciary. Certain methods of search could also be deemed unreasonable under so generous a rationale like this. Cf. *Rochin v. California*, 342 U.S. 165 (1952).

46. *Arizona v. Evans*, 10.

47. Id.

48. See, e.g., Crime Bill of 1990, *Cong. Rec.* H9022 (October 15, 1990). See also Exclusionary Rule Reform Act of 1995, H.R. 666, 101st Cong. (1990).

49. See, e.g., Ariz. Rev. Stat. § 13-3925 (1993); and Colo. Rev. Stat. § 16-3-308 (1994).

50. 18 U.S.C. § 3501 (establishing a rule of voluntariness rather than requiring advance warnings for a custodial confession to be admissible). See *Dickerson v. United States*.

51. 530 U.S. 428 (2000).

52. Id. at 437.

53. Id. at 444 (Scalia, J., dissenting).

54. *Ex parte Banks*, 769 S.W.2d 539 (Tex. Crim. App., 1989), rev'd sub nom. *Banks v. Cockrell*, 48 Fed. Appx. 104 (5th Cir., 2002), rev'd on other grounds sub nom. *Banks v. Dretke*, 124 S.Ct. 1256 (2004).

55. Congress might have tried a different statute. If Congress had adopted a set of alternative warnings, it would have been responding to the invitation in *Miranda*, not contravening it.

56. In *James v. Illinois*, the weighing was rigged from the start the other way.

Affirmative Action: The Use
of Race by Government

WHEN CAN RACE be used by government in America? In the controlling opinion in *University of California Regents v. Bakke*,[1] Justice Powell proposed that a lower than strict standard of review might be appropriate in cases where there had been a "determination by the legislature or a responsible administrative agency that the University engaged in a discriminatory practice requiring remedial efforts."[2] However, there had been no such finding by the legislature or the executive with regard to the University of California's medical school at Davis. Applying the higher strict standard, he found that it had not been met in the case before the Court but that "obtaining the educational benefits that flow from an ethnically diverse student body" might qualify in another case.[3] None of the other asserted benefits,[4] even if proved, would suffice to meet the higher standard.

The question was left open whether findings by a political branch suffice to justify the use of race. The next case to come before the Court on affirmative action dealt with "findings" by private parties. In *Steelworkers v. Weber*,[5] the Court held that a labor union and employer could, under the aegis of Title VII, adopt an affirmative action plan to remedy the history of discrimination they themselves observed in their own behavior. Such private-party action, of course, did not involve Fifth or Fourteenth Amendment standards, but it did occasion a search for congressional intent in the 1964 Civil Rights Act, which applied (in Title VII) to private parties and was at issue in *Bakke* through Title VI (applying to recipients of federal assistance). In upholding the use of race, essentially by consent of the parties, the Court might have been ready to signal that, a fortiori, a branch of government could justify the use of race. The question came to the fore the next year, in *Fullilove v. Klutznick*,[6] where the Court in 1980 held the Constitution did not bar Congress from authorizing the use of race in federal contracts. The Court did not even apply strict scrutiny, deferring to the congressional determination as that of a "co-equal branch."[7] Seven years later, however, the Court refused to extend the same deference to a unit of state government. A county had to make a much more specific finding of its own discriminatory past regarding the groups now favored,[8] and a city would, likewise, have a heavy burden to meet of showing its own discriminatory past.[9] Within six years, the deference given to Congress in its use of race was almost completely taken away,[10] and all political branches, state or federal, appeared suspect in their use of race.

Federal courts, of course, could order race-specific action by state and local governments as remedies to findings of constitutional violations.[11] This was quite different from a unit of state, federal, or local government confessing its own past wrongdoing and then proposing to fix it by race-conscious action. Under a court's supervision—even in a consent decree—a factual basis had to be established that the past discrimination in fact happened and that its consequences could be remedied by the proposed decree. Without a court's supervision, neither need be there. That is, legislatures or executives could "confess" to a discriminatory past and propose race-conscious remedies to seek modern political advantage—even if there were no such past or no monitoring of the proposed remedy to stay within the bounds of correcting that past. That possibility was rife with potential political use of race.

This was the suspicion motivating the Supreme Court's opinion in *City of Richmond v. J. A. Croson Co.*,[12] written by Justice O'Connor, the only justice to have been a state legislator, showing the same suspicion of legislative actions she showed in *Illinois v. Krull*:[13] "Absent searching judicial inquiry into the justification for such race-based measures, there is simply no way of determining what classifications are 'benign' or 'remedial' and what classifications are in fact motivated by illegitimate notions of racial inferiority or simple racial politics."[14]

Richmond had fallen far short of proving the need to remedy past racial discrimination. The Court singled out as particularly vulnerable the 30 percent set-aside as imprecise.[15] The seeming breadth of *Bakke's* dictum had now been cut back: there, a finding "by the legislature or a responsible administrative agency" of past discrimination might have justified less than strict scrutiny. Now, the Court was applying strict scrutiny to just such a finding. "Reliance on the disparity between the number of prime contracts awarded to minority firms and the minority population of the city of Richmond is similarly misplaced."[16] This was because the contracts required particular skills and experiences, which should not be assumed to be present in all racial communities in the same proportion each bore to the general population.

However valid that might be as a basis to reject a prima facie showing under Title VII, that would not have been a valid basis for rejecting the 30 percent set-aside under minimal scrutiny. Suppose the city simply wanted to increase the percentage of contracts going to minorities. Whether or not 30 percent was the proper end-number, it was an entirely rational number to use to get to the end of increased minority percentage. With a black population of 50 percent,[17] a 30 percent set-aside ran some, but no logically absolute, risk of overshooting the target.

Hence, *Croson* (and *Johnson v. Transportation Agency of Santa Clara County, California*)[18] was a major repudiation of the role of local governments in authorizing the use of race. There is reason to believe the Court's repudiation would today apply to Congress.[19] Certainly, *Adarand Constructors, Inc. v. Pena* announced a strict, not minimal, level of scrutiny to congressional set-asides.[20]

The key to the current state of the law, and the structural analysis I am attempting in this book, is Justice O'Connor's use of the phrase "racial politics," a concept that would apply equally to federal and state legislatures. The use of race is, quite literally, suspect. She noted that the Richmond City Council included five black council members out of nine.[21] Racial politics is not only helping one's own race, it's using race to curry votes; and half the population of Richmond was black. Dean John Hart Ely's general approach was quoted: to defer to decisions made by groups capable of representing themselves in the political process but to suspect such decisions disadvantaging other races, "Of course it works both ways: a law that favors Blacks over Whites would be suspect if it were enacted by a predominantly Black legislature."[22]

In *Grutter v. University of Michigan*, Justice O'Connor returned to this posture of suspicion, even as she upheld the University of Michigan law school's affirmative action plan. She repeated her language from *Croson* about the fear of racial politics and added, "Strict scrutiny is designed to provide a framework for carefully examining the importance and the *sincerity* of the reasons advanced by the governmental decision-maker for the use of race in that particular context."[23] Her degree of deference, however, was markedly greater for the law school at the

University of Michigan than it was for the city council of Richmond. "The Law School's educational judgment that such diversity is essential to its education mission is one to which we defer. . . . Our holding today is in keeping with our tradition of giving a degree of deference to a university's academic decisions, within constitutionally prescribed limits. See Regents of Univ. of Mich. v. Ewing, . . . Board of Curators of the Univ. of Mo. v. Horowitz . . . ; Bakke."[24] In fact, the degree of deference was unprecedented in any of those cited opinions. *Ewing*[25] and *Horowitz*[26] upheld pedagogical decisions challenged on procedural due process grounds. Neither *Ewing* nor *Horowitz* granted a university the right to make a distinction challengeable on equal protection grounds. Had the student in *Ewing* claimed that only students of his race had been denied the right to retake a test or the student in *Horowitz* claimed that only students of her race had been failed on the clinical component of medical school, there is absolutely nothing in those opinions to suggest the Court would have granted deference to those university decisions, but instead the Court would in all likelihood have applied the highest standard of scrutiny. And as to *Bakke*, the Court's holding actually overturned a university's decision; it was only in dicta that the Court referred to deference, and none of the cases cited in *Bakke* for that proposition involved the explicit use of race by an agency of state government.

The special deference granted to a university in *Grutter* has two possible sources. The first is a quasi–First Amendment status to university decisions regarding how academic discussion is to be conducted, which other agencies of government might not enjoy. The second is the insulation of a state university from the temptation of racial politics.

On the first point, "The freedom of a university to make its own judgments as to education includes the selection of its student body," Justice Powell opined in *Bakke*, and Justice O'Connor quoted in *Grutter*.[27] The immediately preceding language in *Bakke* was: "The fourth goal asserted by the petition is the attainment of a diverse student body. This clearly is a constitutionally permissible goal for an institution of higher education. Academic freedom, though not a specifically enumerated constitutional right, long has been viewed as a special concern of the First Amendment."[28]

In referring to the First Amendment rights of the university, Justices Powell and O'Connor assume that an agency of state government itself can possess First Amendment rights, and they hold that the exercise of those rights includes not only the right to speak but the right to choose the racial composition of the speakers. It is helpful for defenders of affirmative action to make this extension from a public policy interest to a constitutionally protected right. The person who does not receive the affirmative action at a state university has a constitutional claim—that the government denied him or her a benefit based on his or her race. No mere interest, or value, espoused by the state or federal government could overcome such a claim; only a compelling state interest, or a competing constitutional principle, could. In *Bakke*, Justice Powell tried to escape this by denying the plaintiff had suffered a constitutional deprivation;[29] in *Grutter*, Justice O'Connor found that, even granting a constitutional deprivation, the state interest was compelling. Both justices also found it helpful to rely upon the quasi-constitutional First Amendment interest of the state.

There is deference granted here to a state university that would be granted to no other agency of government. Justice O'Connor goes on to say, "Our conclusion that the Law School has a compelling interest in a diverse student body is informed by our view that attaining a diverse student body is at the heart of the Law School's proper institutional mission, and that 'good faith' on the part of a university is 'presumed' absent 'a showing to the contrary' [citing *Bakke*]."[30] The "proper institutional mission" of a state university is to craft terms of academic discussion; that would not be true of the other governmental actors with which the affirmative action cases have dealt (for example, a city council or Congress).

As for the presumption of good faith, the citation to *Bakke*, on which Justice O'Connor relies for this proposition, proves how path-breaking this proposition is. Justice Powell's statement about presuming good faith cites three cases: *Arlington Heights v. Metropolitan Housing Development Corporation*,[31] *Washington v. Davis*,[32] and *Swain v. Alabama*.[33] None of these cases, however, dealt with the explicit use of race. *Arlington Heights* permitted zoning with racial impact but no proved racial discriminatory intent; *Davis* upheld a police academy exam with disparate impact in the absence of proof of intent; and *Swain* (since overturned)[34] upheld a prosecutor's use of preemptory challenges that excluded jury members of the defendant's race where the defendant had failed to prove discriminatory intent. Each case was explicitly decided on the basis that intentional use of race had *not* been shown. These cases' ability to support the proposition, therefore, that deference is entitled to a state university's *intentional* use of race is limited in the extreme. It is fairer to say that Justice Powell had no authority for his proposition that state agencies are entitled to deference in a decision to use race; and Justice O'Connor had no authority other than Justice Powell's dictum.

So, it must be the fact that the affirmative action was practiced not by just any state agency but by a state university that is significant—because of the quasi–First Amendment nature of a university's control over discourse on campus.

The second basis on which a state university might be treated differently for the purpose of making use of race has to do with the temptation to racial politics, on which Justice O'Connor premised so much of her concern in *Croson*. Let me begin a contrast between the use of race by a university regarding admissions and the use of race by a legislature with an example from my own experience in the latter context.

In 1994, California expanded its minority contract set-aside program to include Portuguese and Iberian Peninsula Spanish. The bill was introduced by a state senator of Portuguese American ancestry.[35] The state senate passed the bill with every Democratic vote and two Republican votes. I asked one of the two Republicans why he voted as he did, and he replied that he had many Portuguese American dairy farmers in his district. I asked the other, and she replied that she anticipated running for statewide office. In debate on the state senate floor, I quoted *Croson*'s requirement for a finding of past discrimination. I asked the bill's sponsor if there had been any study done documenting that Portuguese Americans had been excluded from state contracts in California. He replied that an appropriate impact study could be done—once the bill passed.[36]

From this personally observed episode, I offer some validation of Justice O'Connor's suspicion. The political branches will be greatly tempted to use race for political advantage if permitted to do so. And it was difficult to call this use of race benign. The inclusion of Portuguese Americans in California set-asides actually took away benefits from African Americans, Native Americans, and New World Hispanic-Americans, since the total number of contracts available for affirmative action remained the same.

What governmental decision-maker might be relatively immune to such temptation to use race to further electoral politics? A federal court is one; a university might be another.

The advantages of the federal judiciary in making use of race are two: insulation from politics and experience with monitoring remedies. Let us focus on the second and contrast how a court would oversee the use of race until a specific objective is achieved (as they did in so many school-busing decrees), as opposed to how a legislature would act. When affirmative action is placed into a statute, it need have no natural termination date. Some subsequent legislature might repeal it, but there's no requirement to do so. Indeed, the effort to repeal a racially based preference would always be construable by a political opponent as evidence of discriminatory intent against the racial group favored by the preference—even if it had long since achieved its goal. I know of no racial preference set in statute that has subsequently been repealed by a legislature. By contrast, a court, in administering a remedy, will constantly take evidence on whether it is having the desired effect. Eventually, its time will run out.

When there has not been an actual finding of discrimination, however, a court is ill suited to determine when the time for the remedy is at an end. But the majority in *Grutter* felt the need to create some such closure; hence, the statement by Justice O'Connor that "race-conscious admissions policies must be limited in time. . . . In the context of higher education, the durational requirement can be met by sunset provisions in race-conscious admissions policies and periodic reviews to determine whether racial preferences are still necessary to achieve student body diversity. . . . We expect that 25 years from now, the use of racial preferences will no longer be necessary to further the interest approved today."[37]

A court is institutionally inclined, and structurally equipped, to monitor remedial measures, following a finding of actual discrimination. If Justice O'Connor's words were not pure dicta, she was holding that, to avoid violating the Constitution, Michigan's affirmative action would have to have some similar kind of monitoring device like a sunset clause. In fact, the university's plan had no such provision for when it would phase out, so Justice O'Connor imposed one of her own making. It is a fascinating hybrid: the Court deferred to the University of Michigan for the fact-finding that affirmative action was a compelling necessity, but it imposed its own time limit in a manner more typically connected with judicial monitoring of a remedy in a lawsuit. It attempted to use a courtlike function to limit a legislative-like finding.

It was also inappropriate. The Court's function is to say whether an affirmative action plan, at the time of its challenge, is constitutional. In suggesting a sunset clause, the Court was acting as though it were reviewing a lower court's imposition of a remedial decree, when there had been no lower court judicial finding of a law violation. Rather, the findings were all made by the University of Michigan. The Court had no business guessing what those findings might be in the year 2028.[38] The Court should simply have said, "The fact that today we uphold the University of Michigan's judgment that educational diversity requires affirmative action is no prediction that we will do so should subsequent challenges be brought under different circumstances."

The twenty-five-year issue should not obscure the important point, however, that the Court recognized another branch of government could make findings on which the explicit use of race could be based. The University of Michigan's findings of educational benefit were allowed to justify a continuing use of race unmonitored by a court (at least until twenty-five years have passed). The *Grutter* Court grants a presumption of good faith to those findings and a huge amount of deference to how the University of Michigan law school chooses to act upon those findings.

There is a useful point to be observed here between what the University of Michigan can do and how a court could act in applying affirmative action in a remedial setting. In a remedy case, a court would make the finding of wrong and then determine how much affirmative use of race would be sufficient, and for how long, to undo it. By contrast, in the absence of a finding of wrong, a court would be at sea in determining how much affirmative action is appropriate.[39]

The branch of government most able to judge the educational value of the diversity of the student body is the university itself, and, structurally, it is the more appropriate agency of government to implement what it decides. In some state constitutions, the state university is virtually its own branch of government. In California, for instance, the independence of the university is constitutionally mandated.[40] Its management is given to a board of regents, selected by the governor and confirmed by the state senate, for terms of such extraordinary length[41] as to underline the framers' desire to insulate regents from politics once appointed. The legislature votes on the overall budget of the university but may not dictate any line item.

Such a structure lends itself to deference. There is insulation from the temptation to use race for political purposes,[42] the fear identified by Justice O'Connor in *Croson*. There is a decision on educational effect to be made by those whose only governmental role is an educational one: to administer the state university. Structurally, therefore, the politically insulated state university might be trusted with the choices involving the use of race.

This, plus the quasi–First Amendment nature of the decision about whom to admit, qualifies state universities as governmental actors with significantly different characteristics than any other government agencies attempting to use race. Complete deference is not appropriate; the Court's striking down of the Virginia Military Institute's (VMI) all-male admission rule demonstrated that, as the dissent of Justice Thomas, in which Justice Scalia joined, in *Grutter* observed.[43] The governing board of VMI, however, had adopted an absolute prohibition: in that sense, it was like UC-Davis in *Bakke*, and, deference or no, an absolute prohibition on the basis of race, or gender, would not be permitted. But in judging a system of relative preference, the insulation from electoral politics and the quasi–First Amendment nature of the enterprise constitute a sufficient answer to Justice Scalia's question in *Grutter*: if deference to the University of Michigan is appropriate, why not deference to some racial preference in the Michigan civil service system?[44] A state university *is* different from another agency of state government.

In sum, race is a dangerous factor in American government. The inherent advantage of a court is to limit the use of race to the achievement of a specific remedial goal, premised upon a specific finding of fact, and then to stop. The use of race for broader purposes has been attempted by Congress, state legislatures, local governments, and state universities. Congress does not bear the stigma of the Fourteenth Amendment's mistrust of the states on racial matters, but the Supreme Court has all but eviscerated that distinction. All elected political branches, to which judgments of policy are normally entrusted, are potentially flawed by the attraction and salience of racial politics.

The implication of the structural analysis developed in this chapter is to limit any governmental use of race to (1) a court supervising, and eventually eliminating, a remedial decree addressed to correcting a specific racial imbalance caused by a law violation, or (2) an agency of government uniquely insulated from electoral politics and enjoying a claim of right to consider race that draws from another provision of the Constitution. So far, only state universities, claiming First Amendment privilege, have been held to qualify in the latter category.

NOTES

1. 438 U.S. 265 (1978).

2. Id. at 305. This possible category was left untouched in *Grutter v. Bollinger*, 2003 U.S. Lexis 4800, and *Gratz v. Bollinger*, 2003 U.S. Lexis 4801.

3. The California Supreme Court, in *Bakke*, had ruled that race could not be used to justify the affirmative action program at UC-Davis. It would have sur-

prised that court to learn that a state interest as seemingly weak as the "educational benefits" that flow from a racially diverse student body would be sufficient to withstand strict scrutiny. Indeed, Justice Powell himself did not find that interest sufficient at UC-Davis to justify the use of race as a determinative factor; it was only powerful enough to defend the use of race as one factor among others.

No other justice joined Justice Powell in that determination: that race was permitted as one factor but not the determining factor. Four justices held that the remedial nature was enough to defend the use of race by the state; four others held that Title VI of the 1964 Civil Rights Act barred affirmative action by the university. So only Justice Powell held that a little use of race was permissible but a lot wasn't. The Harvard plan was attached as an appendix to Justice Powell's opinion as an example of how race could be used as a "plus factor," so long as it was not determinative.

This distinction is vacuous. If one student of a favored minority race is admitted and another functionally equivalent student, but of a disfavored minority or majority race, is not, then the "plus factor" has become the determining factor. If both would be admitted anyway, or neither would be admitted anyway, there is no discrimination to attract the Court's attention. In *Bakke*, eight of the nine justices failed to follow Justice Powell's formulation: four because it wasn't necessary (remedial intent being sufficient to uphold affirmative action), four because it wasn't persuasive (as against Title VI's explicit prohibition on discriminating based on race).

In *Grutter*, seven of the nine justices would similarly not grant the distinction between using race a little and using race a lot to achieve diversity in higher education. Four justices dissented in *Grutter* and joined the majority in *Gratz*, holding that diversity was not a compelling state interest (no matter how it was accomplished). Three justices dissented in *Gratz*, two holding that, since diversity was a compelling state interest, the University of Michigan was within its rights to use a point system in its undergraduate school to do so, and one (Justice Stevens) holding the plaintiffs lacked standing. Only Justice O'Connor explicitly embraced the distinction between *Gratz* and *Grutter*: that diversity is a compelling state interest when used as part of a particularized inquiry in law school admissions but not when used to grant 20 out of 150 points in a college admissions program. (Justice Breyer appeared to agree with her. *Gratz v. Bollinger*, 67–68.)

We might be condemned to repeat history. Twenty-five years of *Bakke* brought great controversy in deciding how much use of race by government was acceptable and how much was too much—an enterprise engendered by the opinion of only one justice. Another twenty-five years have now been announced in *Grutter*, during which affirmative action will be allowed to continue but only in a subjective, not objective, calculus—an enterprise engendered by the opinion of only two justices.

4. The Court listed "(i) 'reducing the historic deficit of traditionally disfavored minorities in medical schools and in the medical profession'; (ii) counter-

ing the effects of societal discrimination; [and] (iii) increasing the number of physicians who will practice in communities currently underserved" as the three other justifications proffered by the university that were not accepted by the Court. 438 U.S. at 306.

5. 443 U.S. 193 (1979).

6. 448 U.S. 448, 476 (1980).

7. Id. at 472. See characterization of the *Fullilove* majority opinion in *City of Richmond v. J. A. Croson Co.*, 488 U.S. 469, 477 (1989).

8. *Johnson v. Transportation Agency, Santa Clara County, California*, 480 U.S. 616 (1987).

9. *Richmond v. J. A. Croson Co.*

10. *Adarand Constructors, Inc. v. Pena*, 515 U.S. 200, 217 (1995). This came after a brief reaffirmance of an easier standard for congressional use of race in *Metro Broadcasting, Inc. v. FCC*, 497 U.S. 547 (1990), a position the *Adarand* Court characterized as "a surprising turn." 515 U.S. at 225.

11. This was the rationale for the school desegregation cases. See *Green v. County School Board*, 391 U.S. 430 (1968), and discussion in *Bakke* at 305.

12. 488 U.S. 469 (1989).

13. 480 U.S. 340 (1987). See discussion in Chapter 7.

14. 488 U.S. at 493.

15. "The 30% quota cannot in any realistic sense be tied to any injury suffered by anyone." 469 U.S. at 499.

16. 488 U.S. at 469.

17. Id. at 495.

18. 480 U.S. 616 (1987).

19. Indeed, following *Croson* and *City of Boerne v. Flores*, 521 U.S. 507 (1997), it would be hard to defend the *Fullilove* outcome today. *Boerne* held the proposed use of congressional authority under the fifth clause of the Fourteenth Amendment had to be "congruent" and "proportional" to the Court's own interpretation of the constitutional right in question. How could 10 percent be ruled to be congruent and proportionate to a constitutional violation Congress supposedly found? If 10 percent was proportionate, would 20 percent have been? If so, what does "proportionate" mean?

20. 515 U.S. 200, 217 (1995).

21. 469 U.S. at 495.

22. 488 U.S. at 496, quoting J. Ely, "The Constitutionality of Reverse Racial Discrimination," 41 *U. Chi. L. Rev.* 723, 739, n. 58 (1974).

23. 2003 U.S. Lexis 4800 at 34, 36 (emphasis added).

24. Id. at 37–38 (citations omitted).

25. *Regents of Univ. of Mich. v. Ewing*, 474 U.S. 214 (1985).

26. *Board of Curators of the Univ. of Mo. v. Horowitz*, 435 U.S. 78 (1978).

27. *Bakke*, 312, quoted in *Grutter v. Bollinger*, 39.

28. 438 U.S. at 312.

29. To avoid this consequence, Justice Powell attempted to distinguish the claim of Alan Bakke—the student excluded from the UC-Davis medical

school's fifteen slots reserved for minorities—from those of others excluded by affirmative action plans like Harvard's, which included race as a factor but had no absolute number of set-asides. Alan Bakke was denied equal protection because he was white, Justice Powell reasoned, but the student rejected by Harvard was not. Scales applied with a racial thumb against an applicant did not implicate a constitutional right; being barred from the scales entirely did. Sophistic as the distinction was, Justice Powell had to embrace it since there were not five votes for the proposition that diversity alone was a compelling state interest. He had to water down the excluded majority race student's claim to below constitutional intensity. In *Grutter*, by contrast, five justices found that higher educational diversity was a compelling state interest, sufficient to overcome the plaintiff's constitutional claim.

30. *Grutter v. Bollinger*, 39.

31. 429 U.S. 252 (1977).

32. 426 U.S. 229 (1976).

33. 380 U.S. 202 (1965).

34. See *Batson v. Kentucky*, 476 U.S. 79 (1986).

35. SB 1426 (introduced February 8, 1994).

36. The quote is from memory; no transcript was kept of floor debates in the California State Senate at the time I served there.

37. *Grutter v. Bollinger*, 61, 62, 64.

38. Justice Thomas holds Justice O'Connor to this twenty-five-year maximum by his explicit "Concurrence in part," characterizing her statement as a holding that only an affirmative action plan of less than twenty-five years' duration from 2003 would be constitutional. "I agree with the Court's holding that racial discrimination in higher education admissions will be illegal in 25 years." *Grutter v. Bollinger*, 105. I cannot agree that it is a holding. How could it be, when the facts of the University of Michigan Law School as of 2028 were not before the Court? Justice Thomas's tactic, however, highlights the inappropriate, nonjudicial nature of this part of the majority opinion.

39. This is demonstrated by the intractable distinction the Court's two opinions make. It is hard to see how a court, in a remediation case, could order or administer a standard like the dual opinions in *Gratz* and *Grutter* dictate. *Grutter* holds that race can make the difference at the margin of law school admissions; but *Gratz* holds that race cannot be given 20 points out of 150 in considering college admissions. Justice Souter is right to complain, "Since college admission is not left entirely to inarticulate intuition, it is hard to see what is inappropriate in assigning some stated value to a relevant characteristic, whether it be reasoning ability, writing style, running speed, or minority race. Justice Powell's plus factors necessarily are assigned some values." *Gratz v. Bollinger*, 90. The deference announced in *Grutter* should extend to *Gratz* or else the deference should never have been extended in *Grutter*.

40. Cal. Const. art. IX, § 9(f).

41. Cal. Const. art. IX, § 9(b). (Eighteen regents serve twelve-year terms; seven regents serve ex officio; and a student regent serves a one-year term.)

42. The insulation is not complete. Regents can be (and some believe have been) denied confirmation by the state senate because of their policy views. In the same light, however, a nominee for a federal judgeship could be rejected by the U.S. Senate because of her or his policy views. The nomination and confirmation processes are inherently political. By insulation from politics, I mean during the term once chosen. Life tenure for federal judges goes as far as one can to guarantee that quality; twelve-year terms are a close second.

43. *Grutter v. Bollinger*, 131–32 (Thomas, J. dissenting), citing *United States v. Virginia*, 518 U.S. 515 (1996).

44. Id. at 100 (Scalia, J., with Thomas, J., dissenting).

The Fiesta Bowl: Unintended Consequences
of Judicial and Legislative Activism

THE INHERENT advantages of the executive branch include the decision when to prosecute or initiate other executive action. The Courts lack this power of initiative. Congress lacks the power to make its initiatives effective. A law may pass, but it is the executive who will decide whether to enforce it. This power to initiate action carries the negative power not to initiate, and, where there is no private right of action, the power not to initiate is absolute.[1]

In 1977, the federal Department of Education required Grove City College, a private college, to file a certificate of compliance with Title IX regulations regarding nondiscrimination on the basis of gender in any of the school's "programs" or "activities." There was no evidence that Grove City did, in fact, discriminate on the basis of gender. The Department of Education's demand was purely administrative. It wanted to have a certificate of compliance "on file." When the college refused, on principle, the department threatened to terminate the Basic Education Opportunity Grants (BEOGs) that its students had received. The students, and the college, sought relief from the federal courts. The question was whether the receipt of BEOGs by its students constituted a sufficient trigger to bring the college under the rules promulgated by the federal Department of Education.[2]

The U.S. Supreme Court ruled that it did. The words of the statute were:

Each Federal department and agency which is empowered to extend Federal financial assistance to any education program or activity, by way of grant, loan, or contract other than a contract of insurance or guaranty, is authorized and directed to effectuate the provisions of section [901] with respect to such program or activity by issuing rules, regulations or orders of general applicability.[3]

The Court held that indirect assistance through BEOGs to students constituted assistance to the college. However, the statute limited the means of ensuring compliance, to

the termination of or refusal to grant or to continue assistance under such program or activity to any recipient as to whom there has been an express finding on the record, after opportunity for hearing, of a failure to comply with such requirement, but such termination or refusal shall be limited to the particular political entity, or part thereof, or other recipient as to whom such a finding has been made, and shall be limited in its effect to the particular program or part thereof, in which such noncompliance has been so found.[4]

Here was a problem of drafting. The students received the BEOGs directly from the Department of Education. Where was the "program or activity"?

The college didn't get the check from the federal government, the students did; but they used some or all of the money for their education. Two outcomes were logical. The first would be to rule that the statutory scheme of BEOGs did not fit within Title IX, at least if the money went directly to the student rather than to the school. That was the district court's opinion.[5] The second was to say the entire school benefited from the BEOGs, hence, the entire school had to comply with Title IX, and compliance could be assured by threat of terminating the BEOGs to all the students. Though harsh on the students, it would give them an incentive not to go to Grove City College and, indirectly, put pressure on Grove City to comply with Title IX. That was the Third Circuit's approach.[6]

The Supreme Court chose something in between. It ruled that the admissions process at Grove City College, not the entire school, constituted the program or activity that received federal financial aid.[7] Hence, the admissions and financial aid office could be compelled to file a certificate about its own observance of the Title IX regulations. (Normally, Title IX violations are sought and found in programs, like sports, that are open to students differentially depending on their sex.) The compulsion was the cutoff of the BEOGs.

The middle ground sought by the Court had an apparent compassionate goal for schools like Grove City which, having chosen to minimize their interaction with the federal government, should suffer minimal intrusion into their affairs. But the Court, in attempting to fashion a middle ground for this situation, made a new rule that the statute did not anticipate. Either of the lower federal courts' opinions, by contrast, was consistent with what the statute said: find a recipient, threaten that recipient with cutoff of funds, and thereby compel that same recipient to follow the regulations. The district court said there is no program or activity receiving federal funds. The Third Circuit said the college is the program or activity receiving federal funds.

Instead, the Supreme Court said the admissions and financial aid program at Grove City, by receiving money even indirectly, constituted itself a program or activity that triggered Title IX. Hence, that office had to submit a certificate of compliance under Title IX with regard to its own activities; but no other part of the college did. If the admissions and financial aid office didn't comply, however, all BEOGs could be cut off.

This was illogical. The financial aid office did not receive a dime of federal money, at least not in more or less proportion than any other department of Grove City College. It was not the "program or activity" receiving financial assistance. The Court should have held, consistent with grammar as well as logic, that either the student or the college was the recipient. If the student, then the statute did not apply. If, however, the college was the "program or activity," then the entire college came under scrutiny. It made no sense to cut off all BEOGs, since they went to the college generally, yet hold that only the admissions and financial aid office came under Title IX's jurisdiction.

What makes this case of interest to our purposes here is what Congress did in response to the Court's ruling.

It is useful for a moment to consider the simplicity of what Congress might have done. It could simply have enacted a law to say: "If any student receives federal financial assistance to attend a college, that college is subjected to the requirements of Title IX and its regulations." That would have reversed the holding in *Grove City*, with no unanticipated collateral results.

Congress, however, was bent on making a political point against the Supreme Court. With correcting the Supreme Court as its goal, Congress considered it important for polemic purposes to use as much of the existing statutory structure as it could, simply "correcting" the Court's misinterpretation of the words "program or activity."[8]

In the Civil Rights Restoration Act of 1987, Congress said, "program or activity" means "all the operations of . . . a college, university, or other postsecondary institution, or a public system of higher education."[9] It was as though Congress was saying, "This is what we meant by 'program or activity' when we used the phrase in 1972 (Title IX) and 1964 (Title VI), as any court could plainly have seen, except a court biased against civil rights."

Instead of writing a new statute, Congress kept that part of the Supreme Court's holding in *Grove City College* with which it agreed, that receipt of scholarship funds could constitute a program or activity, and changed the part with which it didn't agree—that "program or activity" had a narrow meaning in terms of which branch of a college or university had to come under compliance.

When the Supreme Court had been willing to find a "program or activity" in the receipt of scholarship money, however, it contemplated that the consequences would be very narrow: this would serve as a trigger for federal supervision of the admissions and aid office. The receipt of scholarship money did not turn the terms of the scholarship itself into an appropriate subject for discrimination inquiry. But now Congress has used the same words, "program or activity," to encompass the terms of the scholarship itself and the entire school whose students received the scholarship. So, if a scholarship itself discriminated in some way, even if granted by a private source, the use of that scholarship by a student at a college or university would cause that institution to lose all its federal money. Literally, that's what the 1987 law did to Title IX of the 1972 Educational Amendments and Title VI of the 1964 Civil Rights Act.

That result would not have followed from *Grove City* alone. It's true the Court held that receipt of funds indirectly through students' scholarships turned the admissions and financial aid office into a program. But the only consequence was that the admissions and financial aid office would have to submit itself to the nondiscrimination rules of Title IX or Title VI. The Court did not subject the scholarships (in *Grove City*, BEOGs) to discrimination scrutiny. That distinction, however, was lost in the Civil Rights Restoration Act of 1987. Title IX, as well as Title VI of the 1964 Civil Rights Act, was triggered by discrimination in any program, and the sanction was cutoff of federal funds from all other programs.[10]

Many private charitable gifts discriminate on the basis of race or gender. At the end of the Cold War, for instance, it was discovered that Rumania had a huge number of orphans. A donor might want to establish a scholarship to send orphans from Rumania to college in America.

National-origin discrimination would not even occur to most in considering such an act of charity—but the receipt of such a scholarship by a Rumanian student could now strip any university that accepted him or her of all its federal money.

All that remained was an officer within the executive branch prepared to pull this trigger.

In 1990, Arizona rejected making Dr. Martin Luther King Jr.'s birthday a state holiday. This led to criticism of colleges participating in the Fiesta Bowl, held in Arizona. In response, the Fiesta Bowl organization proposed a $100,000 scholarship to both schools participating in the event, to be used by a minority-race student and to be called a Martin Luther King Jr. scholarship. The proposal received much attention, including that of the Office for Civil Rights within the U.S. Department of Education.

The assistant secretary for that office, on December 4, 1990, wrote to the Fiesta Bowl's executive director, informing him of the applicability of Title VI of the 1964 Civil Rights Act to the two universities that would receive the race-based scholarship. The scholarships (now that their use by a school constituted a "program or activity" of the recipient schools themselves, thanks to the 1987 statute) constituted preference on the basis of race. None of the exceptions applied, since the scholarships were entirely unrelated to current racial conditions or history of discrimination at each school. Indeed, the only qualification was having a football team good enough to garner an invitation to the Fiesta Bowl.[11]

The assistant secretary's decision was reversed in less than two weeks. The Department of Education announced that it had no intention of disciplining universities for admitting students who had received private scholarships that were race-exclusive. "ED has decided that the Title VI regulations will be enforced in such a way as to permit universities receiving federal funds to administer scholarships established and funded entirely by private persons or entities where the donor restricts eligibility for such scholarships to minority students. Under Title VI, however, private universities receiving federal funds may not fund race-exclusive scholarships with their own funds."[12]

In other words, "the Department of Education hereby today suspends the effectiveness of the Civil Rights Restoration Act of 1987 with regard to receipt of private scholarships." There could be no private enforcement of Title VI's ban on race preference in this fact situation, since the university had no role in setting up the scholarship.[13] The discrimination was done entirely by the private party who set up the scholarship. So, in announcing it wouldn't bring complaints, the department was announcing the law was, in this regard, a dead letter.

The department news release went further, to deal even with scholarships that were state funded and established:

Race-exclusive scholarships funded by state and local governments are covered by the Supreme Court's decisions construing the Constitution and thus cannot be addressed administratively. Given the evident confusion among the universities on the preceding point, ED will provide universities a four-year transition period in order to permit universities to review their programs under Title VI, and to assure that any students under scholarship, or being evaluated for scholarship, do not suffer.[14]

Unless a plaintiff with private standing could be found, the executive was thus also suspending the applicability of Title VI of the Civil Rights Act for four years. That went far beyond failing to enforce the unanticipated effect of the Civil Rights Restoration Act upon private scholarships. In the pre-*Grutter* world of 1990, government funds used to help only members of some racial groups would have been illegal.[15]

When President Clinton succeeded President Bush, the new secretary of education pushed the nonenforcement policy further. Even beyond the four-year moratorium, the new regulations announced that scholarships, including those using public money, would not be the subject of enforcement action if they were intended to reverse past discrimination, even in the absence of a finding of such past discrimination by a court or administrative agency.[16]

To summarize, the Court wrote a poor opinion in *Grove City College* by ignoring the structure of the phrases Congress used in Title IX, in an attempt to ameliorate the consequences of the Court's own interpretation of "program or activity." Congress acted poorly in choosing not to write a comprehensive and simple statement of what it intended but, instead, to deal with the words the Court used as a means of demonstrating the Court's errors and possible anti–civil rights animus. The executive acted poorly at first, then well, drawing upon its institutional ability to move quickly, to correct errors when made, and to provide through regulation advance word of enforcement policy so as to create a measure of certainty that Congress and the Court had sacrificed in their action. That a subsequent executive went even further and used the regulations as a means of advancing a theory to uphold affirmative action not yet ruled upon by the Court does not detract from a favorable evaluation of the executive in this matter. Part of the executive function, and inherent advantage, is to seize opportunities to create a record so as to persuade the Court, when ripe to do so, of its own views on constitutional questions. The hapless assistant secretary for Civil Rights in 1990 should go down as an example of a slight downside in the executive branch: that constitutionally, it has but one voice, yet not everyone is clear on what the message is, and action can happen without deliberation. For all the criticism Congress receives when it acts in the heat of crisis, there is always deliberation in floor debate and, almost always, recorded dissent in the vote taken. So also with the Supreme Court, with dissenting votes and opinions. There is no such guarantee, however, for a far-flung executive branch with delegated authority. The executive branch error, however, was quickly corrected— far faster than one could expect a comparable change of judgment to be implemented by the Court or Congress.

Appendix

Text of letter by Assistant Secretary of Education, December 4, 1990.

UNITED STATES DEPARTMENT OF EDUCATION
OFFICE FOR CIVIL RIGHTS
THE ASSISTANT SECRETARY

DEC. 4, 1990

Mr. John Junker
Executive Director
C/o Fiesta Bowl
120 South Ash Avenue
Tempe, Arizona 85281

Dear Mr. Junker:

Recent news reports have indicated that the Fiesta Bowl intends to contribute $100,000 to each of this year's participants to create a Martin Luther King Jr. scholarship fund for minority students. I commend your efforts at advancing minority opportunities in education. However, you should be aware of certain civil rights obligations of these participating universities under Title VI of the Civil Rights Act of 1964, which is enforced by the Office for Civil Rights (OCR).

Title VI prohibits discrimination on the ground of race, color, or national origin in any program or activity receiving Federal financial assistance. OCR enforces this statute and the Title VI regulation of the Department of Education (ED) with respect to recipients of Federal education funds. The Title VI regulation includes several provisions that prohibit recipients of ED funding from denying, restricting, or providing different or segregated financial aid or other program benefits on the basis of race, color, or national origin. 34 CFR ss 100.3(b)(1)-(5)(1989). OCR interprets these provisions as generally prohibiting race-exclusive scholarships. However, a recipient may adopt or participate in a race-exclusive financial aid program when mandated to do so by a court or administrative order, corrective action plan, or settlement agreement. *See* 34 CFR s 110.3(b)(6).

While these prohibitions apply to recipient universities, the Title VI statute and regulation do not apply to the Fiesta Bowl. Assuming that the Fiesta Bowl is a strictly private entity that receives no Federal financial assistance, it can award race-exclusive scholarships directly to students. However, the universities that those students attend may not directly, or through contractual or other arrangements, assist the Fiesta Bowl in the award of those scholarships unless they are subject to a desegregation plan that mandates such scholarships. Examples of such university assistance would include soliciting, listing, approving, or providing facilities or other services in connection with a race-exclusive [scholarship] . . . .

Page 2—Mr. John Junker

Consequently, assuming that participants in the Fiesta Bowl are recipients of Federal education funds, they could permit the sponsors of the Fiesta Bowl to provide their students with race-exclusive scholarships or other financial aid, but could not receive [or] disperse such scholarship funds or otherwise assist the Fiesta Bowl sponsors unless subject to a desegregation plan that includes such scholarships.

Alternatively, you may wish to consider changing the Martin Luther King Jr. scholars fund from a race-exclusive program to (1) a program in which race is considered a positive factor amongst similarly qualified individuals if the institution is one where there has been limited participation of a particular race. See 34 CFR s 100.3(b)(6)(ii) or (2) a program that utilizes race-neutral criteria. For example, eligibility to participate in a race-neutral scholarship program could be limited to students who are disadvantaged because of economic status (students from low-income families), educational status (students from poor school districts), or social status (students from single-parent families, or families in which few or no members ever attended a postsecondary institution).

Jeannette J. Lim, a senior attorney on my staff, will contact you in the near future to provide you assistance in designing and implementing the Martin Luther King Jr. scholarship program in a manner which will accomplish the goals you wish to achieve. If you wish, you may contact her at (202) 732-1645.

Sincerely,

/s/

Michael L. Williams

Assistant Secretary
for Civil Rights

cc: Lillian Gutierrez, Regional Civil Rights Director, Region VIII

NOTES

1. In *Alexander v. Sandoval*, 531 U.S. 1049 (2001), the U.S. Supreme Court ruled that there is no private right of action for Title VI violations, unless premised on intentional action by the recipient of federal funds. The reach of "disparate impact" theory beyond Title VII of the 1964 Civil Rights Act, therefore, is entirely within the executive's discretion to enforce.

2. *Grove City College v. Bell*, 465 U.S. 555 (1984). The Supreme Court noted that there were two options: the money could go to the school for disbursement, or the money could go to the individual student. It was the latter that Grove City opted for, utilizing a procedure that the Court described as one used by institutions that "wish to minimize their involvement in the administration of the BEOG program." Id. at 560 n. 6. As a result, no money came to the college itself; the checks went directly to the students.

3. 20 U.S.C. § 1682, quoted at 465 U.S. at 558, n. 2.

4. Id.

5. 500 F. Supp. 253 (W.D. Penn., 1980).

6. 687 F.2d 684 (3rd Cir., 1982).

7. 465 U.S. at 573–74.

8. The findings section of the statute, codified at 20 U.S.C. § 1687 note, state: "The Congress finds that—(1) certain aspects of recent decisions and opinions of the Supreme Court have unduly narrowed or cast doubt upon the broad application of title IX of the Education Amendments of 1972, section 504 of the Rehabilitation Act of 1973, the Age Discrimination Act of 1975, and title VI of the Civil Rights Act of 1964; and (2) legislative action is necessary to restore the prior consistent and long-standing executive branch interpretation and broad, institution-wide application of those laws as previously administered."

9. Section 3 of the Civil Rights Restoration Act of 1987, codified at 20 U.S.C. § 1687.

10. The Civil Rights Restoration Act explicitly amended Title VI of the Civil Rights Act of 1964 as well, to maintain the parallel structure between Title IX and Title VI. See Section 6 of the Civil Rights Restoration Act of 1987, codified at 42 U.S.C. § 2000d-4a.

11. The assistant secretary's letter actually was more generous than a literal reading of *Grove City College* and the Civil Rights Restoration Act would have suggested. The universities, he wrote, "could permit the sponsors of the Fiesta Bowl to provide their students with race-exclusive scholarships or other financial aid, but could not receive or disperse such scholarship funds or otherwise

assist the Fiesta Bowl sponsors unless subject to a desegregation plan that includes such scholarships." This was generous because, following *Grove City*, simply having a financial aid office would have been enough to constitute a program. The assistant secretary's letter appears as an appendix to this chapter.

12. Press Release, U.S. Department of Education, December 18, 1990, "Department Issues Policy Statement On Race-Exclusive Scholarships."

13. *Alexander v. Sandoval* requires proof of specific intent to discriminate by the recipient of federal aid in order to premise a private enforcement action against that recipient.

14. See letter of assistant secretary of education, page 2, points 3 and 4 (accompanying Press Release, note 12, *supra*). Scholarships set up by state or local government with racial requirements would be intentional and hence could still be challenged by private parties, assuming one were found with standing.

15. In *Podberesky v. Kirwan*, 38 F.3d 147 (4th Cir., 1995), the Fourth Circuit struck down such scholarships.

16. Press Release, U.S. Department of Education, January 17, 1994, principles 2 and 3, "Secretary Riley Issues Final Policy Guidance on Race-Targeted Aid."

CHAPTER 10

Defining Constitutional Rights: *Roe v. Wade*

IN ROE V. WADE, the U.S. Supreme Court held "the word 'person,' as used in the Fourteenth Amendment, does not include the unborn."[1] As a result, the issue of government restrictions on abortion was to be analyzed purely from the point of view of the woman and the state.[2] The state had an interest in health and an interest in potential life. The latter became compelling at the end of the second trimester, the former after the first trimester. Up until the end of the first trimester, the state had no compelling interest. The woman, by contrast, had a privacy interest in her own body throughout the time period of any pregnancy. The result of this matrix of interests was to overturn all state laws banning abortion during the first trimester and all those banning abortion for reasons other than health of the mother during the first two trimesters.

Justice Blackmun claimed, "We need not resolve the difficult question of when life begins."[3] Yet, for constitutional purposes, he did. He defined the unborn[4] child or fetus as not a person. Hence, personhood begins at birth. That's all that matters for constitutional purposes.

Was it necessary for the U.S. Supreme Court to do so?

If a state were free to decide that an unborn child was a person, then it could outlaw the killing of one person by another. This is true even though the right to privacy is a constitutionally protected right against government intrusion. It would not be a question of one right giving way to another[5] but, rather, a compelling state interest being found adequate to burden a constitutionally protected right. Saving a specific life, with absolute certainty, not just a statistical likelihood, would, almost always, qualify as a compelling state interest.[6]

On the other hand, if a state burdened a woman's right to privacy for insubstantial reasons, it would violate the Fourteenth Amendment.

The decision of whether an unborn child or fetus is a person thus is a predicate to any analysis of whether the state can outlaw abortion. If personhood attaches at conception, then a restriction on abortion would be permitted.

In our constitutional scheme, it is appropriate for the U.S. Supreme Court to define the terms essential to detailing our guarantees of rights. Before the Court ruled, Congress could have tried an answer;[7] so could state legislatures. In case of dispute, however, someone has to be the final arbiter.

The alternative rule would give the states the right to define who is a person. This, however, would run contrary to the entire purpose of the Fourteenth Amendment, which was to overturn the way states had dealt with one class of persons. Left to itself, a state might deny due process of law to some persons, either by the state's own definition of what process was due or even its definition of who a person was. In the immediate aftermath of slavery, this was not a mere conjecture. Where rights guaranteed to all American citizens, or persons residing in America, were at issue, the Fourteenth Amendment makes it inconceivable that the Court could simply defer to each state's differing definition of who a person is or what liberty entails.

Hence, while one may quarrel with where *Roe* drew the line, it had to fall to the Court to do so. Justice Blackmun's statement that the *Roe* Court did not need to resolve when life begins is disingenuous. Given how he construed the case—as a conflict between the woman's privacy right to terminate a pregnancy and the state's asserted interests—he did have to decide when life began.

The consequences, however, were monumental. Had the *Roe* Court defined a person as beginning in the third trimester, the state would have a compelling interest in stopping murder, and its power to ban abortion would be easy to defend. By denying personhood to the unborn child throughout pregnancy, however, the *Roe* Court had only the state's interest in preserving potential life as running contrary to the woman's right of privacy. An interest in potential life appears no greater than the interest the state would assert to improve water quality or nutrition. Indeed, it's a wonder that so vague an interest would trump that right of privacy even in the third trimester.[8]

In this interplay, the heart of *Roe*'s greatest difficulty is manifest: the right of privacy the Court found there is exceptionally powerful.[9] It overcomes even a desire to preserve potential life, or, as the Court put it in *Planned Parenthood v. Casey*, "fetal life,"[10] which, whatever that might mean, is a rather strong state interest—stronger, for instance, than the need to preserve the efficiency of a selective service system by mandating the individual possession of draft cards.[11]

The answer, I believe, is not to accept the categories of person, yes or no, and life, yes or no. It would be unavoidable to use those categories if construction of the Fourteenth or Fifth Amendment were necessary: the words appear in each of them. That was not the case in *Roe* or *Planned Parenthood*, however. The unborn child is not asserting a right to be kept alive from state action terminating its life.[12] Rather, action by private parties was at issue. There is no constitutional obligation on a state to pass a law outlawing murder or to provide any other means of protecting one person from the actions of another. Hence, the terms "person" and "life" as used in the Fourteenth Amendment are not at issue. Using its inherent advantage of specifying constitutional rights, the Court could have proceeded more effectively by more carefully defining the right of the woman.

What is at issue is the woman's right of privacy and that, alone, needed to be defined. The *Roe* Court defined a generic right to privacy,[13] which extended in the case of the abortion decision for nine months, yet could be overcome by a mere state interest in potential life or maternal health. Rather, the Court should have defined that the right of *privacy* exists in the abortion context only while the matter was essentially *private*. That is, a right of privacy existed, but the right itself diminished over the time of the pregnancy because privacy defines a zone where only one person is, by right, involved. Once the matter involves another, whether constitutionally a person or not, there was no right to privacy.

This formulation makes use of the inherent advantage of the Court, to determine and define constitutional rights. It is still a substantive due process decision, as the *Planned Parenthood* Court was quite clear in recognizing.[14] However, it might be a little easier to defend against the charge of *Lochner*-izing,[15] since the right recognized has a restriction built directly into its definition, rather than being created as an extension from *Griswold v. Connecticut*.[16]

In the years following *Roe*, the Court dealt with restrictions sought by states and by Congress on the fundamental right of privacy the *Roe* Court had announced. Among those restrictions on which the Court ruled, the vast majority were upheld.[17] It is hard, in reviewing those restrictions, to keep in mind that the right to an abortion was a fundamental right, able to be overcome only by a compelling state interest. In *Planned Parenthood*, the Court went a very far distance along a spectrum of legitimate state restrictions that it allowed to constrict such a fundamental right.[18] It seemed the Court itself recognized it created too strong a right in *Roe*.

Nevertheless, as long as *Roe* remains the law, the powerful right to privacy recognized there created an engine that went right ahead pulling other kinds of freight: such as the right to die. If a woman's privacy overcomes the state's right to preserve some other life ("potential life" in *Roe*; "fetal life" in *Planned Parenthood*), then it might be powerful enough to overcome the state's interest to preserve a person's own life against that person's wishes.

In *Cruzan v. Director, Missouri Department of Health*,[19] the Court so ruled, in the context of an individual's decision to refuse medical treatment. However, it found that the state could impose substantial safeguards to ensure that the choice was actually made by the individual herself or himself, and the Court dodged the implication that the right to privacy created a right to die that overcame the state's law.

When Oregon's voters adopted a right to die by statute, the state's interest and the interest of the individual seeking to die were perfectly aligned. Though this case did not come to the Supreme Court, the district judge's tortured opinion demonstrates a great unease with the implication of a broad right of privacy and hence right to die. The district court held that it was a denial of equal protection to have an easier standard for terminally ill persons to commit suicide than for those not terminally ill.[20] There was no new suspect class of the terminally ill, and the state was not the actor taking away anyone's life. Thus, strict scrutiny was not available. Rather, the district court struck down the initiative under minimal, rational basis, review—that Oregon could not be held to have intended making suicide so easy for the terminally ill. The predicate of state action was held to exist by the mere fact of the initiative to repeal state law and replace it with an easier scheme of registering consent by the terminally ill. "Private medical matters become affairs of government when the state sanctions them," the district court ruled.[21] This is an astounding proposition.

If all it takes to constitute state action is to repeal a law regarding private conduct, then federal courts could overturn virtually any legislative repeal of a criminal law. Indeed, federal courts could sit in judgment on what criminal laws were minimally rational for a state to have; if states failed to have such a law, perhaps an affirmative injunction would issue to compel them to do so. At the least, a negative injunction against repeal would lie. Such are the consequences of the district court ruling in *Lee v. Oregon*. The court of appeals avoided these consequences by reversing on standing. The U.S. Supreme Court has yet to deal with a statutory right-to-die law.

Perhaps, when forced to rule, the circuits or the Supreme Court might develop a rationale without such hugely broad implications; but it will be difficult to do so, because the right of privacy, so powerful as to overcome "potential life" or "fetal life," is very hard to limit judicially.

In review, there was a drawback to the Supreme Court having been the progenitor of the right to privacy. Because it had to rule by category, it created a vessel, the right to privacy, into which it poured both procedural and substantive content.[22] As long as it was dealing with procedure, the Court was utilizing advantages of its branch. Moving into substance was probably not necessary, as the outcomes achieved under that heading could have been achieved using a procedural or equal protection analysis.[23] Once having made that move, however, the Court found that it had to recognize a right broader rather than simply the application before it; and, to uphold that right, it set in train a lot of consequences, such as the unpersonhood of an unborn child and a personal right to die. It created a "super-right,"[24] with which the Supreme Court, and lower federal courts, soon felt uncomfortable.

Such are the consequences of using the judicial branch's power. Its authority is to find constitutional rights and apply them. Its own majesty is its inherent limitation, however. It could not simply announce a right to abortion in the first trimester. It had to find a right to privacy and then balance that right against a state's interest. The state's interest was very strong, so the right the Court found had to be even stronger.

Contrast this approach with how a legislature might have proceeded. A legislature could create a right to abortion in the first trimester in so many words. No other laws would have to be written. As master of words, the legislature could address exactly the problem at hand and attempt to solve it, with no wider ramifications.

In the years before *Roe*, some legislatures did attempt statutory solutions that permitted abortion.[25] Others maintained a prohibition against abortion. The federal legislature stayed silent. Under present jurisprudence, Congress would probably lack a constitutional premise for enacting a law to reach private decisions on abortion. If a state had no law outlawing private abortions, that failure to act would not constitute state action,[26] and state laws outlawing abortion probably do not sufficiently affect interstate commerce.[27]

While Congress could not have acted, the states could—prior to *Roe*. Using the states as the engine for movement in this area would have required tolerance for lack of uniformity across the states and potential change of heart in any given state. Lacking a federal constitutional substantive due process basis, the right to abortion would depend upon the public policy views of the people or legislators of any given state at any given time. This is what is going on now through legislation in the federal Congress[28] and through the common law in the states[29] regarding the punishment for killing an unborn child or fetus in a traffic accident or in the course of a crime. Different states are taking different views about the appropriate augmentation of punishment where an unborn child or fetus is damaged in a tort or crime.

So, suppose *Roe v. Wade* had never been decided—the issue would stay with the states. Is this in keeping with the inherent advantages of state legislatures or initiatives? The answer turns on whether a constitutional right is involved. If not, then one can readily admit the advantage of fifty different solutions, one for each state. Justice Scalia goes further, to praise the very process of seeking an outcome state by state.

In his dissent in *Planned Parenthood v. Casey*,[30] Justice Scalia analogizes the *Roe v. Wade* decision to *Dred Scott v. Sandford*.[31] By denying personhood to the unborn child, Justice Scalia reasoned, and by construing the right of privacy to include abortion, the Supreme Court had taken an issue away from the more salubrious means of resolving it. "[B]y foreclosing all democratic outlets for the deep passions this issue arouses, by banishing the issue from the political forum that gives all participants, even the losers, the satisfaction of a fair hearing and an honest fight, by continuing the imposition of a rigid national rule instead of allowing for regional differences, the Court merely prolongs and intensifies the anguish."[32]

Justice Scalia appears to reflect some of the analysis just set forth: that *Roe* made a matter of constitutional right what had previously been a matter of policy and thus foreclosed all further efforts at whatever consensuses might have emerged from the different political processes in different states.

Using Scalia's own analogy of *Dred Scott*, however, makes me wonder whether Justice Scalia's objection is not so much to the method as to the outcome. The opposite of *Dred Scott* was not the abolition of slavery:

it was the continuation of slavery in the states that had it, in the new states south of the Missouri Compromise line, in such of the territories as Congress might determine, and in such free states as wished to change and implement slavery. That was where slavery stood at the time *Dred Scott* was argued. Is that what Justice Scalia would prefer?

It's true Chief Justice Taney took the issue away from the political process in which it had been engaged. But to one who thinks slavery is abominable, a mighty evil permitted by our nation's founders but a duty to be corrected by their sons and daughters, it was hardly adequate to say "let it live a little longer" or "let each state work out its own answer," so that all sides would have the satisfaction of a fair hearing and an honest fight—all sides, that is, except the slaves.

Would Justice Scalia have joined an opinion, in a properly pleaded case involving abortion at state hospitals arising before *Roe v. Wade*, holding that:

(1) the U.S. constitutional guarantee that no state deprive any person of life without due process of law compelled the Court to determine who a "person" was;

(2) reaching that issue, a person included an unborn child from the moment of conception, as a matter of federal constitutional law;

(3) state hospitals could not, therefore, perform abortions; and, further,

(4) that all states with murder statutes that did not also cover the unborn were guilty of unequal protection of the law with regard to the discrete and insular minority[33] of unborn children.

In such a decision, the matter of abortion would also have been "banished from the political forum that gives all participants, even the losers, the satisfaction of a fair hearing and an honest fight," in Justice Scalia's words.[34]

Perhaps Justice Scalia would have dissented from such a decision, preferring to let the matter continue to percolate among the states. Perhaps in 1856 he would have allowed slavery to continue in the territories as Congress might direct. On its face, that is what Justice Scalia's *Planned Parenthood* dissent implies. I am skeptical, however. Since he analogizes the unborn child to a slave, I suspect Justice Scalia would have sought a way to grant freedom to both the unborn child and to the slave.

The analogy to slavery works both ways, however.

If the woman, rather than the unborn child or fetus, is analogized to the slave, then *Roe v. Wade* is the end of an incident of slavery, the end of a restriction on freedom imposed by government upon a group long subject to discrimination, not even permitted to vote within the memory of some still living today. It would be comparable to a holding in *Dred Scott* that, not only was the Fugitive Slave Law unconstitutional, but slavery itself was unconstitutional. From the point of view of the slave, or the woman, these are wonderful outcomes to be won; and winning them from the Supreme Court's finding of a substantive fundamental right, as opposed to the action of a state legislature, guarantees that the right will be uniform and, at least in main part, will not be taken back.

This discussion, however, is not about what is right. In the abortion context, what is right seems to turn on what one's own conscience says about when life begins. Rather, my focus is on the inherent advantages of the various branches of government to deal with this most intractable of all modern problems. The fundamental problem with the Supreme Court leading the way on this is that Justice Blackmun had to write into the Constitution a substantive right of privacy beyond anything that had gone before. To have reached an analogous outcome in *Dred Scott*, Chief Justice Taney would have had to rewrite the Constitution, since the pre–Civil War Constitution envisioned slavery. As a policy matter, I wish he had done it—if by so doing the slaves could have been freed and the Civil War avoided. But as an institutional matter, how could the pre–Civil War Court have done it?

Either a 100 percent pro-choice outcome or a 100 percent pro-life outcome were both possible results from taking cases to the Supreme Court. Either outcome could lay claim to constitutional principle and, in so doing, cut off the democratic political processes in the several states. The *Planned Parenthood* majority might, indeed, have been guilty of hubris in thinking it could "call the contending sides of national controversy to end their national division by accepting a common mandate rooted in the Constitution," when the opposite outcome could just as easily have been announced, also purporting to be rooted in the Constitution.[35]

Yet, if it's a matter of fundamental right, who else can settle it?

The people can. The national debate can center around a constitutional amendment: pro-life or pro-choice. The virtue of a constitutional amendment, as discussed in the previous material regarding flag burning, is that it can be written specifically to deal with the issue of concern, without creating a broader right (substantive right of privacy) or denigrating other rights (personhood of an unborn child or fetus).

Trimesters, as a rough compromise, could be explicitly written into the proposed amendment, rather than being eked out of a substantive right of privacy, to so much criticism.[36] The right to die could be explicitly left out, for another day's consideration in the courts or another amendment. The political processes would work their fullest, with the salutary effect to which Justice Scalia refers of everyone having her or his day, whether winner or loser. The answer, when it came, would be as permanent as a Supreme Court ruling—indeed, much more so.[37]

The price, however, would be justice delayed. Women in some states would be free to control their own bodies; women in others wouldn't. Unborn children or fetuses would be free to live in some states, but not in others. Whether one analogizes women or unborn children to slaves, slavery would be permitted in some of the states and territories, but not in others, for the number of years it would take until the constitutional amendment was passed.

Making one side or the other follow the constitutional amendment route will seem unfair to that side. However, this result is unavoidable. One side had to be chosen to bear the burden of seeking a constitutional amendment. It was more efficient, from the point of view of this book, that the burden be placed on the pro-life side. The reason is that, to achieve its policy objective, the pro-life side already had to go to the legislatures of each state to seek a law banning abortion. It is no more institutional burden to go to those same legislatures to seek their approval of a constitutional amendment. A majority vote of the legislature is required in each case. By contrast, if the burden of seeking a constitutional amendment had been imposed on the pro-choice side (by the hypothetical opinion discussed above that would strike down abortion in a state hospital), the pro-choice side would have a new burden it would otherwise not have borne.

In this process-oriented sense, *Roe v. Wade* was, thus, the correct decision. The question of abortion in the context of a woman's right to privacy can best be solved, institutionally, through the constitutional amendment process. A definitive ruling by the Supreme Court is necessary to compel that process to start. Otherwise, both sides will continue to seek victory in court adjudication. One side had to lose. The effect of *Roe v. Wade* was to place the burden of the constitutional amendment on the side that would have to recur to the state legislatures anyway.

Too little has been made of the constitutional amendment process in separation of powers thinking. The process has all the beneficial attributes that Justice Scalia ascribes to a legislative battle. In fact, a constitutional amendment is nothing but a legislative battle—to achieve the concurrent majority of the legislatures of thirty-eight states (*not* the supermajority of any one of them). And the result is worth the struggle. It has the highest authority known in our constitutional system. It can trump the Supreme Court on an issue of constitutional law; it can trump Congress or the president on a matter of policy.

In deciding *Roe v. Wade* as it did, the Court hasn't prevented resort to the constitutional amendment process. It has impelled it. While both sides continue to think victory is achievable through a Supreme Court decision (or reversal of an earlier decision), the constitutional amendment route is put on hold.[38] When the Supreme Court route appears settled and closed, however—whichever way—the losing side has the clearest impetus to engage in the constitutional amendment process.

Justice Scalia might respond that before *Roe*, the pro-life side could have argued state by state for a law banning abortions, and this resort to the political system was cut off in any one state by *Roe*. However, all it takes for a constitutional amendment is a majority of each state legislature, the same as would have been required to pass a law in the state—provided the pro-life side obtains thirty-eight such majorities. Even the requirement of a two-thirds majority of each house of Congress can be sidestepped by thirty-eight state legislatures, if they first call for a constitutional convention.[39]

Had they won at the Supreme Court, the pro-life adherents would actually have won no more of a victory than a constitutional amendment would give them. Indeed, it would be far less. At the Supreme Court, the pro-life side could hope that "person" was defined to include an unborn child, so that the state could not deprive that person of life, through abortion at a state-funded facility, without due process of law. To ban abortion everywhere (in all the states and in private hospitals as well as public ones), only a constitutional amendment would do.

It is undeniable that *Roe* took away the pro-life chance for a partial victory—defined as outlawing abortion in thirty-seven or fewer states.[40] But *Roe* simply made the pro-life goal change from getting as many state legislatures as possible to ban abortion to getting thirty-eight state legislatures to ban abortion. (I doubt the pro-life target was ever fewer than all fifty states in the first place, but that is entirely speculative on my part.) *Roe* did not change the process leading to the pro-life goal: it remains, as before *Roe*, through the individual state legislatures.

The result of the Supreme Court ruling, once it is clear it won't be reversed by the present Court or any Court reasonably foreseeable in the near term, is to commence anew recourse to "the political forum that gives all participants, even the losers, the satisfaction of a fair hearing and an honest fight," namely the constitutional amendment process in the fifty states.

Presented with a claim of constitutional right in *Roe v. Wade*, the Supreme Court ruled. That is its job. But in this instance, the judicial method for decision was ill suited to the problem. The Court ruled far too broadly, compelled by the judicial need to fit the right to choose abortion within the broader right of privacy—which itself lacked explicit constitutional moorings. The Court also ruled too narrowly, setting up a trimester regime from which it later retreated. In each respect, a constitutional amendment would have been preferable, because like any legislation, it could be drafted specifically to the issue under focus. The outcome in *Roe* has now put the impetus for a constitutional amendment on the pro-life side. That process might very well call forth an alternative draft from the pro-choice side, with the end result that our nation will, through the process of constitutional amendment, achieve compromise leading to satisfaction that has eluded us for thirty years.[41]

NOTES

1. 410 U.S. 113, 158 (1973).

2. The Court's opinion actually referred to the right of the physician, "in consultation with his patient . . . to determine, without regulation by the State, that, in his medical judgment, the patient's pregnancy should be terminated." 410 U.S. at 163. Elsewhere, however, the Court stated, "This right of privacy . . . is broad enough to encompass a *woman's* decision whether or not to terminate her pregnancy." Id. at 153 (emphasis added). Furthermore, in *Planned Parenthood v. Casey*, 505 U.S. 833 (1992), the Court's decision was based on the woman's right of privacy, and the Court has never based any subsequent decision on the assumed constitutional right of the physician. In *Rust v. Sullivan*, 500 U.S. 173 (1991), for instance, the Court upheld, against a First Amendment challenge, funding restrictions on physicians who performed abortions. If *Roe* had meant to convey a constitutional right on the physician to perform abortions, the *Rust* outcome would have been much more difficult.

3. 410 U.S. at 159.

4. As Justice Blackmun used the word "unborn," I will use it here along with the word "fetus," which Justice Blackmun also used. No legal or policy conclusion is intended by my choice of words. Indeed, in the sentence denying them personhood, Justice Blackmun used "unborn."

5. Popular discourse has pitted a women's right of privacy ("pro-choice")

against the "right to life" of the unborn child or fetus ("pro-life"). This contrast, however, is not constitutionally accurate. There is no constitutional right to life—only a right that the government not deprive a person of life without due process of law. Private action that deprives a person of life is not prohibited, or even addressed, by the Constitution. Abortion at a state or county hospital, however, would implicate a constitutional right, since, if an unborn child or fetus is a person, the state would be taking that person's life. Curiously, Justice Blackman, in dicta, stated otherwise. "If this suggestion of personhood is established . . . the fetus' right to life would then be guaranteed specifically by the Amendment." 410 U.S. at 156–57.

6. A state can prohibit speech where it advocates imminent lawless action. *Brandenburg v. Ohio*, 395 U.S. 444 (1969). If the facts are specific enough and the proof strong enough, an individual's right to speak would give way to the state's interest in protecting the lives of specific citizens. In the case of abortion, the individual whose life would be saved is absolutely clear, identified, and probabilistically close to 100 percent. Hence, it became necessary for Justice Blackmun to deny the personhood of the unborn child or fetus.

7. Congress might attempt to make use of its authority under the fifth clause of the Fourteenth Amendment to define "person" for the sake of enforcing the guarantees of that amendment to all persons. However, any such exercise would have to be congruent and proportional to the documented threat to those rights. *City of Boerne v. Flores*, 521 U.S. 507 (1997). Where, as here, the Supreme Court has already spoken about a definition, it can safely be predicted that the Court would tolerate no different definition from Congress as "congruent and proportional."

Furthermore, the Court's definition of "person" in *Roe v. Wade* was not for purposes of determining who is entitled to the protection of the Fifth and Fourteenth Amendments; rather, it was to determine whether Texas had a compelling state interest to overcome the woman's right to privacy. Putting aside, for the moment, the question of abortions performed at state-run hospitals, therefore, the word "person" as used in the Fifth and Fourteenth Amendments is not at issue in the abortion context. Hence, Congress's attempt to define the word would hardly be "congruent and proportional" to the purposes of those amendments.

From time to time, legislation has been introduced in the Congress to codify, or to overturn, *Roe v. Wade*. The former, such as the Freedom of Choice Act of 1993, H.R. 25 (103rd Cong., 1st Sess.), makes *Roe v. Wade* statutory, by defining "liberty" to include abortion previability. The latter, such as the Human Life Act of 1981, H.R. 900 (97th Cong., 1st Sess.), seeks to overturn *Roe* by defining life as starting at conception. Post-*Boerne*, only the former would survive; and it might have some force in preventing a Supreme Court reversal of *Roe v. Wade*.

Regarding abortions at state-run hospitals, the *Roe* holding that an unborn child or fetus is not a person would preclude Congress from saying to the contrary, following *Boerne*. Had *Roe* never been decided, however, it would have been permissible for Congress to use its section 5 authority to define person and to prohibit the state from taking the life of a person through an abortion at a state-run hospital. In using section 5 of the Fourteenth Amendment, Congress could not, however, have gone beyond the case of state-run hospitals, since state action would be lacking in the case of private abortions. Hence, the pro-life congressional effort was inherently more circumscribed than the pro-choice congressional effort. This asymmetry stems simply from the fact that there is a constitutionally protected right to "liberty" that states can be seen to have infringed by banning abortion, whereas, outside of state hospitals, there is no constitutionally protected right of a person not to be killed by another person.

8. The *Roe* Court speaks of the state's interest growing over the time of the pregnancy. 410 U.S. at 162–63. In reality, it's the probability that an unborn child or fetus is really a person that grows over the time of the pregnancy; the state's interest in "potential life" remains the same. Yet the *Roe* Court couldn't put it that way without overturning its holding that an unborn child or fetus was not a person.

9. Ely observes, "What is unusual about *Roe* is that the liberty involved is accorded a far more stringent protection, so stringent that a desire to preserve the fetus's existence is unable to overcome it—a protection more stringent, I think it fair to say, than that the present Court accords the freedom of the press explicitly guaranteed by the First Amendment [citation omitted]." J. Ely, "The Wages of Crying Wolf: A Comment on *Roe v. Wade*," 82 *Yale L. J.* 935.

10. 505 U.S. at 859.

11. *United States v. O'Brien*, 391 U.S. 367 (1968).

12. That case would be presented regarding abortion in a state hospital, a subcategory not presented in *Roe* or *Planned Parenthood*.

13. Nor did the *Roe* Court bolster confidence in its decision by its own ambiguity as to the constitutional text in which the right could be found. "This right of privacy, whether it be founded in the Fourteenth Amendment's concept of personal liberty and restrictions upon state action, as we feel it is, or, as the District Court determined, in the Ninth Amendment's reservation of rights to the people, is broad enough to encompass a woman's decision whether or not to terminate her pregnancy." 410 U.S. at 153.

14. 505 U.S. at 845–49.

15. See, e.g., Ely's criticism of *Roe*, "The Wages of Crying Wolf."

16. 381 U.S. 479 (1965).

17. The Court held that it is permissible for government to fund some medical needs of women but not nontherapeutic abortion (*Maher v. Roe*, 432 U.S. 464 [1977]); permissible to prevent recipients of federal funds from advising women about their right to an abortion (*Rust v. Sullivan*); and permissible for a state to impose a waiting period, to require the woman to read literature biased against abortion, and to require parental consent (with a judicial bypass) for underage women (*Planned Parenthood v. Casey*).

18. For instance, in *Planned Parenthood*, Pennsylvania had imposed a twenty-four-hour waiting period from the time a woman first presented herself for an abortion and when she could receive the abortion. If there are no abortion clin-

ics within a day's drive from the woman's place of work or home, then the burden on a woman imposed by a twenty-four-hour waiting period could be much more than trivial, and the trial court so found. Pennsylvania also obliged an unmarried woman under eighteen to obtain a parent's consent, though she could go to a court on her own instead. The practicality of an underage woman making use of that right, in that context, might well be more theoretical than real. Furthermore, the distinction between unmarried women under eighteen and married women under eighteen defied any standard above minimal rationality, which a burden on a fundamental right should call forth. The Pennsylvania law required that the woman be provided with information (biased against abortion) to read, "if she chooses to view these materials," and required her to "certify in writing, that the information . . . has been provided." 505 U.S. at 903. If a woman could not make such a certification because she couldn't read, in upholding these conditions the Court would have upheld what it did not uphold in the voting context: a literacy test as a condition on exercising a fundamental right. *Katzenbach v. Morgan*, 384 U.S. 641 (1966). The Court did not even consider that possibility.

If we were speaking of another fundamental right, like voting, simple discouragement of the exercise of the right would constitute an "undue burden." Suppose a state were to broadcast television and radio messages saying, "Whereas it's your right to vote, if you're not well informed about the candidates or the issues, you really shouldn't vote. So, if that's you, please don't vote." Would we be comfortable with the state weighing in so clearly against the exercise of the right to vote? If not, the comfort shown by the *Planned Parenthood* Court in allowing exactly that kind of message regarding a woman's fundamental right to choose to terminate her pregnancy indicates the Court was trying, at the least, to cut back the "super-right" and maybe, even, to accord the right to privacy something less than full "fundamental right" status.

My purpose is not to debate all the conditions upheld in *Planned Parenthood*, but simply to identify that the Court's approval of those conditions substantially undercut the stature of the fundamental right.

19. 497 U.S. 261 (1990).

20. *Lee v. Oregon*, 891 F. Supp. 1429 (D. Ore., 1995), *rev'd on other grounds*, 107 F.3d 1382 (9th Cir., 1997).

21. Id. at 1437.

22. "Although a literal reading of the Clause [14th Amendment's guarantee of liberty] might suggest that it governs only the procedures by which a State may deprive persons of liberty, for at least 105 years, at least since *Mugler v. Kansas* . . . , the Clause has been understood to contain a substantive component as well, one 'barring certain government actions regardless of the fairness of the procedures used to implement them.' " *Planned Parenthood v. Casey*, 846.

23. For instance, in *Griswold v. Connecticut*, 381 U.S. 479 (1965), and *Eisenstadt v. Baird*, 405 U.S. 438 (1970) (upholding the substantive right to use contraceptives), the Court could alternatively have ruled that a search to obtain evidence that a contraceptive was actually being used would in all cases lack reason-

ableness. Prosecutions for use of a contraceptive would essentially be shut down. Similarly, the right to marry was not necessary to recognize as a substantive right of privacy in *Loving v. Virginia*, 388 U.S. 1 (1967), since the Court also based its decision on an equal protection challenge on behalf of interracial couples.

24. See Ely, "The Wages of Crying Wolf," 935–36.

25. New York and California, for instance, had passed laws guaranteeing the right to an abortion before *Roe v. Wade*. California had put a right to privacy into its constitution. Cal. Const. art. 1, sec. 1 (1972). See also N.Y. Penal Law § 125.05 (1970).

26. The district court in *Lee v. Oregon*, however, might hold that such laws constituted state sanctioning of abortion and, hence, adequate state action; however, I believe that expansion of state action doctrine is erroneous. A federal law could have addressed state-run hospitals' abortions or state-financed abortions under the fifth clause of the Fourteenth Amendment. Today, however, *City of Boerne v. Flores* would constrain such a federal law to do little more than repeat *Roe* and *Planned Parenthood*.

27. The fact that some might travel in interstate commerce to obtain abortions they could not obtain in their home state might be suggested as enough effect on interstate commerce to justify federal congressional authority. However, parents might travel between states to find safer schools, and that was not enough to justify congressional authority in *U.S. v. Lopez*, 514 U.S. 549 (1995).

28. Unborn Victims of Violence Act (P.L. 108–212 [2001]), signed into law by President Bush on April 1, 2004, increased penalties for federal criminal statutes when a fetus is killed.

29. See, e.g., the Oklahoma courts' resolutions of this question in the context of the common law "born alive" rule: *Hughes v. Oklahoma*, 868 P.2d 730 (Ok. Crim. App., 1994); see also, *Unborn Child of Julie Starks v. Oklahoma*, 2001 OK 6, 18 P.3d, 342, (2001) (holding that an unborn child or fetus is ineligible for protection by the state from endangerment by its mother, since statutory analysis of the child endangerment statute showed it was written in contemplation of a born child).

30. 505 U.S. at 1001 (Scalia, J., dissenting).

31. 60 U.S. 393 (1856).

32. 505 U.S. at 1001 (Scalia, J., dissenting).

33. *United States v. Caroline Products*, 304 U.S. 144 at n. 4 (1938), and J. Ely, *Democracy and Distrust* (1980).

34. A pro-life outcome, in other words, banishes the issue as much as a pro-choice outcome does.

35. Justice Scalia scolds the majority for making this call. "It is no more realistic for us in this case, than it was for [Chief Justice Taney] in that [*Dred Scott*] to think that an issue of the sort they both involved—an issue involving life and death, freedom and subjugation—can be speedily and finally settled by the Supreme Court, as President James Buchanan in his inaugural address said the issue of slavery in the territories would be." 505 U.S. at 1002.

36. See, e.g., Ely, "The Wages of Crying Wolf," 922, calling the trimester rule akin to "a commissioner's regulations."

37. Only one U.S. constitutional amendment has been undone by a subsequent amendment. The Library of Congress's annotated U.S. Constitution, however, counts 216 times when the Supreme Court has expressly overturned one of its earlier opinions up to 1998. See note 35, Chapter 5. Cf. *Payne v. Tennessee*, 501 U.S. 828 and n. 1, listing Supreme Court reversals of its own constitutional opinions over the last twenty-one years.

38. In the Second Amendment context, I argue in Chapter 13 that the failure of the Court to make a ruling has stymied resort to the amendment process. A clear decision, one way or the other, would send the losing side into the constitutional amendment process with vigor.

39. A state governor's veto may also be sidestepped. Calling for a constitutional convention or ratifying a constitutional amendment each requires the approval only of the state legislature, not the governor, under the U.S. Constitution. Thus, it is actually easier to obtain any one state's approval to ban abortion by constitutional amendment than by individual state law, with the one major proviso that the anti-abortion view would have to prevail in thirty-eight state legislatures for it to prevail in any.

40. It is possible that it would be harder to obtain a state legislator's vote for a constitutional amendment banning abortion than for a state law banning it, perhaps out of that legislator's respect for every other state's right to decide the issue for itself. It is just as likely the converse could be true, however—where, for instance, a legislator felt banning abortion in her or his state alone would be fruitless as the woman would merely travel to another state. That legislator might vote yes for the constitutional amendment but no on the statute.

41. One constitutional amendment possibility that was discussed when I was in Congress, but never introduced, was as follows:

Neither the federal government nor any state shall impose a burden on a woman's decision to have an abortion during the period of her pregnancy up to one month after the time she knows or should reasonably have known she was pregnant. The case of a woman not sufficiently mentally competent to realize she was pregnant within such a time may be dealt with through judicial process. Thereafter, the government or any state may limit or prohibit abortions within its respective jurisdiction.

In no case, however, may the federal government or any state impose a burden on a woman's decision to have an abortion when her life would otherwise be imperiled.

CHAPTER 11

The Civil Rights Act of 1992: The Burden of Proof as a Judicial Function Used to Achieve a Legislative Result

THE ORIGINAL Civil Rights Act of 1964 was a compromise. Assurances were given to the Senate Republicans whose votes were necessary to overcome the southern Democrats and join northern Democrats in a majority. It was important that the newly created right to sue employers would not lead to hiring by the numbers.[1] Employers and unions alike were concerned that employment tests not be upset.[2] Similarly, bona fide seniority plans were to be preserved.[3] The key assurance was that intentional discrimination was the focus, not the myriad of consequences that various employment practices might have had without being designed to have that effect.[4]

It was inevitable that cases would come along where the intent of the employer to discriminate was not overt but might be inferred from circumstances. The Court has dealt with problems like this in the context of other statutory schemes.[5] It is an attribute of the Court's comparative advantage that it can fashion evidentiary presumptions to guide juries in finding intent. When presented with this question in the Title VII context, however, the Supreme Court chose a different approach, an approach of an essentially legislative character. Years later, the Court sought to reverse this legislative result using judicial tools. Congress then reversed the reversal, in part using judicial tools. This remarkable illustration of functional advantages and disadvantages of the Court and Congress is the subject of this chapter.

In *Griggs v. Duke Power Co.*,[6] the Supreme Court dealt with a company that had adopted a requirement for employment in any department other than its lowest paying—the "labor department," which consisted exclusively of black workers before segregation became illegal. This requirement, an aptitude test purportedly designed to measure general intelligence, was put in place on July 2, 1965, the very day after Title VII of the Civil Rights Act of 1964 came into force. There was no attempt to correlate the aptitude test with specific skills required for the job to which an individual might be applying. The trial court had found that, prior to Title VII, the employer, Duke Power Company, had a history of open racial discrimination.

Against such a background, the Court, in traditional manner, could have affirmed an inference of intent to discriminate. The timing of the test alone would have supported such an inference. Had the Court so decided, subsequent Title VII law would have been spared much of the contest over the use of statistics that has ensued.

Instead, the Court held that intent was not a necessary element of a Title VII claim. Rather, the act was designed to prohibit "built-in headwinds," mechanisms that were "fair in form but discriminatory in operation,"[7] for which an employer could not advance a good reason. The way to distinguish whether the employer's reason was valid was described in four different phrases within a single page of text: "the touchstone is business necessity," "related to job performance," "Congress has placed on the employer the burden of showing that any given requirement must have a manifest relationship to the employment in question," whereas an invalid reason was one "unrelated to measuring job capability."[8] Evidently, any one of these tests could be satisfied. Or perhaps they all had to be satisfied. The Court didn't say; yet the four phrases are very different. An intelligence test is "related" to job performance or capability to the extent any job requires comprehending instructions. Yet for many jobs, passing a certain level of such an exam would not be a "necessity" or have a "manifest relationship to the employment in question."

In setting up these alternative tests, the Supreme Court was legislating. Congress, when it legislates, has committee hearings, markup sessions in committee, floor debate, and conference committee deliberations. In any of these settings, four different expressions of the same test could be ironed out into a single test.[9] As master of words, Congress could say what it wanted to say. The Court highlighted its institutional incompetence in this regard by saying a very important thing four different ways. No lower court in a subsequent case could determine definitively which of these alternative phrases was the actual test.

In allocating the burden of proof, however, the Court was on more traditional judicial ground.[10] It is a courtlike function to place the burden on the party most able to bear it—at least in the silence of the legislative branch. In *Griggs*'s fourth formulation, the Court allocated "the burden of showing that any given requirement must have a manifest relationship to the employment in question" upon the employer. That makes sense: the Court allocated the burden of showing the value of an employment test upon the party that imposed the test.

In *Griggs*, even if the Court was legislating a liability formulation that Congress did not put into Title VII, its allocation of the burden of proof was an example of what courts traditionally are well equipped to do. Nineteen years later, it was this allocation of the burden of proof that the Court reversed, in *Ward's Cove Packing Company v. Atonio.*[11] Institutionally, it was right to make use of burden of proof. Having institutional competence and using it properly, however, are two different things.

In *Ward's Cove*, the Court reversed the usual rule that a burden be placed upon the party most able to bear it. The Court held that an employer could merely suggest (burden of production) a "legitimate neutral consideration" for using the device that had the disparate impact.[12] The employee would then have to show that this business justification was invalid.

The employer knows her or his business better than the employee. Nevertheless, following *Ward's Cove*, once the employer simply suggests a supposed business reason for the practice in question, the employee must prove that defense false. If the employee attempts to do so by proffering an alternative device to achieve the asserted neutral goal of the employer, the *Ward's Cove* Court further piles on the burdens: "Of course, any alternative practices which respondents [employees] offer up in this respect must be equally effective as petitioners' [employers'] chosen hiring procedures in achieving petitioners' legitimate employment goals. Moreover, '[f]actors such as the cost or other burdens of proposed alternative selection devices are relevant in determining whether they would be equally as effective as the challenged practice in serving the employer's legitimate business goals.' [Citation omitted]."[13]

The *Ward's Cove* Court was hanging out a sign above the disparate-impact Title VII window, "Employees Need Not Apply."

This result was so palpably unfair as a burden of proof matter as to undermine the Court's professed policy neutrality. This gave tremendous strength to those in Congress seeking to establish the *Griggs* kind of case, "disparate impact," as statutory, as opposed to judge-made, law. In 1964, there had not been sufficient consensus in Congress to out-law disparate-impact violations of Title VII; indeed, the opposite was true.[14] It took the Court's action in *Griggs* to change this. When the Court repented of that action, it imposed an onerous burden of proof,[15] in words so cynical as to lend themselves to the demonization[16] the Court then suffered.

[T]he plaintiff bears the burden of disproving an employer's assertion that the adverse employment action or practice was based solely on a legitimate neutral consideration. [Citations omitted.]

We acknowledge that some of our earlier decisions can be read as suggest-ing otherwise [citations omitted] but to the extent that those cases speak of an employer's "burden of proof" with respect to a legitimate business justification defense, [citations omitted], they should have been understood to mean an em-ployer's production—but not persuasion—burden.[17]

It would be difficult to find a clearer invitation to disrespect an opin-ion of the Court, coming from the Court's own lips, than "We acknowl-edge that some of our earlier decisions can be read as suggesting other-wise [than what we hold today]," and (paraphrasing) "when we said 'burden of proof' we really meant 'burden of production.' " It was easy for members of Congress to say the Court was actually rewriting the law to achieve an anti-civil-rights policy objective. Congress's reaction to *Ward's Cove* was to make statutory for the first time what had been only judge-made law (namely, liability without proof of intent to dis-criminate), to allocate the burden of proof sensibly for all elements of a disparate-impact case, and to use the occasion to address a fundamen-tal criticism of disparate-impact cases not technically presented in *Ward's Cove*.

For the most part, this reaction was an illustration of inherent con-gressional advantages in legislating. In reversing the perverse alloca-tion of burdens of proof in *Ward's Cove*, Congress was participating in a function jointly shared by courts and legislatures. Whereas courts have expertise in allocating burdens of proof, a legislature can coun-termand those allocations through legislation. In so doing, the legisla-ture should, and does, take testimony from trial judges and other ex-perts on the practical effect of allocating burdens of proof. The Federal Rules of Evidence, for instance, mandates a procedure that partakes of this shared responsibility between the federal judicial and legislative branches to decide burdens of proof and other evidentiary rules.[18]

The opportunity to address criticisms technically not presented in the *Ward's Cove* case also illustrates an inherent advantage of the legislative branch. A court must deal with the case before it; any excursions into broader rules are dicta with no binding effect. Institutionally, it is the legislative branch that can survey the field and, whatever the immediate provocation for legislation, create an overall balance that might not be achievable simply from addressing the fact situation that brought the policy matter forward. The Civil Rights Act of 1992 illustrated that legislative function. However, it also illustrated Congress failing in its use of this institutional advantage by using court-made phrases, and referring to Supreme Court opinions, rather than simply writing the law afresh.

Over the years, disparate-impact cases had led to criticisms that they caused employers to hire by the numbers. Cautious employers who never intended to discriminate would nevertheless realize their vulnerability to statistical inference applied to virtually any of their practices. Most dangerous of all, however, was a "system-wide" use of disparate-impact theory. Where an employer used a series of screens in choosing to hire or promote, a plaintiff using a system-wide disparate-impact theory could simply plead the numbers going in and the numbers coming out, and if there were a statistical disparity, the plaintiff would say the system itself was a discriminatory device under *Griggs*. Employees were helped in such litigation by dicta in federal court opinions from the early civil rights era, such as "statistics often tell much, and courts listen,"[19] and "nothing is as emphatic as a zero."[20]

Choose any level of probability of "type 1" error we wish to accept. It is possible to construct an example of several levels of testing, each level of which passes that probability screen but all of which, taken together, do not. An example is given below,[21] but intuitively, this result can be grasped by asking the same question, "What is the probability of the particular outcome occurring by chance?" at each of three screens where we measure outcomes. Suppose the answer is one in ten. If we evaluate disparate impact screen by screen, the employee will lose (assuming the Court has adopted a 5 percent probability as the threshold for statistical inference). No one screen can be shown to have a disparate impact at the required level of probability. Yet the probability of all three screens independently producing a result that could occur by chance only one in ten times is one in a thousand. So we would have a disparate-impact case of the "system-wide" variety. It is to prevent that kind of outcome that a risk-averse employer might simply look at the final numbers and say, "Get me just enough of X minority in the final selection groups so no statistical inference can be made."[22]

Aware of this criticism, Congress undertook a comprehensive reform of system-wide disparate-impact discrimination cases in the Civil Rights Act of 1992. Such cases were substantially restricted.[23] Hiring by the numbers was, by a large margin, the deepest criticism of disparate-impact theory. Had Congress enacted the reforms of the 1992 act regarding this practice prior to *Ward's Cove*, it is possible the Court would not have ruled as it did. That the hiring-by-the-numbers problem was on the Court's mind was made clear in several cases leading up to *Ward's Cove*.[24] However, *Ward's Cove* itself was not a system-wide case.[25] A narrower ground was available to the Court, but in making use, instead, of the procedural device at hand, the allocation of burdens of proof, the Court was able both to bar the plaintiffs' action in *Ward's Cove* and shut down system-wide disparate-impact practice as well.

The comparative advantage of Congress in this enterprise is apparent. The burdens of proof should not have been reallocated. The Court did so because it was the most effective judicial means of shutting down the kind of Title VII case that had been most criticized. An outright reversal of *Griggs* would also have done this—but it would have reached more broadly than the problem most in mind: hiring by the numbers. Congress, by contrast, could address the problem with precision. And, largely, that is what Congress did in the Civil Rights Act of 1992.

There was in the action Congress took following *Ward's Cove*, however, an underappreciation of its own legitimate function in at least one regard: its deference to judge-made phrases. In resetting the burdens of proof for an employee to show an alternative selection device, Congress should simply have said what those burdens were, as it did in the immediately preceding sections of the 1992 act. It could have said, for instance, "An employee can rebut the employer's or union's affirmative defense by showing an alternative employment practice that would have substantially accomplished the asserted purpose of the practice used, that lacked the effect on the employee's protected group, and that was no more than 5 percent more expensive to implement." Yes, I'm making up 5 percent, but that's what Congress is supposed to do. It can, and should, decide exactly how much additional cost it wishes to impose on employers and unions in order to vindicate the objectives of the Civil Rights Act.

Instead, in the Civil Rights Act of 1992, Congress said, "If the respondent demonstrates that a specific employment practice does not cause the disparate impact, the respondent shall not be required to demonstrate that such practice is required by business necessity. The demonstration referred to . . . shall be in accordance with the law as it existed on June 4, 1989, with respect to the concept of 'alternative employment practice.' "[26]

The date of *Ward's Cove* was June 5, 1989.

We can observe a similar approach in the part of the Civil Rights Act of 1992 defining "business necessity": "This subsection is meant to codify the meaning of 'business necessity' as used in *Griggs v. Duke Power Co.* (401 U.S. 424 [1971]) and to overrule the treatment of business necessity as a defense in *Ward's Cove Packing Co., Inc. v. Atonio* (490 U.S. 642 [1989])."[27]

In these two instances, Congress resigned its authority as master of words. Instead, Congress limply referred to the state of the law prior to Supreme Court opinions it doesn't like. This is lazy and potentially harmful. The harm comes from requiring all employers and labor unions, potential respondents under Title VII, to research not the current law but the law as it stood what is now fifteen years ago. It is costly to research legal history, and not particularly fair to those who have no prior experience with the law. Also, this approach cuts off common law development. If the interpretation of "alternative employment practice" could progress with more and more case experience, it is wrong to freeze that progression instead, forever, as of June 5, 1989. And freezing the meaning of "business necessity" as used in *Griggs* actually freezes in an ambiguity, as "business necessity" was used interchangeably with three other formulations in *Griggs*.

Why did the Congress do this?

There came a time in the negotiations where the major parties agreed they wanted to overrule *Ward's Cove* but couldn't agree on every aspect of what they wanted in its place.[28] There were other impasses as well— for example, over retroactivity.[29] In the legislative practice, ambiguity can allow progress to continue on areas of disagreement, rather than making *complete* agreement the prerequisite to *any* agreement. Nevertheless, legislation that simply cites a court opinion by name and says, "that's what we mean," is an abdication of the legislative role and comparative advantage actually to say what the legislature means.

There is one other reason why Congress acted as it did. Several Supreme Court opinions served as the impetus for the Civil Rights Act of 1992, *Patterson v. McLean Credit Union*[30] and *Ward's Cove* chief among them. Congress wanted, explicitly, to condemn those opinions and to characterize the justices in the majority (and their political allies) as insensitive to civil rights. Enacting the previous Supreme Court's opinions served this purpose, as though to say, "Those were the correct interpretations of the law; any departure from that interpretation is so outrageous as to suggest the later Court's lack of respect for civil rights, and to suspect the commitment to civil rights of presidents who appointed the justices in the majority in those opinions, and, maybe even, the commitment to civil rights of other members of the political party of those presidents today." That Supreme Court opinions occasionally figure in, and are distorted by, political battles is no shocking revelation.

So Congress was making a political statement as well as a statutory one. As we saw in the flag-burning arena, there is potential harm whenever a legislature uses its statutory authority to make a point more appropriate for a resolution. There could have been a civil rights resolution, indeed, a joint resolution requiring presidential signature or veto, if Congress intended to put the president on the spot, condemning the U.S. Supreme Court's opinions. There could then have been separate legislation. In combining the two, Congress surrendered, at least in small part, its inherent advantage in drafting law in order to put the prior Supreme Court's formulations under a glaring light. That approach was potentially self-serving and also historically hypocritical in that Congress had failed to muster the votes to accomplish in the Civil Rights Act of 1964 what the Supreme Court had decided in *Griggs* and *Albemarle Paper Co. v. Moody.*[31] Saying that those two opinions were obviously correct allowed Congress to cover up for the fact that Congress lacked the will to make those holdings the law when it drafted the Civil Rights Act in 1964.

NOTES

1. See, e.g., remarks of Sen. Hubert Humphrey: "Contrary to the allegations of some opponents of this title, there is nothing in it that will give any power . . . to require hiring . . . to achieve a certain racial balance." 110 *Cong. Rec.* 6549 (1964). See, generally, legislative history collected in the dissenting opinion of Justice Rehnquist, joined by Chief Justice Burger, in *United Steelworkers of America v. Weber*, 443 U.S. 193 (1979).

2. The Civil Rights Act reflected this judgment in its explicit "safe harbor" for a "professionally developed ability test." Civil Rights Act of 1992, 42 U.S.C. § 2000e-2(h). The legislative history for this provision, the "Tower Amendment," named for Sen. John Tower, is found at 110 *Cong. Rec.* 13,492, 13,724 (1964).

3. See the "safe harbor" for "a bona fide seniority or merit system." 42 U.S.C. § 2000e-2(h).

4. The statute forbade action taken "because of such individual's race." 42

U.S.C. § 2000e-2(h). The safe harbor for employment tests carried the proviso that they not be "designed, intended, or used to discriminate." The words "because of" should dominate the words in a specific exception; and even in the context of that exception, the statutory rule of *ejusdem generis* would support the construction that "used to discriminate" did not swamp all the other words pointing to an intent requirement. Indeed, if "used to discriminate" meant a results-only test, the words "designed" and "intended" in the same proviso would have been superfluous.

5. For example, antitrust law prohibits agreements in restraint of trade but not unilateral action with the same result. *Theatre Enterprises, Inc. v. Paramount Film Distributing Corp.*, 346 U.S. 537 (1954). In searching for evidence of agreement, the Supreme Court has allowed an inference to be formed from parallel conduct (*American Tobacco v. United States*, 328 U.S. 781 [1946]) and from conduct that makes sense only if each actor anticipates that each other actor engages in the same conduct (*Interstate Circuit, Inc. v. City of Dallas*, 390 U.S. 676 [1968]).

6. 401 U.S. 424 (1971).

7. Id. at 431.

8. Id. at 431–32.

9. As an illustration, suppose the following language were to be found in the original version of the bill, as it was submitted for markup in the House Judiciary Committee.

> It shall be an unlawful employment practice for an employer or union to condition a job or benefit upon an applicant's meeting a certain qualification, where applying that qualification resulted in excluding applicants on the basis of race or sex or national origin or religion. But the claim won't be sustained if the qualification
>
> (1) was a necessity for the job, and / or
> (2) was related to performance of the job, and / or
> (3) was related to measuring job capability, and / or
> (4) was manifestly related to the employment.

The first few minutes of a markup session in committee would encounter an inquiry of the author, "Is it 'and' or 'or'?" For our purposes here, it doesn't matter what the answer was; it is my point, simply, that the legislative drafting process would almost surely ask the right question and lead to a clearer statement.

Another question that would also very likely be raised early in a markup would be, what level of proof is required to show applicants were excluded on the basis of race or sex? Statistical proof in social science uses different acceptable probabilities of false positives; 1 percent, 5 percent, and 10 percent are most common. In the 1964 Civil Rights Act, Congress did not specify. This itself is strongly suggestive that Congress expected proof of intent to discriminate to be required, not just a discriminatory effect. Intent was a well-known element of civil and criminal law. Had the statute simply been relying upon proof of intent, the Judiciary Committee would have been comfortable in leaving to judicial interpretation how intent was to be proven. When venturing into proof without need of intent, however, Congress would have had to confront the level of proof required from statistical inference, to demonstrate that the specific "built-in headwind" had been proven to exist.

In the absence of statutory guidance, following *Griggs*, federal courts developed their own standards, sometimes making egregious errors of statistical interpretation. See T. Campbell, "Regression Analysis in Title VII Cases—Minimum Standards, Comparable Worth, and Other Issues Where Law and Statistics Meet," 36 *Stan. L. Rev.* 1299 (1984).

10. Which party has the burden of proof is to be distinguished from the standard of proof. The latter is a legislative function to set. Where evidence is based on probabilities, how much tolerance for a "type 1" error can be allowed and still meet the standard of "preponderance of the evidence" typical of civil cases? If "preponderance" means more likely than not, the ultimate fact can come in at anything under a 50 percent chance of a "type 1" error. That suggests that predicate facts based on statistics can also come in with a "type 1" error of anything less than 50 percent. There is nothing in statistical science, however, that says this is correct; and Congress, had it intended to address the issue of statistical proof, might well have set a different percentage. It is an issue as to which Congress would have institutional advantages: hearings, testimony, and public debate of alternative formulations and their consequences.

11. 490 U.S. 642, 659–60 (1989).

12. Id. at 660.

13. Id. at 661.

14. The professionally developed ability test is the best illustration of this structure. See 110 *Cong. Rec.* 13,492, 13,724 (1964).

15. Three almost insuperable obstacles were now imposed: (1) As just discussed, any employer could suggest a nondiscriminatory reason for a practice, and the employee would have to disprove it; (2) The nondiscriminatory reason did not have to be a necessity anymore, despite that formula among the options in *Griggs*. "The touchstone of this inquiry is a reasoned review of the employer's justification for his use of the challenged practice. . . . [T]here is no requirement that the challenged practice be 'essential' or 'indispensable' to the employer's business for it to pass muster." 490 U.S. at 659; (3) The alternative an employee might suggest to the discriminatory device now had to be equally effective, including cost considerations. (In *Albemarle Paper Co. v. Moody*, 422 U.S. 405, 425 [1975], the Court had only required that such an alternative "would also serve the employer's legitimate interest.")

16. See, e.g., the "Purposes" section of the act, "to respond to the Supreme Court's recent decisions by restoring the civil rights protections that were dramatically limited by those decisions." Civil Rights Act of 1992, § 2.

17. 490 U.S. at 660.

18. Fed. R. Evid. 301 (burden of proof).

19. *Alabama v. United States*, 304 F.2d 583, 586 (5th Cir., 1962).

20. *United States v. Hinds County School Board*, 417 F.2d 852, 858 (5th Cir., 1969). See also *Hazelwood School District, v. United States*, 433 U.S. 299 (1977). The jury discrimination cases from the 1950s and 1960s gave plaintiffs quite a boost here. The context was very different, but the language of the Court, in accepting inference of discrimination from numbers, was very supportive. When citizens were summoned for grand jury service and all the African American potential jurors were excluded, the Supreme Court was willing to infer intentional discrimination. No special skill is required to serve on a grand jury; so plaintiffs were not obliged to show what part of the screening process to serve on a jury resulted in the discriminatory exclusion of blacks. Logically, this kind of inference should not apply to a hiring process that involves several good faith substantive requirements, but judges not particularly skilled in statistical inference were not the most vigilant guardians against this trend. Hence, the system-wide disparate-impact kind of case born in the jury-discrimination area gained footing in employment discrimination cases. See Campbell, "Regression Analysis in Title VII Cases," n. 9.

21. Cumulative effect of selective screens:

	B	W	Total	"Expected" B	Lower Range of "Expected" B
Number surviving each screen	B	W	T	E	L
(1) Apply	50	50	100		
(2) Initial interview	30	35	65	32.5	28
(3) Reference check	17	33	50	23	16
(4) Probationary period rating	5	20	25	8.5	4
(5) Validated skill test	1	14	15	3	.06
(6) Selected	1	14	15	7.5	3.8

B = Number of minority race at each level.
W = Number of nonminority race at each level.

$T = B + W;$

$E_{ROW} = (B/T)_{IN\ PREVIOUS\ ROW} \times T_{ROW}$ except ROW 6,

where $E = (50/100)(15)$

and $L = E - 1.9 \sqrt{15(50/100)(50/100)}$.

For all other rows, $L = E - 1.9\sigma,$

where $\sigma_{ROW} = \sqrt{(T)_{ROW} \times (B/T)_{IN\ PREVIOUS\ ROW} \times (W/T)_{IN\ PREVIOUS\ ROW}}$.

22. Such conduct might itself constitute reverse discrimination; except that the employer might allege he or she was engaging in self-policing and correc-

tion, as the Supreme Court has permitted private employers to do in *Steel Workers v. Weber*, 443 U.S. 193 (1979), and has said public employers might be able to do in *Johnson v. Transportation Agency, Santa Clara County, California* 480 U.S. 616 (1987), and *City of Richmond v. J. A. Croson Co.*, 488 U.S. 469 (1989).

23. Civil Rights Act of 1992, § 105(B)(i):

> With respect to demonstrating that a particular employment practices causes a disparate impact as described in subparagraph (A)(i), the complaining party shall demonstrate that each particular challenged employment practice causes a disparate impact, except that if the complaining party can demonstrate to the court that the elements of a respondent's decision making process are not capable of separation for analysis, the decision making process may be analyzed as one employment practice.

24. *Hazelwood School District v. United States; Texas Department of Community Affairs v. Burdine*, 450 U.S. 248, 251 (1981); *Watson v. Fort Worth Bank & Trust*, 487 U.S. 977, 991 (1988) (plurality opinion).

25. The plaintiff had alleged a statistically significant disparity between the number of nonwhite workers in two kinds of job: cannery and noncannery. 490 U.S. at 650. This is similar to, but not the same as, a case that alleged an applicant pool and a decision group differed significantly in minority representation. The Court could simply have stopped its decision with its holding that the two groups were not comparable, nor were they in a feeder relationship to each other; hence, plaintiffs had not proven either a traditional disparate-impact case or a system-wide disparate impact case. As the Court stated, "For reasons explained below, the degree of disparity between these groups is not relevant to our decision here." Id. at 660 n. 5.

26. 42 U.S.C. § 2000e-2(k)(1)(B)(ii) and 2(k)(1)(C).

27. 42 U.S.C. § 2000e(o)(3).

28. There is no public record of these deliberations, but I and Congressman Hamilton Fish of New York and I were the Republican House Judiciary Committee members who participated in them.

29. This ambiguity was eventually resolved by the U.S. Supreme Court ten years later. Critics of the Civil Rights Act of 1992 complained that retroactivity would enrich particular plaintiffs and their attorneys in pending litigation. Defenders of the act did not want to deny its benefits to pending litigants but preferred to remove the debate from focusing upon particular individuals. Hence, the matter was left open.

As a general matter, Congress will leave potentially controversial issues, not necessary for resolution, to the courts when there is general confidence in how the courts will rule. When that confidence is less, Congress tends to spell more out in statutory language. There were many ambiguities in the 1964 Civil Rights Act, but the federal courts, in the wake of their record following *Brown v. Board of Education*, were generally trusted to resolve them. By contrast, the Congress that passed the Civil Rights Act of 1992 explicitly mistrusted the federal courts. As a result, the Civil Rights Act of 1992 took up more pages in the U.S.

Code to deal with only one section of the 1964 statute than the entire 1964 statute had comprised (twenty-nine versus twenty-seven pages, as measured in the text portion of U.S. Code Annotated).

30. 491 U.S. 164 (1989).
31. 422 U.S. 405 (1975).

CHAPTER 12

Two Statutes, a Hundred Years Apart: When Court Interpretation Changes between and after Two Separate Legislative Acts

THE INTERPLAY between the Congress and the Supreme Court can sometimes yield results that leapfrog each other. The Civil Rights Acts present several illustrations of this process. Studying these illustrations points out the benefit of reliability and clarity in what the Supreme Court does and the desirability of Congress making use of its authority to write words for specific circumstances. Instead of finding these attributes, we will see the Supreme Court shifting opinions after Congress has acted in reliance on an earlier interpretation; and we will see, again, Congress responding to Court opinions by correcting the Court's own words, as though tutoring an erring student, rather than stating what it wishes the law to be. And both institutions have been guilty of claiming they never changed their positions at all. This unwillingness to confront a changed interpretation with candor has resulted in confusion and grossly unanticipated results.

In 1866, the Congress enacted a civil rights law guaranteeing,

All persons within the jurisdiction of the United States shall have the same right in every State and Territory to make and enforce contracts, to sue, be parties, give evidence, and to the full and equal benefit of all laws and proceedings for the security of persons and property as is enjoyed by white citizens.[1]

A separate law from the same era included a prohibition against racial discrimination in the sale or rental of property.[2]

For more than a hundred years, those laws were applied by the Court to guarantee no more than equal access to the agencies of government, without regard to race. Then, in 1968, in *Jones v. Alfred H.*

Mayer,[3] the U.S. Supreme Court ruled that the Civil War–era statutes actually intended to outlaw private discrimination, at least in so far as the clause dealing with the sale or rental of property was concerned.

At the time of this decision, the Open Housing Act was pending before the U.S. Congress. If the century-earlier statute really reached private discrimination in rental and leasing of property, the 1968 Open Housing Act would have been largely unnecessary. The *Jones* Court, however, did not let the pendency of the new federal law affect its decision. In this, the Court turned away from an accommodation between the branches that might have avoided later conflict. Instead, both the Court and Congress went ahead, and the Court reversed its long-standing, narrow interpretation,[4] almost contemporaneously with the enactment of the new Open Housing Act.

Needing a jurisdictional base that would cover private real estate not involved in interstate commerce, the Court found it in the Thirteenth Amendment, holding that Congress had the authority to overturn "badges of servitude," lingering since the termination of slavery in America.[5] Two different statutes were now available for a private party to sue alleging racial discrimination in housing, a hundred years apart.

Eight years later, the Court was presented with extending the Civil War civil rights statutes once again—this time to the context of private contract unrelated to property. The fact situation was compelling: a private primary school in Virginia had denied admission to two students simply because they were black. The Court upheld a private right of action to redress this private form of discrimination. That result was unsurprising given *Jones* and might actually be held up as an example of a positive judicial attribute, to seek consistency across relatively parallel legislative schemes, whenever possible.[6] The two rulings are instructive, however, for the interaction between the Court and Congress that ensued.

At the time of *Jones*, the Supreme Court could have waited for the outcome of the Open Housing bill. If the bill passed, the Court could have dismissed the certiorari petition in *Jones*, allowing the plaintiffs to bring an action under the new scheme arranged by Congress. If it did not pass, the Court could then have taken the case and decided whether to expand its interpretation of the earlier act of Congress. The result of such caution would have been that the Court and the Congress would be working in harness, not against each other.

However attractive that alternative might have been, by the time *Runyon v. McCrary*[7] was decided twelve years later, Congress had already acted. In the 1964 Civil Rights Act, Congress created a right of action for discrimination in employment: Title VII.[8] Congress chose not to create a right of action for other forms of discrimination.[9] If the earlier civil rights statute, 42 U.S.C. § 1981, reached all private contracts, then Title VII (and Title VI) would have been superfluous, as to victims of race discrimination. What Congress did in 1964 was necessary precisely because the earlier civil rights statute did not reach private action.

In *Runyon*, the Court leapfrogged Congress. It held that the remedies of 42 U.S.C. § 1981 did apply to the decision to bar two black children from a private school. Of necessity, this meant the remedies of 42 U.S.C. § 1981 also applied to employment discrimination; the qualifying criterion was a "contract," and employment involves a contract.

In the employment discrimination context, the practical result was totally unanticipated by Congress—either in 1866, 1964, or 1976. Because 42 U.S.C. § 1981 reached racial discrimination, plaintiffs in employment-related race cases could collect punitive damages. Victims of gender, religious, or national origin discrimination in employment, however, could not. Punitive damages had been implied into the 1866 Civil Rights Act many years before under the theory that, if a federal tortlike statute were created, the state remedies for tort applied in the venue of the case.[10] The 1964 Civil Rights Act, by contrast, had no punitive damages provision. Employment cases based on race also would be entitled to jury trials, even though Title VII cases were not.[11]

So matters stood for another thirteen years. Congress was willing to allow the disparity to continue. There was never a question of taking away the rights newly found in 42 U.S.C. § 1981. A one-way ratchet was at work in the legislative branch. Even though the 1866 or 1964 Congress might well not have intended to grant a particular right, it was impossible to take it away once granted by the Court. Congress was constrained by expectations of constituents; to take away a right once enjoyed is immensely harder than simply to refuse to grant the right in the first place.[12] The Court, by contrast, unconstrained by constituent expectations, has shown no difficulty in taking back what it had at one time granted. And that is just what it did in *Patterson v. McLean Credit Union*.[13]

While not affected by the one-way ratchet of settled expectations of a right, the Court has peculiar attributes of its own decision-making process that lead to imperfections in our constitutional scheme. Key among these is a desire not to overrule an earlier case outright but, rather, to find some controlling difference between the two cases.[14] In *Patterson*, the Court allowed this attribute to bring about an absurdity. Rather than simply saying, "*Runyon* is reversed, there is no remedy under 42 U.S.C. § 1981 for private discriminatory acts, the statute only bears upon governmental agencies, as everyone thought for a hundred years until 1976," the Court created a tortured reading that only discrimination at the formation stage of a private contract was covered. The statute guarantees that all persons have the same right "to make *and enforce* contracts . . . as is enjoyed by white citizens" [emphasis added].[15] Mrs. Patterson claimed she'd been racially harassed on the job and then fired from her job because of her race. Justice Kennedy held this was not enough. Had her employer offered her a contract at signing time giving him the right to harass her on the job, she could sue. Had the employer tendered her a contract giving him the right to fire her for her race, she could sue. But because her employer was, allegedly, a hypocrite, offering her a contract that did not include provisions for how she would actually be treated but then acting as though there were such contract terms, she had no cause of action. Such bizarre results are occasionally unavoidable in reconciling differing statutes. But the Court here was interpreting a single statute, indeed, a single phrase within it, "make and enforce contracts."

Patterson demonstrates the Court at its comparative worst. Striving to appear consistent, it only succeeded in appearing petty.

Congress, by contrast, took the occasion to move, when no previous stimulus had provided such an impetus. Though content to leave victims of race and gender discrimination with unequal remedies for thirteen years, and content to leave both of them without any remedies for ninety-nine years after the end of slavery and forty-three years after women's suffrage,[16] Congress now had someone to demonize: the "reactionary Supreme Court." In taking back what it had itself granted only twelve years earlier and leaving everything else (all that Congress had done in the Equal Pay Act and the Civil Rights Act) completely intact, the Court had exposed a weakness that Congress, then under Democratic control, was able to exploit. There had been three new justices appointed between *Runyon* and *Patterson*, all by President Reagan and all voting to cut back *Runyon*, whereas the justices they replaced had each voted with the majority in *Runyon*. These three new justices, O'Connor, Kennedy, and Scalia, joined the two dissenters from *Runyon*, Rehnquist and White, to effectuate the change in a new five-to-four balance. Characterizing the *Patterson* case as a gross denial of civil rights made better politics than observing, as Justice Stevens did, that it was *Runyon* that effectuated the departure from settled law and from what Congress itself, at the time of *Runyon*, thought the law to be.[17] The superficiality of the distinction made by Justice Kennedy strongly added to the force of the charge that the Court was simply set on reversing civil rights gains. Had Justice Kennedy reversed *Runyon* outright, he could not have done as much harm to his cause as did his Dickensian distinctions between making, enforcing, and acting under a contract.

This political potential, an attribute, obviously, of Congress more than of the Court, provided the stimulus to review and make consistent the body of federal statutory law concerning employment discrimination. In the 1992 Civil Rights Act, Congress reversed *Runyon*, and all victims of employment discrimination, whether based on race, gender, religion, or national origin, were given access to the same treatment with regard to damages and jury trial. This denouement showed Congress at its best,[18] drawing upon its unique ability to write policy specific to the problems it saw. For example, in granting new rights to bring breach of contract actions, Congress also imposed caps on the damages that could be sought, based on the size of the employer.[19] Obviously, such a compromise between expanded liability and prevention of ruinous awards was beyond the power of the Court to have crafted. Congress took the problem, rather than the case, under consideration. It showed none of the Court's hesitation simply to reverse what had gone before. But for all these demonstrated advantages of Congress, it took the Supreme Court's action, first in *Jones* and then in *Patterson*, to start Congress on this path. Had neither case been decided, the 1964 Civil Rights Act might well have remained the only route to recovery for employment discrimination.

NOTES

1. 42 U.S.C. § 1981.
2. Id.
3. 392 U.S. 409 (1968).
4. Justice Stevens, however, concurring in *Runyon v. McCrary*, 427 U.S. 160 (1976), stated that the interpretation of the 1866 law that prevailed for a hundred years was the correct one: "There is no doubt in my mind that that construction of the statute would have amazed the legislators who voted for it. Both its language and the historical setting in which it was enacted convince me that Congress intended only to guarantee all citizens the same legal capacity to

make and enforce contracts, to obtain, own, and convey property, and to litigate and give evidence." Id. at 189 (Stevens, J., concurring).

5. 392 U.S. at 424.

6. 427 U.S. at 192 (White, joined by Rehnquist, J.J., dissenting). Justice White attempted to distinguish the statutory genesis of 42 U.S.C. § 1982, at issue in *Jones*, from 42 U.S.C. § 1981, now presented in *Runyon*, in that the former was based on the Thirteenth Amendment and the latter on the Fourteenth Amendment. But he garnered only one other vote, and the majority construed the two sections identically.

7. 427 U.S. 160 (1976).

8. 42 U.S.C. § 2000e et seq.

9. Congressional intent to grant a private right of action under Title VI to victims of discrimination in programs that received federal money was discerned many years later by the Court, in *Cannon v. University of Chicago*, 441 U.S. 677 (1979).

10. 42 U.S.C. § 1981(a).

11. 42 U.S.C. § 1981(b).

12. See M. Kelman, "Market Discrimination and Groups," 53 *Stan. L. Rev.* 833 (2001).

13. 491 U.S. 164 (1989).

14. E. Levi, *An Introduction to Legal Reasoning* 2 (1948).

15. 491 U.S. at 164 citing 42 U.S.C. § 1981.

16. The Equal Pay Act of 1963 can be called the first comprehensive congressional effort to ameliorate workplace discrimination based on sex; the Nineteenth Amendment was ratified in 1920.

17. "For me the problem in these cases is whether to follow a line of authority which I firmly believe to have been incorrectly decided." 427 U.S. at 189 (opinion of Stevens, J. concurring).

18. The president also showed flexibility. Originally threatening a veto of the 1991 Civil Rights Act, President George H. W. Bush eventually signed the 1992 Civil Rights Act, a bill with only cosmetic changes over the 1991 version. What had happened in between was the nomination of David Duke as the Republican candidate for governor of Louisiana. The Republican president recognized that vetoing the Civil Rights Act created symbolism impossible to overcome if he wished to escape being identified with Duke, the former Grand Wizard of the Ku Klux Klan.

19. 42 U.S.C. § 1981a (b).

CHAPTER 13

When the Supreme Court Does Not Do
Its Job: The Second Amendment

IT IS THE RIGHT of the U.S. Supreme Court to announce constitutional protections. It is also its duty. When the Court does not perform this duty, the other branches of the federal government, and the states, do not remain inactive.

In the context of the war power, to be discussed later in this book, the lower federal courts, and the U.S. Supreme Court in denying certiorari, have permitted the executive prosecution of war to continue unchallenged by the branch to which the Constitution gives the explicit right to declare war. The result has been that one branch, the executive, won over the legislative, by reason of the executive's greater flexibility of action.

In the context of personal liberties, the consequence of the Court not exercising its duty is, once again, that the executive wins out, this time over an individual. The laws enforced against the individual that are alleged to be unconstitutional were, obviously, passed by Congress, but the executive chooses when and whether to enforce them. Thus, the consequence of the Court not performing its function is not, as the Court glibly says, that the matter will be resolved by the "political branches." The matter, rather, is resolved, often by severe cost to an individual's freedom or property, by the executive, who in a second term is unanswerable to the electorate[1] and whose actions cannot be constrained by Congress short of a veto-proof two-thirds consensus of both houses. That is the consequence of judicial abstention.

Convictions under federal firearms laws have been common.[2] The U.S. Supreme Court, however, has been silent on the constitutional provision most important to challenge such laws, since 1939.[3] The lower federal courts have been obliged to hear appeals from firearms convictions, including challenges to the constitutionality of the underlying federal firearms statutes. In all instances but one (which was reversed on appeal), these lower federal courts have ruled in favor of the constitutionality of the statute being challenged.[4] Their rationales, however, have not been consistent. Some circuits have held that there is no private right under the Second Amendment, that it adheres only to the state and its militia.[5] Other circuits have held that the Fourteenth Amendment does not incorporate the Second Amendment; hence, a state can do what it wants regarding private ownership or use of firearms.[6] Most recently, the Fifth Circuit has ruled that there is, indeed, a private right of firearms ownership, though one of the judges on the panel characterized this conclusion as dicta.[7]

The silence of the U.S. Supreme Court, in the absence of a circuit conflict, might be interpreted as acquiescence in the lower courts' decisions.[8] Unlike in the cases involving the declaration of war, the lower federal courts have rendered decisions on the merits. The danger, therefore, is not that an important constitutional claim has not been decided upon by the judiciary. The danger is more subtle; it is that the sphinx-like silence of the U.S. Supreme Court, after some reasonable time, has moved from a source of stability to one of concern, even diffidence. The implication is all the more strong when the announced rationale for the last opinion rendered by the Court, in 1939, has been superceded in parallel contexts of constitutional law. Eventually, there is a duty for the Court to rule, even if only to affirm what the lower federal courts have been doing. This is one of the hardest obligations to crystallize. The closest analogy is to the president's duty to take care that the laws be faithfully executed. Congress, by contrast, has virtually no constitutional obligation to legislate. It's entirely acceptable for Congress to decide not to change the status quo or to be deadlocked so that no majority of both houses emerges to do so. The branch that has taken unto itself the duty to state what the law is, however, after some period of time must do so.

The last time the U.S. Supreme Court gave our country guidance on the meaning of the Second Amendment was in *U.S. v. Miller* in 1939.[9] The Court held it could not take judicial notice of the fact that a sawed-off shotgun was a weapon useful to the militia. The defendant, a Mr. Miller, was absent. No counsel was appointed to represent him. The argument before the U.S. Supreme Court was ex parte. The trial court had dismissed the indictment under the Second Amendment. Miller, evidently, chose the occasion to go to ground.

In a footnote, the Court cited its earlier opinion in *Presser v. Illinois*,[10] but it did not rely on *Presser*. Nevertheless, federal circuits hearing subsequent cases have resurrected *Presser*'s holding, that the Fourteenth Amendment did not incorporate the Second Amendment.[11] However, in 1886, when *Presser* was decided, the Court had not incorporated any of the Bill of Rights. It was not until thirty-nine years later that the First Amendment was deemed incorporated,[12] and other incorporations came after that.[13] So, in citing Supreme Court precedent from *Miller* relying on *Presser*, that the Second Amendment was not incorporated, modern circuits do nothing to disprove the claim of individuals who assert that, had the Supreme Court the obligation to take a modern case, it would have to incorporate the Second Amendment as it had so many other parts of the Bill of Rights.

There is no absolute rule I can propose for when the Supreme Court has been silent too long. The continued legitimacy of the premises underlying its earlier ruling certainly is one factor: here, the premise of nonincorporation as of 1886 (or 1939) is very much in doubt. The procedural setting of that earlier case is another factor: here, Miller was not present, and no one presented the arguments about the Second Amendment that an actual defendant (or even a court-invited amicus curiae) could.[14]

Furthermore, the Court's actual basis in *Miller*, that his weapon had not been shown to be related to the militia, and the Court chose not to take judicial notice that it was, is so narrow as to offer practically no guidance for any future cases. If a sawed-off shotgun were used by the militia, would Miller have been acquitted? An ancient case, decided on idiosyncratic grounds, whose premises have been undermined and that was decided without benefit of adverse argument: all these factors call out for the Court to rule anew. A sense of outrage[15] is felt by those who observe criminals receiving protection of other provisions of the Bill of Rights yet are denied their chance to make their case before the U.S. Supreme Court (and have been since 1886, since the 1939 argument was ex parte).

In the absence of such a ruling, members of Congress and the state legislatures are presented with firearms control bills on a regular basis. Each member of the state legislature, preliminarily, has to decide whether the Second Amendment applies to the state. Assuming that it does, members then have to decide whether the bill before them constitutes an abridgement of those rights or merely a not "undue burden" on these rights.[16] If the abridgement is serious, the legislator must then consider whether the state's interest is compelling.

For federal firearms legislation, each member of Congress has to start by asking if the Second Amendment creates an individual or a collective right. If individual, then the same questions as for a state legislator would ensue. If collective, then the member of Congress would still have to ascertain whether the proposed restriction interfered with the right of the state to train the militia.[17]

These questions are not likely to be asked by legislators. In Chapter 3, I discussed the obligations of a legislator to apply the Constitution to her or his own official acts. Even if the oath requirement were taken at its strongest, however, the institutional arrangements of a legislature do not readily afford the means to rule on these questions in a thoughtful and deliberate manner.[18]

Nor does the text of the Second Amendment itself offer sufficient guidance. Of many difficult constitutional phrasings, that in the Second Amendment is among the least clear. The uncertainty stems from the sentence structure and punctuation—including what seems to be an entirely superfluous final comma, which was present in some versions of the Second Amendment as it came back from the various state legislatures and not in others.[19]

One other institutional impediment stands in the way of the nonjudicial branches' resolution of this issue: members of Congress, state legislators, governors, and presidents bring to office their own views on firearms legislation. It is one thing for a public policy matter to be subjected to a rather arcane constitutional provision, such as whether the commerce clause is broad enough to support a particular proposed piece of federal legislation. The elected official can be expected to have a view on the desirability of the underlying policy; but few, if any, will have put their views on the commerce clause on record or had them considered by the voters in deciding whether to vote for them. In such a case, it is plausible that conclusions from a legislative hearing or presidential commission would be respected and followed when it reported back that the policy goal, however laudable, could not be achieved without violating the Constitution. In the case of firearms legislation, however, the elected official's position on the public policy and the Constitution are linked. One will ask a candidate what her or his views on the Second Amendment are, just as one will ask a candidate whether she or he believes abortion is constitutionally protected. As a result, it is unrealistic to expect a legislator or executive to be open to changing her or his mind upon hearing argument and evidence—either on the policy or on its constitutionality. Unlike a federal judge, a U.S. representative or state legislator pays a personal price for "flip-flopping." To decide an issue of constitutional law in a fair manner, however, one has to be willing to accept a determination contrary to one's policy preference. Otherwise, the Constitution has no force.

The result I reach is that such circumstances compel the U.S. Supreme Court to take a case on the Second Amendment and decide it in as clear a manner as it is able. Too much time has passed since the last time it did so; too much doctrine has changed; the issue is too important; and the other branches institutionally cannot be expected to handle the constitutional issues. There is occasionally a duty to rule; this is such an occasion.

NOTES

1. For the last twenty years of the twentieth century, the executive authority was in the hands of a president not responsible to the electorate for 40 percent of the time.

2. Bureau of Justice Statistics, Special Report: Federal Firearm Offenders 1992–98, John Scalia. 1998 convictions: 4,180; 1997 convictions: 5,849.

3. Its last ruling was *U.S. v. Miller*, 307 U.S. 174 (1939).

4. The one exception is *U.S. v. Emerson*, 46 F. Supp. 2d 598 (N.D. Tex. 1999), *rev'd*, 270 F.3d 203 (5th Cir., 2001). Since then, some litigants have argued the Court has, *sub silentio*, affirmed the absence of an individual right under the Second Amendment (see, e.g., Brief for Appellant, *U.S. v. Emerson*, 270 F.3d 203 [5th Cir., 2001]) (available at http://www.saf.org/pub/rkba/Legal/EmersonCenterToPreventHandgunViolencebrief.htm).

5. See, e.g., *U.S. v. Warin*, 530 F.2d 103 (6th Cir., 1976). There is language in *U.S. v. Miller* to sustain this view. 307 U.S. at 178–79.

6. See, e.g., *Silviera v. Lockyer*, 312 F.3d 1052 (9th Cir., 2003), and *Quilici v. Village of Morton Grove*, 695 F.2d 261 (7th Cir., 1982).

7. *U.S. v. Emerson*, 270 F.3d 203, 272 (5th Cir., 2001) (Parker, J., concurring). All three judges agreed that, even if there were a private right to ownership of a firearm, it should be held to yield to a federal statute denying that right to an individual subject to a court order in a domestic dispute involving violence.

8. With the Fifth Circuit's ruling in *Emerson*, the inference that Supreme Court silence meant approval of the lower courts decisions is still available, though a bit strained, since the circuits point in such different directions. The Court might, silently, be of the view that there is no constitutional right to an individual to keep and bear arms, but, if there were, it would yield, just as other rights in the Bill of Rights, to compelling state interests, which can be defined in

terms not antithetical to the right itself. Content with the outcome in *Emerson*, the Supreme Court might not be content with the circuit court's reasoning but also not interested in setting the matter for argument.

9. 307 U.S. 174 (1939).

10. Id. at 182, citing *Presser v. Illinois*, 116 U.S. 252 (1886).

11. See, e.g., *Quilici v. Village of Morton Grove*, 269.

12. *Gitlow v. New York*, 268 U.S. 652 (1925).

13. The Fourth Amendment was deemed incorporated in 1961 (*Mapp v. Ohio*, 367 U.S. 643 [1961]); the First Amendment was incorporated in 1925 (*Gitlow v. New York*); the Fifth Amendment was deemed incorporated in 1886 (*Boyd v. U.S.*, 116 U.S. 616 [1886]); and the Sixth Amendment in 1963 (*Gideon v. Wainwright*, 372 U.S. 335 [1963]).

14. See, e.g., *INS v. Chadha*, 462 U.S. 919 (1983) (Congress allowed to intervene to defend one-house veto), and *U.S. v. Dickerson*, 530 U.S. 428 (2000) (Professor—now Judge—Paul Cassell appointed to defend statute's constitutionality when executive refused).

15. Cf. S. Levinson, "The Embarrassing Second Amendment," 99 *Yale L. J.* 637 (1989). Professor Levinson points out how civil libertarians, particularly on major law school faculties, seem to shy away from vindicating Second Amendment rights the way they fight to vindicate other parts of the Bill of Rights.

16. Cf. *Planned Parenthood v. Casey*, 505 U.S. 833 (1992).

17. Article I, section 5, clause 16, grants to Congress the right "to provide for organizing, arming, and disciplining, the Militia" but reserves to the states the right to train the militia, according to the discipline set down by Congress.

18. Some legislatures allow for interim hearings, divorced from any specific bill, during which advocates from both sides of this constitutional debate could present their testimony and following which the committee could release a report. The procedures for such a hearing could be made to mimic those of an appellate or trial court. The U.S. Congress could do the same. For some policy issues of importance, Congress has created commissions, with instructions to report back conclusions after a specific amount of time. Presidential commissions are also common. In the absence of a Supreme Court ruling, the other branches could have summoned advice in this manner. What would be lacking, however, is finality to any determinations of such hearings or commissions. Further, there is an inherent bias. If a majority of legislators are disinclined to support a specific piece of firearms legislation, then it won't happen, so why hold a hearing? If a majority of legislators are inclined to support the legislation, then why learn that they can't do so? The inherent bias comes from being both advocate for a public policy position and arbiter of its constitutionality.

19. See undated letter from Library of Congress to Congressman T. Campbell (1989 by author's recollection):

Punctuation in the Second Amendment to the Constitution

The language of the Second Amendment has been the focus of much controversy in the on-going debate over the nature of the constitutionally guaranteed right "to keep and bear arms." Oddly, this amendment may be found in various reliable reference works to contain one, two, or three commas. This inconsistency in the placement of the punctuation occurs at the following places in the language:

A well regulated Militia, (1) being necessary to the security of a free State, (2) the right of the people to keep and bear Arms, (3) shall not be infringed.

The Bill of Rights, as passed by both houses of Congress, contained twelve articles. The first two articles failed of ratification, and thus it was article four which ultimately became the Second Amendment. The "official copy of the Joint Resolution of Congress proposing articles to the Legislatures of the States," as exhibited at the National Archives Building contains all three commas. However, to facilitate ratification of the proposed amendments, 13 copies were made by hand for forwarding to the states. At least one of these documents (viewed at the National Archives Building) omitted the final comma. In conveying notice of ratification, some states (e.g. Delaware) merely attached the official state action to the copy received. Other states (e.g. New York) recopied the text of the amendments in its notification. The New York ratification document of March 27, 1790 contains only one comma in the 4th article.

It would seem that the critical documents for final determination of proper punctuation would be the official engrossed copy of the joint resolution as passed by Congress and the document agreed to by each ratifying state. However, the multitude of handwritten copies relied on in the amendment process makes it impossible to determine what the "official" punctuation would be. While there may, in fact, be no "official" punctuation, few have structured their arguments concerning the true intentions of the framers of this amendment around the placement of these commas. The proper use or omission of punctuation may therefore be of little moment in this instance.

Kent M. Ronhovde

Legislative Attorney

CHAPTER 14

Methods of Solving Disputes between (and within) the Branches of Government

WHICH BRANCH of government should be called upon to tailor the application of a legislative rule to fit the circumstances of a particular situation that seems to have been unanticipated in the statute? One approach is for the legislation itself to anticipate the possibility of exceptions and to provide a mechanism for granting them. That was the eventual outcome of the dispute pitting preservation of habitat for endangered species against nearly complete federal projects. The Endangered Species Act prohibits any federal agency action that would "result in the destruction or modification of habitat of such species which is determined by the Secretary, after consultation as appropriate with the affected States, to be critical."[1] The statute appeared to have no discretion: if the species were listed and the secretary of interior determined some habitat was critical to that species,[2] then no federal project that modified that habitat could go ahead.

Resort was first made to the courts as repository of the discretion needed to make the Endangered Species Act work in harmony with the completion of federal projects commenced before the effective date of the act. For federal projects commenced thereafter, there still might be a need to accommodate from a pragmatic sense if an endangered species turned up that due diligence had not been able to locate in advance; however, most cases of conflict would be resolved at the time the project itself was approved.[3] In the case of the Tellico Dam on the Little Tennessee River, however, the project had been started and nearly completed before the effective date of the Endangered Species Act. Individuals with standing sued to block the completion of this dam, and the Tennessee Valley Authority (TVA) responded in favor of finishing the dam. The district court denied the injunction, relying on its equitable jurisdiction to weigh the effective forfeiture of $53 million against the damage to the habitat of one endangered species, the snail darter.[4] The U.S. Court of Appeals reversed,[5] and the case went to the U.S. Supreme Court.

The argument before the Supreme Court was remarkable for a number of reasons. The United States was on both sides of the case: the TVA favored the dam, the Environmental Protection Agency (EPA) favored the fish. The attorney general of the United States, former judge Griffin Bell, presented the case for the TVA. He commenced his oral argument by producing from his coat pocket a vial of formaldehyde in which was immersed a snail darter. Judge Bell observed that the fish was rather small to be the cause of such a large controversy, prompting Justice Powell to ask if the case would be any different were it a larger fish. Another justice asked if the fish were "good for anything, could it be used for bait, for example," a definition of "good" that might have surprised those who drafted the Endangered Species Act.

Fundamentally, the case dealt with the power of the court, not the worth of a fish. The trial judge seemed to have acted entirely within the traditional bounds of a court sitting in equity. An injunction, the relief sought by the plaintiffs, was an equitable remedy. A judge sitting in equity should follow the rules of equity, one of which is "that a court of equity will not lend its aid actively to enforce a forfeiture."[6] To stop the dam when it was over 80 percent completed would result in "nonrecoverable obligations" of $53 million.[7] Of course, one might respond that a species once extinct was gone forever, but the plaintiffs were not arguing, and the facts did not support, that the snail darter would become extinct. The standard, rather, was the one passed by Congress—that no federal project could proceed that modified critical habitat for the species. In the plaintiffs' view, not even moving the snail darter population from the Little Tennessee River to a more hospitable environment would be permitted under the act.

The U.S. Supreme Court agreed with plaintiffs, and the dam had to be stopped. This was not necessary. The Court could have ruled that, at least for projects long since started, it was within the contemplation of Congress that, in setting up what appeared to be an absolute rule, it was not intending to repeal the equitable jurisdiction of federal courts or the rules under which that jurisdiction was traditionally exercised. The Court could have given an *in futuro* only application to the Endangered Species Act. Had it done so, the U.S. Supreme Court would have been vindicating the comparative advantage of the judicial branch, to take into account the circumstances of an actual application of a statutory regime and to help make it work. Federal courts perform this task routinely, for example, in reconciling potentially conflicting federal statutory regimes, where literal application of both would be impossible.[8] The Court could have done this without denying that if Congress really meant the more Draconian interpretation, Congress could have it—provided Congress was explicit about it.[9] Instead, the U.S. Supreme Court appeared to remove from the arsenal of federal trial courts the ability to deny retroactive application of a statute when the statute itself is silent. In subsequent years, the Court was to reconsider this restriction and engaged quite readily in considering whether it would be equitable to apply a statute's provisions to cases pending at the time of its enactment, where the statute itself was silent.[10] A broader ability, apart from the retroactive situation, to exempt from application of a statute a class of persons or cases that a court believes was not foreseen by Congress, remains in doubt.[11]

Besides the judiciary, the executive branch also has an inherent advantage to perform such a task. As we saw in the context of the Fiesta Bowl and Title VI regulations for race-based scholarships, the executive chooses cases to prosecute. Through its choice of such cases and, even more directly, by announcing what it would not prosecute, the executive branch can effectively make an act of Congress work within circumstances Congress did not anticipate. Private plaintiffs, however, can proceed in court even if the executive does not—so if the statute in question permits standing for nongovernmental parties, the executive branch advantage of discretion is less availing. From the other direction, if such standing is not allowed by the statute, there is no check upon the executive choosing never to enforce a statute. By contrast, the courts will only have the one case before them, and their exercise of judgment won't present this danger.

In the wake of the U.S. Supreme Court's decision in *TVA v. Hill*,[12] Congress stepped in with its own statutory solution. A joint committee was created, including the federal agency in question, the governor of the state where the action was to occur, and the heads of several cabinet departments, to consider applications on a case-by-case basis for exemption from the Endangered Species Act's prohibition on government actions that modified critical habit of endangered species.[13] The statutory amendment explicitly refers to "reasonable mitigation and enhancement measures, including, but not limited to, live propagation, transplantation, and habit acquisition and improvement."[14]

This statutory amendment allows an opportunity for a hearing and emphasizes conciliation and possible compromise. Officially, it does not say that damage to any species can be traded off for other concerns. In practice, however, that is what it commands, since, if an alternative could have been arranged at reasonable cost that would not have harmed the critical habitat of an endangered species, the agency should have pursued it under the terms of the original unamended Endangered Species Act. What we see in this post–*TVA v. Hill* amendment is a politically acceptable route toward making a compromise with the fundamental purpose of the Endangered Species Act. That could not have been accomplished by a court sitting in equity; and, since the executive cannot control private parties bringing suit, it could not have been accomplished by exercise of the executive branch's prosecutorial discretion. As a legislative creation, the committee can issue decisions as valid as the Endangered Species Act itself and incapable of being overturned provided they are based on the record and are not arbitrary or capricious.[15]

A court sitting in equity and an explicit congressionally created committee of executive agency officials are ways to deal with fitting a statutory scheme to unanticipated circumstances. Another way is to bring the matter back to Congress itself. This route is fully explored in *INS v. Chadha*,[16] the case challenging the legislative veto. In this device, Congress sought control over a wealth of decisions made by the executive. *Chadha* struck down the constitutionality of this device; Justice White's dissent argues strongly for its constitutionality and effectiveness. In Justice White's view, the growth of the administrative arm of the federal government, the "fourth branch" of government, was balanced by the retention, by Congress, of oversight ability through the legislative veto. The ability retained by Congress to review executive regulations, arms sales, and decisions to extend clemency in immigration matters was intrinsically related to the grant of greater authority to the executive branch by Congress. Every action made by an administrative agency could be made by Congress, with the possible exception of those so targeted to the detriment of an individual that it could constitute a bill of attainder. Instead, Congress said, let the administrative process go forward, but if one house of Congress disagrees, then that particular instance of delegated authority is blocked. It takes two houses of Congress to agree to legislation in the first place; hence, any one house should be able to block the result of a specific delegation.

The logic in favor of the constitutionality of the one-house veto is powerful; so powerful that its detractors argued it would also justify a committee veto—a result so absurd, the detractors believe, as to point out the unconstitutionality of the entire idea. There is an important distinction, however, that familiarity with the legislative process demonstrates. A bill cannot become law without the approval of both houses. A bill can, however, become law without the approval of any single committee. In the House, a majority of members and, in the Senate, any senator may bring to the floor a motion to discharge a committee of further consideration of a bill.[17] So, the argument does not prove too much. A system allowing a single house of Congress to vitiate administrative action that that house could have prevented in the first place does not compel granting the same power to a committee.

As Justice White predicted, the demise of the legislative veto has led to accommodations to congressional demands for oversight that are far less democratic than the legislative veto. The clearest of these is the power exercised by the Appropriations Committees. Of necessity, appropriations bills are broad in scope. They could be more detailed, constitutionally, but the complexity of the modern federal government makes more precise legislation impractical. What happens instead is that an agency recites to the relevant Appropriations subcommittee its plans for spending the money appropriated on an annual basis. When, over the year, an agency seeks to spend money in a way that departs from that plan, it submits a "reprogramming request" to the relevant subcommittee. If the chair of that subcommittee approves of the reprogramming request, it goes ahead. If he or she does not, then the agency proceeds at its tremendous peril; for the next year, the agency knows, the subcommittee will write in specific language to the appropriations bill reversing the decision, and other punishments in the form of lower expenditure, or in an even more targeted way, lower limits for the cabinet official's personal office, will be included. Majority and minority alike participate in this process, as it enhances the power of the committee on which they serve; and the minority party hopes its minority status is temporary.

The result is that, instead of having oversight exercised by a majority of one house, a far more democratic process, oversight has become lodged in the discretion of a single individual, the chair of the Appropriations subcommittee dealing with the federal agency in question or, at most, the members of that subcommittee.

After *Chadha*, Congress passed the Congressional Review Act in 1996 as a way of supervising agency rule-making. This act is really only an expedited rule for legislation to overturn a regulation.[18] Legislation overturning a particular rule would, in the most common course, be vetoed by the president, however; so it amounts to a very weak review indeed—one requiring two-thirds of both houses to implement. When the executive branch changes political hands, however, there is the possibility of a regulation approved by the previous administration not being approved by the next administration. Then, the Congressional Review Act actually can have some teeth, in providing a means of reversing the regulation without having to build an administrative case for a new rule. That actually happened in 2001 with the ergonomics rule promulgated by the Occupational Safety and Health Administration (OSHA).[19] This one illustration, the first time the act had been used, demonstrates the general lack of adequacy of this statute for congressional oversight: barring an internal fight within the executive branch, where the president disagrees with one of the agency heads the president had appointed, the act will only be effective regarding regulations (1) promulgated fewer than sixty days before the end of an administration that is (2) followed by an administration of a different persuasion on the rule and (3) with which Congress agrees. In any other case, the act has no effect unless two-thirds of both houses of Congress oppose a rule; but against two-thirds of both houses, no law, regulation, or executive action capable of being reversed by statute can stand.[20]

Of the three methods of fitting a general statute to specific circumstances that we have considered, the amendment to the Endangered Species Act draws upon the greatest institutional advantages of the relevant branch. A more general law, based on that model, might raise the question long dormant since *Schechter Poultry Co. v. United States*[21] of excessive delegation of legislative power. The criteria for creating exceptions were specific to the Endangered Species Act. Should other statutes prove amenable to this kind of specific exemption process, then institutionally, the best course would be to create, by statute, other committees of executive branch officials capable of making such particularized exceptions.[22]

I believe it would have been better to leave a broader role for the other branches in this adjustment process. Courts should have been allowed to exercise equitable jurisdiction, even beyond the case of retroactivity; and it would have been better to leave the one-house legislative veto functioning. However, after *TVA v. Hill* and *INS v. Chadha*, both routes have been foreclosed. Our governmental systems have, to that degree, lost a valuable element of flexibility that could have drawn upon the advantages of all three branches, not merely those of the executive.

NOTES

1. 16 U.S.C. § 1536 (2001).

2. Of course, the secretary of interior might be tempted to be a bit lenient on deciding whether a particular habitat was, indeed, critical, where the consequences of such a determination were devastating to a worthwhile federal project. However, to invite the secretary to do so would invite her or him to act in an ultra vires manner; and we should not be content with a system that relies for its flexibility on encouragement of sub-rosa law violation by federal officials.

3. The resolution would be in favor of the endangered species if the statutory criteria were met. No federal money, however, would be wasted, as the project would not be commenced.

4. *TVA v. Hill*, 419 F. Supp. 753 (E.D. Tenn., 1976), *rev'd*, 437 U.S. 153 (1978).

5. *TVA v. Hill*, 549 F.2d 1064 (6th Cir., 1977), *aff'd*, 437 U.S. 153 (1978).

6. G. Bispham, *The Principles of Equity: A Treatise on the System of Justice Administered in Courts of Chancery* 238 (1887).

7. 419 F. Supp. at 759.

8. See, e.g., the power exercised by federal courts to create exemptions from the federal antitrust laws when necessary to make some other statutory scheme effective. *New York Stock Exchange v. Silver*, 373 U.S. 341 (1963).

9. The Supreme Court's opinion in *TVA v. Hill* can be interpreted as saying that Congress was so explicit. However, Justice Powell's dissent carefully rebuts that conclusion; and no citation to the statute itself deals with projects started before the effective date of the act. While claiming not to rely on legislative history, since the "statute . . . is plain and unambiguous on its face," 437 U.S. at 185, n. 29, the majority nevertheless presents an extensive amount of legislative research to bolster the conclusion that ongoing federal government practices would have to be stopped. Id. at 186–87.

10. See, e.g., *Landgraf v. USI Film Products*, 511 U.S. 244 (1994) (retroactive application denied for compensatory and punitive damages and jury trial in 1991 amendments to Civil Rights Act).

11. Justice Powell, at 437 U.S. at 204, relied on *Church of the Holy Trinity v. United States*, 143 U.S. 457 (1892), for such authority; the majority limited the implications of *Church of the Holy Trinity* to the context where Congress had made explicit that it wanted the courts to exercise such judgment. Id. at 189, n. 33.

12. 473 U.S. 153 (1978).

13. 16 U.S.C. § 1536. The committee is irreverently called "the God Squad,"

since it deals with the existence of species. Technically, the committee is not charged with balancing the value of a species with the value of a particular project; the committee's authority is limited to balancing the proposed agency action against alternative courses of action, "consistent with conserving the species or its critical habitat." 16 U.S.C. § 1536(h)(1)(A)(ii).

14. 16 U.S.C. § 1536(h)(1)(B).

15. 5 U.S.C. § 556(d). See also *Universal Camera Corp. v. NLRB*, 340 U.S. 474 (1951).

16. 462 U.S. 919 (1983).

17. House Rule X. In the Senate, the Rules Committee does not function the same way as it does in the House, and, barring a unanimous consent agreement in place, any senator may at any time amend the bill on the Senate floor with the text of another bill.

18. 5 U.S.C. § 801–8. While following *Chadha* generally, there is one small aspect in which the Congressional Review Act gives power to the actions of a single house, and that might, therefore, prove unconstitutional. In general, the law provides that agency rules are stayed for sixty days while Congress can propose and vote on a joint resolution of disapproval. To be effective, once passing both houses, such a joint resolution has to be submitted to the president for signature or veto. When a resolution disapproving a rule has been defeated by a single house, however, the rule goes into effect at once, even before the statutory sixty days have elapsed. 5 U.S.C. § 801(a)(5). That's logical, since the defeat of the joint resolution by a single house means it has no chance of passage; but, in making an outcome (even of a few days' sooner effective date) turn on the action of a single house, this provision probably violates *Chadha*.

19. 69 U.S.L.W. 2493 (Feb. 20, 2001). Had President Clinton's OSHA promulgated the rule earlier than in the very final days of his administration, the sixty days would have run before President George W. Bush took office, and the Congressional Review Act would have returned to its status as ineffectual.

20. One other slight advantage is that the act provides for consideration of the motion of disapproval in the Senate without possibility of a filibuster. 5 U.S.C. § 802(d)(2).

21. 295 U.S. 495 (1935).

22. As in the Endangered Species Act itself, officers of state government could also be included. To include federal legislators, however, would create a *Chadha* challenge.

CHAPTER 15

Another Method of Solving Interbranch Disputes: Legislators Going to Court to Sue the Executive Branch

THE STANDING of members of Congress to challenge presidential action on constitutional grounds has been cut almost to an empty set.[1] This was done through development of a rule that is internally illogical and undesirable for the smooth functioning of our government. A workable rule for standing can be developed that would afford the possibility of a hearing of legislators' constitutional claims in categories of cases important to separation of powers concerns, yet prevent the use of the courts to fight anew every lost legislative battle.

The Desirability of Allowing Legislators' Standing

If the Congress and the president have a disagreement, a fundamental, on-the-merits difference of opinion on a matter of constitutional prerogative, the courts should be available to resolve the dispute. This is already the case if a private individual suffering particularized harm from an action of the president or Congress brings a lawsuit to enjoin the harm. However, not all issues can be addressed through suits brought by private individuals. The harm of which the member of Congress complains may be of a different kind than the harm of which a private plaintiff would complain.[2] In other cases, where a private plaintiff may eventually be found, the time for action may have passed.[3] Further, the private individual will not have suffered the same kind of harm that the president, or Congress, has endured from a usurpation of constitutional authority by one branch from the other; and in any analysis of whether a foray by one branch into the powers of another is actually a usurpation, the branch alleging the invasion ought to be able to tell its own story as to how much it has been harmed, rather than having to wait for a private plaintiff to do so, and to do so possibly ineffectually.

If we grant there are such cases where private individuals with particularized harm cannot be counted on to bring suit in time or at all, or with the proper kind of claim, then court adjudication of the dispute has significant advantages over leaving the "political" branches to battle between themselves. Under the doctrine of "political question," the Supreme Court has developed circumstances where such combat is unavoidable.[4] However, not all disputes between the political branches fit the Supreme Court's criteria for the political question doctrine.[5] Those are the cases that, by definition, could be resolved without encountering insuperable impediments to a court's exercise of equity jurisdiction but where the court chooses not to intervene.

When a court could act, but chooses not to do so, the warfare between president and Congress that ensues has several undesirable aspects.

First, there is no guarantee the battle will be confined to the context of the good faith dispute. For instance, a hold on a presidential nominee might be exacted in retribution for an executive agreement that some senator believes should have been submitted for ratification as a treaty.[6] Escalation of a dispute results when the offenses and responses cannot be restricted in kind. In the most extreme illustration of this tendency, one judge has suggested, seemingly seriously, that it would be preferable for the effective working of our government for Congress to conduct an impeachment and trial of a president who in good faith insisted on a specific interpretation of presidential constitutional prerogatives, rather than have a court decide the issue.[7]

The invitation to a political branch battle also misapprehends that the legislators bringing suit are capable of defending their constitutional interests just as well through the legislative process. The president has a huge tactical advantage over Congress simply in acting, unilaterally, rather than waiting for legislation to pass, and this advantage can be used to usurp congressional authority.[8] To overturn a president's unilateral action, far more legislators would be needed than the group claiming a constitutional prerogative that has been usurped.

To illustrate this latter point, consider a claim that a particular treaty should have been ratified by the Senate. One-third plus one of the senators should be entitled to that right. A good example was presented in *Goldwater v. Carter.*[9] Senator Goldwater complained that the treaty with Taiwan could not be abrogated without the approval of two-thirds of the Senate, just as it could not have been adopted without their approval. If he were right (and, at the stage of determining standing, he should be assumed to be right), then he and thirty-three other senators should have had the right to prevent the abrogation of the Taiwan treaty, which act President Carter undertook on his own.

Yet the Supreme Court dismissed his case, evidently because Goldwater had his remedy in the political arena.[10] How? He couldn't even get a Sense of the Senate Resolution passed if he had only thirty-four votes. It's true he could have his remedy by an appropriation rider if sixty-seven senators and 290 House members agreed with him; but his claim was one of a right that inhered in thirty-four senators, even if every other member of Congress, House and Senate, disagreed with them.[11]

Reliance on cutting off appropriations, as a legislative remedy alternative to litigation, is equally unavailing. The president can veto the bill cutting off appropriations; so a majority vote of one house, sufficient to stop positive legislation from being enacted, gives way to a two-thirds majority of both houses, the vote necessary to override a veto, as the minimum sufficient way for Congress to effectuate its will against some result whose adoption or not is given to the Congress to decide. An additional reason exists, in the context of the war power, for the inadequacy of an appropriations remedy. Defense appropriations are so large, and American involvement in modern wars often so short, that appropriations votes are not for the war in question at all. All the expenditures have been appropriated the year before and are in the pipeline. The typical supplemental appropriations bill during a time American troops are engaged in combat is to replenish the supplies (for cruise missiles, for instance) that have already been used in the U.S. involvement. Thus, quite literally, Congress could not cut off funds for a short war. The vote, rather, is whether to keep America's weapons stockpile empty or full for the next crisis.[12]

Similarly misguided is the Court's statement in *Raines v. Byrd*[13] that the plaintiffs, who had voted against the legislation conferring the line-item veto on the president, simply were complaining about losing a vote in Congress, the vote that established the line-item veto.[14] Senator Byrd and his colleagues in *Raines* complained that a majority of each house of Congress, with the willing complicity of the president, had effectuated a diminution of every member's influence on appropriations matters because of the line-item veto. Assuming the line-item veto was unconstitutional, as we must for determining standing, this response to Senator Byrd was equivalent to telling a student in a segregated public school that objecting to the harm he or she suffered was just complaining about not having enough votes on the school board when segregation was approved. That Senator Byrd was in the Congress that passed the line-item veto doesn't change in the slightest how he was hurt by the action of his colleagues in passing an (assumedly) unconstitutional law.

Another illustration is the statement in the opinion for the D.C. Circuit in *Campbell v. Clinton*, the litigation complaining that the Kosovo war had not been approved by Congress: "Of course, Congress always retains appropriations authority and could have cut off funds for the American role in the conflict."[15] Yes, but the president could veto the bill cutting off appropriations. So, it would take two-thirds of both houses to utilize this weapon in the battle of the political branches. The right being asserted, by contrast, was the right of a majority of one house of Congress to prevent war from being declared. There was nothing that the majority of only one house could do legislatively to vindicate its right.

Like Senator Goldwater regarding the Taiwan treaty, the members of Congress who blocked a declaration of war over Kosovo were told their case could not be heard because, if they obtained a hugely greater degree of support than the Constitution said they needed (taking plaintiffs' well-pleaded allegations as correct), they might have had enough pressure to stop the president's unconstitutional usurpation of power without having to come to court.

Imagine a shareholder being told her or his derivative action had to be dismissed because, if she or he actually controlled the board, the corporate action could be reversed, hence, the case would be committed to the "corporate branches," rather than to the court, for battle.[16] At least before *Raines*, it was accepted doctrine that legislators were not to be treated any worse for standing purposes than nonlegislators.[17]

So, it is simply not true that, because a matter can be sent to the "political branches," the constitutional rights at issue are, even roughly, guaranteed anything like a fair fight.[18] Very often, if not always, the alternative legislative relief will require much more than the Constitution does to vindicate the rights of the legislator plaintiffs, taking their pleadings as correct.

For the foregoing reasons, therefore, it is desirable for the courts to hear and resolve a dispute between the president and Congress, at least where the case is otherwise justiciable (including, specifically, that it is not caught up in the political question doctrine). Nevertheless, it has been the dominant trend in case and commentary to look with disfavor upon such suits,[19] and especially so since *Raines*.[20] I believe a more accommodating attitude toward legislators' standing is appropriate and can be developed without realizing the fears of critics that legislators' standing will simply open up the courts to a reenactment of lost legislative battles.

Toward a Coherent Rule on Legislators' Standing

A Case or Controversy Requires Some Action by Congress

What restraints should be placed on such lawsuits? The "case or controversy" requirement of personal and real injury must still apply.[21] In the case of a congressional plaintiff, that means, at the least, that a constitutional authority that she or he possesses must have been usurped by the president.

This introduces an important issue of breadth. Anything the president does, for which the president does not have inherent constitutional authority but which power the president could exercise if Congress explicitly gave the president such authority, can be asserted to be such a wrong. In *Chenoweth v. Clinton*,[22] Congresswoman Chenoweth and two of her colleagues sued the president for taking action through executive order with regard to wild and scenic rivers. She alleged that he had acted beyond his inherent unilateral authority, and Congress had passed no law to give him additional authority.

The D.C. Circuit upheld a denial of standing to Congresswoman Chenoweth and her two colleagues. The court held that if she were granted standing, any member of Congress would have standing to complain of any action by the president, not based on an explicit statutory grant of authority. By requiring some congressional action as a predicate to bring a lawsuit of this kind, courts would prevent overuse of the judicial remedy. This will be discussed below. In *Chenoweth*, there had been no such action by Congress.

Dellums v. Bush[23] presented a contravention of a concrete constitutional provision, the war powers clause. Judge Harold Greene entertained Congressman Dellums and his colleagues' lawsuit against President Bush in the context of Desert Shield (the buildup of American troops in Saudi Arabia prior to their engaging Iraqi forces in Kuwait in 1991). Judge Greene held the matter to be justiciable. It was, to him, not a political question. However, it was not ripe. Judge Greene saw two kinds of ripeness problems. First, at the time of the suit, U.S. troops were still gathering in Saudi Arabia. The president had not committed them to combat. Second, Congress had not acted to show its agreement with Congressman Dellums and his colleagues.

On the first point, Judge Greene was undoubtedly right. Judge Greene noted that war might still be averted (reflecting the hope of many at the time that Saddam Hussein might be pressured diplomatically into leaving Kuwait on his own). He observed that negotiations were still under way, and, as matters developed, the relief Congressman Dellums sought—a vote in Congress—eventually took place as Desert Shield turned into Desert Storm.[24]

It is the second point in *Dellums*, however, that holds the key to *Chenoweth*. In *Chenoweth*, the president had acted, but Congress had not. Nor had Congress acted in *Dellums*. Unlike the president, who constitutes an entire branch in one person, neither Congressman Dellums nor Congresswoman Chenoweth spoke for the legislative branch.

Why should this matter? First, on normal equitable grounds, a court in equity will strive to put parties in precisely the relationship they should have been but for the wrong suffered.[25] If Congresswoman Chenoweth had the right to vote on a bill giving the president power over scenic rivers, she might nevertheless find herself on the losing end of that vote. In seeking to enjoin the president from acting, she was seeking more than would flow, necessarily, simply from giving her a vote.

There is another sense, however, in which both Congressman Dellums and Congresswoman Chenoweth, and the plaintiffs in *Raines v. Byrd*, alleged harm regardless of the substantive outcome of the policy matter in question. Dellums and Chenoweth both alleged they had a right to vote on a matter. Similarly, Senator Byrd and his coplaintiffs alleged they had the right to an appropriations process unencumbered by the president's threat of a line-item veto. In other words, each could have made a claim to process, not to an outcome. It was this claim that the Supreme Court found too ephemeral to warrant standing in *Raines v. Byrd*. Indeed, it would be difficult to articulate exactly how Senator Byrd was compelled to behave differently than he normally would by reason of the fear of an, as yet, untested line-item veto. The Court was right that the harm alleged was not specific and tangible enough to grant standing. Dellums and Chenoweth could point to their desire to go on record with a vote—whether each was on the winning side or not. That desire, however, could be easily met by a public statement inserted into the *Congressional Record*. The claim to process, qua process, seems likely always to fall into one or the other of these categories (insufficiently tangible or easily correctable) so as to deny standing.

There is another reason why a vote of the relevant house of Congress, when possible to obtain, should be a requisite to standing. Congress (or a subset of members of Congress) may have rights but choose not to exercise them. It is natural in any contest for antagonists to choose their best moment to press a point. That attribute would be lost to Congress if any single member could raise the issue of a congressional prerogative in any context of her or his own choosing. Perhaps the ergonomics rule went farther beyond the executive branch's authority than did the wild and scenic river executive order; or perhaps they were equally excessive, but the public strongly supported the one and not the other. Is it not fair to reserve to Congress, as a body, the decision of whether to challenge the president over ergonomics or wild and scenic rivers?

Under one approach, it would be enough to show that that percentage of members of Congress able to exercise the authority asserted have chosen to do so. Normally, this would be proved by a vote that took place on the floor. There was no vote in *Chenoweth* or, at the time, in *Dellums*. Had the Scenic Rivers Act been debated on the floor of the House, however, and been defeated, following which President Clinton had implemented its provisions anyway through executive order, then Congresswoman Chenoweth should have been allowed to proceed. (Remember, *arguendo*, she is assumed to be correct that the executive order went beyond the president's implicit powers.) In *Dellums*, similarly, once the vote on Desert Storm had been taken, had authorization for war been voted down, Congressman Dellums could have proceeded.

On the night of April 28, 1999, the U.S. Air Force was dropping bombs on Yugoslavia, and the House of Representatives went on record voting down authorization to do so.[26] Had Judge Greene to rule, his opinion in *Dellums* would have required a holding of standing in *Campbell*, the Kosovo case.[27]

In denying standing in *Campbell*, the district judge noted that Congress had not spoken clearly enough, since it had also failed to vote to withdraw the troops and had authorized appropriations for the war.[28] Let us test that holding under the two rationales for requiring Congress to act, first, the rule that kept Congresswoman Chenoweth from having standing. Would a court be giving a plaintiff member of Congress more than that to which she or he was entitled? No. Congress showed that it would not vote to go to war or to authorize the bombing. That was exactly voted on, it was not a matter of doubt. Hence, if the court enjoined the president from going to war, the effect would not be undone by an immediate congressional declaration of war. There was no danger that the court would be entertaining a remedy in vain, as there was in *Chenoweth*. Second, the plaintiffs in *Campbell* were not seeking simply a procedural right to vote. Their house of Congress had voted, and the effect of its vote had been stymied. This was a harm greater than what could be cured by a statement in the *Congressional Record*.

On the third ground, however—would Congress have wished the thirty-one plaintiffs in *Campbell* to represent all of them? There was no Sense of the House Resolution of authority to go to court. The district judge noted that a majority of the House, while failing to authorize the bombing, had also voted against withdrawing the troops. So it could be that, as an institution, the group of members possessing the right assertedly being infringed upon, half of the House, preferred to fight this battle with the president some other way or some other day.[29]

This interpretation of the district court holding in *Campbell* presents a more coherent basis for building a general rule on legislators' standing than did its alternate ground (the appropriation votes)[30] or any of the rationales of the several opinions of the three-judge court of appeals panel.[31] However, it is still ultimately unsatisfactory. The plaintiffs in *Campbell* sought declaratory relief only, that the court announce the rights of Congress in the context of the Kosovo war. That a majority of the House did not favor immediate withdrawal said nothing to undo the position of 50 percent of the House against authorizing what had happened or to overturn a presumption that the same 50 percent would want a court to declare their rights.

Action Must Be by a Sufficient Number of Legislators

The approach is to ask who possesses the constitutional right being asserted. In *Goldwater*, the answer is thirty-four senators possess the right, since one-third plus one of the senators can stop a treaty from being ratified.[32] In *Campbell*, *Dellums*, and *Chenoweth*, the answer is half the number of House members.

If a member of Congress plaintiff can get a vote on the floor of the House or Senate, he or she must. This step prevents the Court from doing a vain thing, if the Congress would grant the authority to the president anyway. The plaintiffs in *Campbell* obtained the requisite vote—half the House would not authorize the bombing of Yugoslavia, and all but two House members would not vote for war. These House members had the procedural means to obtain a vote by reason of the War Powers Act.[33] (It is nonetheless possible that the House members who voted against the Kosovo war might have not wanted to challenge in court President Clinton's going ahead anyway. However, for those members of Congress to obtain a separate vote approving litigation might not have been procedurally possible—the War Powers Act does not grant a right to that kind of vote, as it does to a vote on the merits. And exactly 50 percent of the House of Representatives [and not a member more]—the vote on the Kosovo resolution—could not effectuate a discharge petition on a resolution to authorize litigation.) Congresswoman Chenoweth's case presents the other situation: she had no procedural means to obtain a vote (though the harm she suffered remained quite ephemeral). Similarly, a senator opposing a presidential appointee acting without having been confirmed, or a presidential action in enforcing a treaty without having submitted it for ratification, would lack guaranteed procedural means to obtain a vote, since thirty-four senators cannot put a matter on the Senate floor for a vote.[34] In those cases where there was no means of obtaining a recorded vote,[35] then the only way to demonstrate that the relevant group wishes to pursue litigation is by joining them as plaintiffs. This was what Judge Greene hinted at in *Dellums*. It was hinted at again in *Raines v. Byrd*,[36] but the Court did not base its decision on Senator Byrd's failure to have fifty other senators as plaintiffs.

Allegation That the Legislators' Vote Was "Completely Nullified"

These preliminary requirements were all met in the one case of legislators' standing the U.S. Supreme Court explicitly preserved in *Raines v. Byrd*: *Coleman v. Miller*.[37] In *Coleman*, the plaintiffs included the very twenty Kansas state senators who voted against ratifying an amendment to the U.S. Constitution. The vote was twenty to twenty, the lieutenant governor voted in favor, and the lower house of the Kansas legislature had already approved. The twenty state senators then sued to order the secretary of the senate to erase the entry of passage and not to send the constitutional amendment along to the governor for conveyance to the U.S. Congress. They claimed the lieutenant governor could not break a tie over a constitutional amendment. The plaintiff class was perfect; it included all twenty state senators who had voted no.[38]

The *Raines* Court held that the plaintiffs in *Coleman* had had their constitutional authority "completely nullified." The Court construed *Coleman* as holding (at most) "that legislators whose votes would have been sufficient to defeat (or enact) a specific legislative act have standing to sue if that legislative action goes into effect (or does not go into effect) on the ground that their votes have been completely nullified."[39] As it reads, that formulation is consistent with what I am recommending here.

The D.C. Circuit, however, distinguished *Coleman* in *Campbell*. It construed the words "completely nullified" to refer to the very rare case where there was literally nothing more the plaintiffs could do, even with unanimous support from their institution.[40] The *Miller* Court had noted that, once a state had ratified a U.S. constitutional amendment, that action might not have been able to be rescinded.[41] By contrast, the D.C. Circuit held, in the Kosovo case, that Congress could (with two-thirds of each house) vote to cut off funds at once.

That distinction is a poor one. First, the *Miller* Court did not hold that a U.S. constitutional amendment, once ratified by a state, could not be rescinded. It expressly left that question for Congress to decide. Hence, it was quite possible that the twenty-one senators could introduce a senate resolution in the Kansas State Senate ordering the secretary of the senate of Kansas (Miller, the named defendant) to enter the word "Rejected" on the U.S. constitutional amendment in the senate's journal and ordering him not to send the amendment on to the governor. Indeed, that was part of the relief prayed for in the original mandamus action filed in the Kansas Supreme Court. Hence, there was plenty for the *Coleman* plaintiffs to do, short of going to court. They could have obtained relief without going outside their own legislative body.[42]

The plaintiffs in *Miller* complained that their vote had been nullified, and the U.S. Supreme Court agreed, but that couldn't have been because the state senators had no other recourse than to go to court. The *Raines* Court's attempt to squeeze *Coleman* into this rubric is an example of the weakness of the way the judicial branch operates, similar to what we saw in Chapter 7 on the exclusionary rule. The Court at the time of *Coleman* would permit legislators' suits; by the time of *Raines*, the Court had changed its membership and its mind on this. A new president, or a new Congress, would simply have said so. A new Supreme Court felt it could not; hence, it cited *Coleman* in *Raines*, leaving it to the D.C. Circuit to find what was not present: a coherent rationale explaining both opinions.[43]

The D.C. Circuit's observation that the plaintiffs in the context of Kosovo had other legislative paths to relief was erroneous not only because so did the plaintiffs in *Coleman* but also because the alternative legislative paths still available in the Kosovo case all required more votes than were necessary to defeat the war resolution in the first place. The logical question should have been whether the subset of the legislative branch, whose rights were, assertedly, being infringed upon, could do anything else. To require a majority of one house to get two-thirds of both houses is to nullify their constitutional right as a majority of one house.

In sum, the requirement of *Coleman*, for legislators' standing, should be deemed met when, as the U.S. Supreme Court phrased it in *Raines*, "legislators whose votes would have been sufficient to defeat . . . a specific legislative Act have standing to sue if that legislative action goes into effect."[44]

Are the Legislators Seeking Action or Inaction by the Executive?

Returning to the effort to establish a coherent rule for legislators' standing, and assuming the previous screens have been passed, litigation by members of Congress against the executive[45] should be subjected to an additional hurdle: whether the complaint demands the executive branch to take action, or whether the complaint demands the executive branch to desist from unilateral action that the Congress alone has the authority to order and has not yet ordered.[46] This distinction was not imposed in *Raines*; indeed, the Court was explicit in saying both situations would be treated the same.[47] Nevertheless, there is good merit to consider such a screen.

If it is an order to the executive to desist that is sought, the Court can fashion a clear remedy: an injunction against the action. The president is ordered to stop prosecuting a war in Yugoslavia, or Kuwait, consistent with the safe removal of our troops.

Other examples occurring before *Raines* include *Edwards v. Carter*.[48] In that case, the plaintiff sought an order restraining the president from turning over the Panama Canal property to the Republic of Panama. That is the heart of a simple negative injunction: Don't do what you are planning to do.

In other cases, however, the complaint is that the president has failed to act, and so the relief requests an affirmative step. In *Riegle v. Federal Reserve Open Market Committee*,[49] a senator complained about the fact that the president had not submitted the names of seven of the twelve members of the Federal Reserve Board's Open Market Committee to the Senate for confirmation, bypassing the Senate's constitutional right to advise and consent. (These were the members appointed by the member banks.) The remedy of ordering those individuals to step down would only accomplish half of what Senator Riegle wanted. It would leave vacancies on the board.

The further remedy, ordering the president to send a nomination to the Senate, would involve ordering affirmative relief. Suppose the president would rather leave the board understaffed? A court order insisting on a presidential nominee unquestionably would intrude on the president's prerogative of when to appoint, a right as much in the president's authority as the prerogative of whom to appoint.

Raines and *Kennedy* present the problem even more starkly. In the eyes of the plaintiff members of Congress, the president should not have been able to veto an appropriation line-item (*Raines*) or to pocket veto an item (*Kennedy*). The remedy is to order the president to spend the appropriation that had been vetoed. Suppose the president doesn't believe the economic conditions are right for such an expenditure? How much, and for what contracts, will a court order the president to spend?[50] And suppose the vetoed measure was more complex than simply spending money?

In *Goldwater v. Carter*, the remedy would be to order the president to act as though the treaty had not been abrogated. That presents a severe impracticality in international law and diplomacy, given that presidents often, and should, act with more or less fidelity to treaty obligations depending upon how the other party is acting toward us. No one challenges that the latter power is constitutionally vested in the president. How, then, would a court distinguish between such behavior and the action of a president who wants to treat a foreign nation as though a treaty between our country and it had been terminated?

There is an additional reason to restrict legislators' standing to cases requesting relief of a nature to compel the executive branch to desist rather than to act. The Congress that seeks such relief has been wronged. The action taken by the president that is to be stopped, while it continues, offends the constitutional prerogative of the sitting Congress. When the relief requested is of an affirmative nature, however, because the president has failed to do something, it is an earlier Congress whose rights are offended. The earlier Congress passed the law requiring presidential action. There is no certainty at all that the current Congress would have done so. Many statutes, having coalitions at one time, lack them at a later time. The affirmative relief requested, therefore, might not be the wish of the majority of the institution on whose behalf relief is being sought.[51] In seeking to force the executive to desist from an action that infringes upon congressional prerogative, there could well be many members of Congress, perhaps a majority, who don't wish to sue; but it cannot be denied that, taking the pleadings as true, the present Congress as an institution has been harmed.

Through all these examples, we see a rather simple rule at work: the relief sought by the members of the Congress against the executive must be of a kind that can be ordered by a court. It's the simple rule of equity, not to order that which could not effectuate a remedy.[52] As such, the concept need not be incorporated formally into the doctrine of legislators' standing. Where the Court is asked to issue an injunction against the executive, the Court will ask whether its doing so will likely lead to meaningful relief. If not, the Court should abstain. As a general though not absolute rule, this will eliminate cases where the relief is to force the president to do an affirmative act, as opposed to restrain the president from doing a specific act.[53]

From these screens, legislative standing still emerges with an important function. When there is a conscientious disagreement between the president and Congress regarding constitutional power, and the Court can make a resolution of that conflict stick, the Court should resolve it, rather than leaving it to the battle of the political branches.

Applying the Rule Reciprocally to the Executive

There will be less occasion to use this formulation when the president seeks to sue Congress, but the doctrine should be fully reciprocal. Since the executive has the broader scope of activity, it will more likely be Congress that sues to restrain the president than vice versa. It may be illuminating in testing this formulation of standing for congressional plaintiffs to engage in a thought experiment of symmetric cases arising with the president as plaintiff.

INS v. Chadha[54] was such a case. The president wanted to rid his dealings with Congress of the noxious legislative veto. He stood to gain, measurably, in constitutional balance by forcing Congress to delegate broad authority to the executive rather than maintaining the legislative-veto method of subjecting that authority to particularized congressional oversight. The Supreme Court delivered him a major victory.

The president obtained this result by having his attorney general put Chadha in such legal limbo that Chadha brought suit. To satisfy the "case or controversy" requirement, since Chadha and the attorney general were in agreement he should not be deported, the Supreme Court pointed to the fact that Congress had sought leave to intervene and was permitted to do so.[55] Note what this means: when the executive branch initiated the litigation (practically speaking), the Court got around the case or controversy problem by allowing the Congress to intervene.[56]

Now, for the thought experiment. If the president could initiate a judicial branch resolution of a presidential-congressional dispute, could, in the same fact situation, Congress do so? The answer must be yes or else the president would be given an entirely unwarranted advantage over a supposedly coequal branch.

Chadha's presence in the case did not change the standing issue; the Court felt reassured there was a case or controversy only when Congress intervened. However, to grant Congress the right to initiate litigation in the *Chadha* fact pattern would require a reversal of the construction given to *Raines* by the D.C. Circuit in *Campbell*. The congressional plaintiffs "could" pass an appropriation rider, by a two-thirds vote of each body, preventing the Department of Justice from spending money to stay Chadha's deportation order.[57] Hence, the House's power to affect Chadha's case had not been "completely nullified."[58] I conclude that the *Raines* and *Chadha* decisions allow the president, but not Congress, to sue to resolve the identical constitutional issue. (Of course, just as in lawsuits brought by members of Congress, so also in lawsuits brought by the president the political question doctrine continues to apply.)[59]

Alternative Approaches to Legislators' Standing

There are two remaining alternatives to consider as rules for legislators' standing. The first would be to deny all standing to legislators as legislators,[60] and to the executive as executive, when one sues the other. The rule of abstention would be absolute. This could be accomplished by expanding the political question doctrine beyond the constraints imposed in *Baker v. Carr*.[61] The undesirability of this approach was considered above in the first section of this chapter. The consequences to the stability of our nation, from an increase in battles between the political branches with no referee, would have to be considered against whatever institutional harm the judiciary might fear from following a standing rule of the kind proposed here.

Should the Court adopt such an approach, it would, in essence, have made a fundamentally selfish choice. It would have put protection of the Court's own interest in avoiding the kind of criticism that always attaches when it engages in issues of political content above the good it can do by ruling in an authoritative way when different sources of governmental authority in our nation would otherwise be propelled toward conflict.

An almost opposite alternative is to dispense with all the screens proposed above and all the "jurisprudential" constraints on hearing a case and grant standing whenever a majority of either house, by resolution, authorized the bringing of an action (provided the case or controversy requirement is met).[62] This would *not* be the same thing as the practice of some European governments empowering the legislature to put a question to a constitutional court, though Chief Justice Rehnquist attempted to conflate the two in *Raines*.

There would be nothing irrational about a system that granted standing in these cases; some European constitutional courts operate under one or another variant of such a regime. . . . But it is obviously not the regime that has obtained under our Constitution to date. Our regime contemplates a more restricted role for Article III courts, well expressed by Justice Powell in his concurring opinion in United States v. Richardson, 418 U.S. 166 (1974):

"The irreplaceable value of the power articulated by Mr. Chief Justice Marshall [in *Marbury v. Madison*, 1 Cranch 137 (1803)], lies in the protection it has afforded the constitutional rights and liberties of individual citizens and minority groups against oppressive or discriminatory government action. It is this role, not some amorphous general supervision of the operations of government, that has maintained public esteem for the federal courts and has permitted the peaceful coexistence of the countermajoritarian implications of judicial review and the democratic principles upon which our Federal government in the final analysis rests." Id., at 192.[63]

The citation to Justice Powell's criticism is curiously inapt. Justice Powell says that the power manifest in *Marbury v. Madison* was a "triumph for the protection of individual citizens and minority groups against oppressive or discriminatory government action." It was nothing of the sort. Subsequent courts may, indeed, have used the power of judicial review to achieve such a triumph. But *Marbury* was not a case about "individual citizens and minority groups." Rather, *Marbury* was a case calling on powers very much closer to those raised in lawsuits by legislators.

Marbury was testing President Jefferson's authority to ignore Article I judicial appointments made by his Federalist predecessor, John Adams. It was a clash between the legislative and the executive branches on the question of how a statutory scheme (the creation and then the appointment of District of Columbia judges) was to operate. It was also a clash between the judicial (albeit Article I) and the executive branches as to when an individual became a federal judge. It was a clash between political parties, Federalist and Jeffersonian. Chief Justice Marshall ruled for Jefferson, but he did so in a manner least likely to enhance Jefferson's authority in future conflicts.[64]

Marbury v. Madison was a challenge of just the kind Powell criticized. Although not "amorphous," the case called for the Court to exercise "supervision of the operations of government."[65]

A rule that granted legislative standing for real cases or controversies whenever a majority of either house of Congress sought it would not abrogate the constitutional constraints on judicial authority.[66] Legislative standing in such a situation would not overturn the case or controversy requirement. Congress could not simply send interesting questions to the Court for advisory opinions. What we are dealing with here are real, very important disputes between the branches—but which are, nevertheless, not being resolved by the courts under existing standing rules because the plaintiff is suing as a member of Congress rather than as a private citizen.

The Court's prestige is not sacrificed by taking such a case, especially upon the request of a majority of both houses, whose members are seeking a neutral adjudication of an important point of dispute, rather than a potentially escalating conflict, spilling over into unrelated areas, that would result from political warfare between the branches.[67] It is refusing to take such a case, not taking it, that diminishes the Court's prestige.[68]

This simpler alternative does have a drawback, if the rule that a majority of both houses has to agree to go to court is necessary as well as sufficient for standing in an otherwise justiciable case. There are members of the House or Senate who are much more sensitive than their colleagues to constitutional prerogative. Should such a plaintiff be prevented from vindicating constitutional issues because a majority of that member's colleagues lacked that member's willingness to fight?

This difficulty will be especially acute where the right being asserted belongs to less than a majority of both houses, so that one could have the agreement of numbers adequate to assert the right and still not be permitted to do so through the courts.[69]

Conclusion

Standing should not be an additional barrier to bringing an otherwise justiciable action because the action is between members of Congress and the executive branch. The current rules on legislators' standing, interpreting *Raines v. Byrd*, have reduced legislators' standing almost to a null set. This is undesirable because neutral resolution of principled interbranch disputes can often be superior to political warfare. Political warfare between the branches tends to expand rather than contain a dispute, and such warfare is not an even contest because of the president's ability to act, essentially unconstrained, until money runs out. Sensible rules on standing can restrict the Court from being forced to enter vain orders while still permitting sincere constitutional disputes to be resolved. At least two such sets of rules can be envisioned and have been set forth above. Either is superior to the present state of the law on legislators' standing, for many reasons, but in one setting more poignant than most others—the case of war.

That wars will be fought, and people die, on the decision of one person alone was an evil the founders explicitly sought to avert. A careful student of the history of the founders observed: "Kings had always been involving and impoverishing their people in wars, pretending generally, if not always, that the good of the people was the object. This our [constitutional] convention understood to be the most oppressive of all kingly oppressions; and they resolved to so frame the Constitution that no one man should hold the power of bringing this oppression upon us."[70] By denying legislators' standing, the Court has allowed precisely this kingly oppression to be imposed. If a president wishes to initiate war, one half of one house of Congress should be able to prevent it.[71] That was the check imposed by the founders. If the Court will not permit those members of Congress to invoke the Court's authority for this end, for what more important task is the Court preserving its authority?

NOTES

Some of the arguments in this chapter appeared in the brief for plaintiffs and petitioners in *Campbell v. Clinton*, 203 F.3d 19 (D.C. Cir., 2000). I was a plaintiff in that case and participated in the drafting of these briefs. The attorneys of record were Jules Lobel, Michael Ratner, Franklin Siegel, William Goodman, Jennifer Green, Joel Starr, H. Lee Halterman, and James Klimaski. To them, I owe a scholarly debt and, what is more, a debt of gratitude for attempting to defend the separation of powers in our Constitution. See H. Halterman, J. Lobel, J. Starr, M. Ratner, J. Klimaski, "War Powers Revisited: Commentary: The Fog of War (Powers)," 37 *Stan. J. Int'l. L.* 197 (2001).

1. *Raines v. Byrd*, 521 U.S. 811 (1997), announced a rule denying legislators' standing unless the legislators could show "that they voted for a specific bill, that there were sufficient votes to pass the bill, and that the bill was nonetheless deemed defeated" or, possibly, that "legislators whose votes would have been sufficient to defeat (or enact) a specific legislative Act have standing to sue if that legislative action goes into effect (or does not go into effect), on the ground that their votes have been completely nullified." Id. at 824, 823. The Court further appeared to hold that no standing would be granted if Congress could "repeal the Act or exempt appropriations bills from its reach." Id. at 829. The one Supreme Court case granting legislators' standing, *Coleman v. Miller*, 307 U.S. 433 (1939), was read to require the legislators' votes be "completely nullified." Id. at 823. The D.C. Circuit, in interpreting that phrase in the only two cases since *Raines*, has held a vote is not completely nullified while Congress could pass a new law or appropriation bill dealing with the issue in question. *Chenoweth v. Clinton*, 181 F.3d 112 (D.C. Cir., 1999); *Campbell v. Clinton*, 203 F.3d 19 (D.C. Cir., 2000).

2. In *Raines*, the member of Congress plaintiffs alleged that the existence of the line-item veto itself had altered the negotiation position of Congress and the president regarding appropriations, apart from any specific application of this power. This kind of harm is not the same as that felt by a private citizen who might eventually seek standing to sue over a particular appropriation favorable to him or her that had been line-item vetoed. Again, in *Riegle v. Federal Open Market Committee*, 656 F.2d 873, 879 (D.C. Cir., 1981), the plaintiff senator complained that decisions of the Open Market Committee were being made by twelve individuals, only seven of whom had been confirmed by the Senate. The harm of which Senator Riegle complained was not being able to vote on the five. Eventually, someone adversely affected by a decision of the committee might challenge such a decision on the basis that five members were illegally appointed. Such a plaintiff would be complaining of the decision in question, however, not the harm to the senator being deprived of the right to vote to confirm all twelve members. And in either case, while a private plaintiff might eventually get the case to court, in the interim, Senators Byrd and Riegle and their colleagues would have to endure the harm particular to their status as members of Congress. In denying them standing, a court would be telling them to endure that harm for so long as it took for someone else, totally unrelated, to bring a suit to set matters right. Further, each would be denied the chance to provide useful briefing on the case, except by leave of court to intervene, instead of as a right in a matter that so concerns their duties.

Lastly, it is not so much the rights of an individual senator or representative that matters. It is the fact that, by insisting upon their constitutional rights, they protect all of us. The separation of powers is fundamentally a protection against government overreaching. By denying legislators' standing, a court postpones the day that protection will be made effective. Speaking of the founders, Gerhardt Casper concluded, "The only matter on which agreement existed was what it meant not to have separation of powers: it meant tyranny." G. Casper, *Separating Power* 22 (1997). See also G. Gunther, "The Subtle Vices of the 'Passive Virtues': A Comment on Public Principle and Expediency in Judicial Review," 64 *Colum. L. Rev.* 1, 17 (1964) (regarding the Court's duty to rule).

3. Cases challenging presidential exercise of war-making authority will often fall in this category, particularly in more modern times when presidential use of force was over in less than the sixty days granted the president by the War Powers Act. Every case of the use of force since the passage of the War Powers Act in 1973 took less than sixty days, with four exceptions: Iraq-Kuwait, Iraq 2003, Afghanistan (where, in each case, the President asked for and obtained congressional approval), and Kosovo (where Yugoslavia was bombed for seventy-nine days without congressional approval). The private party who might eventually bring suit would either be a soldier, concerned about being ordered into an unconstitutional war, or a person with a financial stake that turns on the existence or nonexistence of war. One of the earliest of the latter such cases is *Bas v. Tingy*, 4 U.S. (4 Dall.) 37 (1800) (regarding whether war existed, in the absence of a declaration, between France and the United States). There, obviously, the

war would already have started before injury was suffered; so, for purposes of obtaining the relief that the war not be entered into, private party action subsequent to the war would be completely unavailing. The same is true about a soldier bringing suit. A soldier could not sue during a military buildup because the case would not yet be ripe. Cf. *Dellums v. Bush*, 752 F. Supp. 1141 (D.D.C. 1990). The placement of U.S. armed forces overseas for possible action is a legitimate exercise of the diplomatic power of the president and might actually prevent the necessity of relying upon the war-making power. So, the soldier litigant would have to sue during the conduct of the hostilities, not before; hence, her or his action would also be entirely unavailing to stop the constitutional harm complained of: the commencement of a war without the approval of the people's legislative representatives.

4. The criteria are set out in *Baker v. Carr*, 369 U.S. 186 (1962). The first is a "textually demonstrable constitutional commitment of the issue to a coordinate political department." 369 U.S. at 369. This criterion should have appended "that has not yet ruled," since, if the Constitution clearly commits the issue to one of the branches, and that branch has ruled, a decision by the Court affirming that judgment would be utterly noncontroversial. If the Constitution has language committing the issue to both of the other branches, then the fundamental advantage that courts possess, by training and experience, to reconcile apparently conflicting language, would also recommend the Court to act. The other criteria, however, would stand in the way of the Court doing so effectively: "lack of judicially discoverable and manageable standards for resolving [the dispute]"; "the impossibility of deciding without an initial policy determination of a kind clearly for nonjudicial discretion"; "the impossibility of a court's undertaking independent resolution without expressing lack of the respect due coordinate branches of government"; "an unusual need for unquestioning adherence to a political decision already made"; or "the potentiality of embarrassment from multifarious pronouncements by various departments on one question." Each of these concerns would figure normally in an equity court's decision to enter an injunction; they are hardly unique facets of an interbranch dispute. A court ought to be able to enter some disputes and not others based on whether its equity powers can effectively be invoked.

5. Judges Silberman and Tatel disputed with each other whether a president's actions putting our country into war constituted such a political question. See separate opinions of each in *Campbell v. Clinton*, 24, 37. See also *Mitchell v. Laird*, 488 F.2d 6112 (D.C. Cir. 1973) (dismissing challenge to Vietnam War as a political question).

6. Even this power might be ineffectual. The authority not to confirm a president's appointees seems to be exercisable by a majority of one Senate committee, backed up by as few as forty-one senators (acting together to filibuster a discharge petition from a Senate committee). Senate Rule XXII, 2, printed in S. Doc. No. 106-15. However, the president may have all his or her major appointees already in office at the time the conflict with the Congress arises; and, furthermore, the instance of Acting Assistant Attorney General for Civil Rights

Bill Lan Lee, who served for three years by sequential recess appointments in the Clinton administration, demonstrates that even the threat of not confirming an appointee can be hollow. In such a case, the retaliation might escalate.

7. See *Campbell v. Clinton*, 23.

8. To undo unilateral presidential action requires much more of Congress than to effectuate its own will, as has been recognized in the political science literature. See, e.g., T. Moe and W. Howell, "Unilateral Action and Presidential Power: A Theory," 29 *Presidential Stud. Q.* 850, 856–57 (1999).

> In this simple scenario, consider what happens when policy is generated according to classic constitutional rules: Congress makes the laws, the president gets to veto. If the original status quo were at [a point on a continuum], Congress would simply pass new legislation imposing [a new point on the continuum] as the new policy, and the president—although he would like a further shift to the right—would have to accept this outcome. Both would be better off, and Congress would actually get its ideal point. Now compare what happens when the president is able to take unilateral action. . . . Here, the president can act on his own to move policy and this new policy would be an equilibrium outcome. Congress would like to move policy back . . . but any move in that direction would be successfully vetoed by the president. Thus, the power of unilateral action allows the president to achieve legislative outcomes much closer to his ideal point, while Congress is correspondingly worse off.

9. 444 U.S. 996 (1979).

10. This has to be inferred, since the Court did not issue an opinion. The Court granted certiorari, vacated the D.C. Circuit's decision, and remanded with instructions to dismiss the complaint, all without even oral argument. Separate opinions in favor of this action were filed by Justices Powell and Rehnquist. Justice Brennan dissented, saying that certiorari should not even have been granted. Justices Blackmun and White dissented in part, agreeing that certiorari should be granted but seeing an issue compelling full briefing and oral argument.

11. In the facts of that particular case, Senator Goldwater had called up a Sense of the Senate Resolution expressing the view that Senate approval was necessary before terminating a treaty and obtained a fifty-nine-to-thirty-five vote in favor, immediately after learning the district court had dismissed the case as not yet ripe. The district court thereupon allowed the case to proceed and entered judgment for the plaintiffs. The U.S. Court of Appeals affirmed on standing but reversed on the merits. See *Goldwater v. Carter*, 617 F.2d 697, 702 (D.C. Cir. 1979). My main point is that, structurally, Senator Goldwater and thirty-three colleagues would not be able to guarantee having such a vote, even though it actually occurred in that case. Nor did it seem to matter much that it did: Justice Powell, in his concurrence from the order vacating the judgment, held that the Senate action was not final and that, thus, "Congress has taken no official action." 444 U.S. at 998. What more could have been done by the thirty-

four senators? The D.C. Circuit realized nothing more could be done—by the thirty-four senators who might have been able to defeat the motion to ratify the treaty had it been properly presented. 617 F.2d at 703.

12. What Congress might be able to do, however, would be to cut off all funds for some agency running a current account deficit. Whether such a threat would be effective would depend upon the importance of that agency to the president at the time. Furthermore, this is precisely the kind of harm to be avoided by the Court settling a dispute between Congress and the president when it is presented: the harm that a conflict will, by not being settled, escalate into a confrontation in unrelated areas.

13. 521 U.S. 811 (1997).

14. The plaintiffs were themselves partly to blame for this. They might have waited for the actual exercise of that line-item veto and then sued, claiming that the president's veto took away their constitutional authority to enact the particular item being vetoed. They sued in advance of any exercise of the veto power, arguing that the very process of negotiating with the president had been measurably altered because the power was "on the books"; but that effect was a bit too inchoate for the Court to appreciate.

15. *Campbell v. Clinton*, 23 (2000) (suit by members of the House asserting the president needed the assent of Congress to the NATO bombings in Yugoslavia). See also *Dellums v. Bush*, 752 F. Supp. at 1151.

16. It might be answered that separation of powers concerns keep courts from assessing the likelihood or adequacy of legislative remedies, concerns that would not be present when inquiring into the likelihood or adequacy of corporate remedies. That response would be wrong. There is no intrusion into what Congress does to ask whether the group asserting a constitutional right could have relief. It is a structural question alone: one-third of the Senate cannot pass an appropriation rider. One-half of the House cannot pass a law. There is no intrusion of any kind in reaching those structural conclusions. Nor is the question of likelihood ever presented.

17. "This principle is a departure from traditional standing analysis because it violates the principle of equality between legislators and private plaintiffs; non-legislator plaintiffs are not routinely denied standing because of the presence of an alternative remedy." *Riegle v. Federal Open Market Committee*, 879. Nevertheless, the D.C. Circuit created the doctrine of "equitable discretion" in deciding whether to hear suits, otherwise justiciable, if brought by members of Congress. See A. Arend and C. Lotrionte, "Congress Goes to Court: The Past, Present and Future of Legislative Standing," 25 *Harv. J. L. & Pub. Pol.* 209, 234ff. (2001). See also L. Fisher, *Constitutional Dialogues* 32 (1988).

18. Moe and Howell, "Unilateral Action," 858.

19. Why does a federal court refuse to hear a legislator's challenge to presidential action? Moe and Howell have recently set forward two principal reasons: (1) all presidents appoint judges with pro-executive-branch predilections, to the extent these can be measured in advance; and (2) all courts are concerned about their institutional respect in making orders that are followed—with the

president heading up the enforcement branch of government, this makes courts quite hesitant to order the president to take action. Moe and Howell, "Unilateral Action," 871. Moe and Howell predict that courts will often reflect these influences by declining to rule, rather than ruling against the president. The court can simply avoid deciding many issues that arise about institutional power, arguing that these are matters that the president and Congress have to resolve on their own. This protects the court from the risk of alienating presidents. It is also an indirect way of giving presidents what they want, because Congress is not equipped to win this kind of struggle. Id. at 872.

To this might be added the one additional point that all presidents, of whatever political party, would be disinclined to elevate a district court judge to the court of appeals, an appellate court judge to the Supreme Court, or a Supreme Court associate justice to chief justice, who has displayed a willingness to curb presidential power in a high-profile case. It is inconceivable such a ruling would be ignored in subsequent consideration, even by another president of a different party, of whether to elevate a specific judge.

20. Prior to *Raines*, the D.C. Circuit had developed an integrated approach to proceeding with lawsuits by legislators, incorporating standing, ripeness, and political question doctrines under the heading of "equitable discretion." See, e.g., C. McGowan, "Congressmen in Court: The New Plaintiffs," 15 *Ga. L. Rev.* 241 (1981); and *Riegle v. Federal Open Market Committee*. Judge McGowan, while keeping open the possibility of the occasional legislators' lawsuit, expressed a general aversion to them. "The problems are multiplied when the plaintiff could have obtained relief from Congress the substantial equivalent of the judicial relief sought, because in such cases the Court is asked to intrude into the internal functionings of the legislative branch itself." McGowan, "Congressmen in Court," 242. After *Raines*, the D.C. Circuit has never granted legislators' standing, although in *Chenoweth v. Clinton* the court claimed that the facts of *Kennedy v. Sampson*, 511 F.2d 430 (D.C. Cir., 1974) (challenge to pocket veto by senators who had voted in favor of the legislative measure), would still support standing.

21. See *Riegle v. Federal Open Market Committee*, 878–79, citing *Warth v. Seldin*, 442 U.S. 490, 498–99 (1975) ("the plaintiff must allege 'such a personal stake in the outcome of the controversy' as to warrant *his* invocation of federal-court jurisdiction and to justify exercise of the court's remedial powers on his behalf.").

22. 181 F.3d 112 (D.C. Cir., 1999).

23. 752 F. Supp. 1141 (D.D.C. 1990).

24. Thirteen years later, just before the start of the second Persian Gulf war, a suit by members of Congress (joined by service personnel and their families) was dismissed for similar ripeness grounds. *Doe v. Bush*, 2003 U.S. App. Lexis 4477 (1st Cir., 2003).

25. G. Bispham, *Principles of Equity* 67 (1887),

[E]quity acts specifically, and not by way of compensation; which embodies a general principle running through the whole system of chancery jurisprudence. This principle is that equity aims at putting the parties exactly in the position which they ought to occupy, giving them in specie what they are entitled to enjoy . . . [t]hus, equity decrees the performance of a contract, and does not give damages for its breach.

This is an application of what is known as the twelfth maxim of equity. Id.

26. The House disapproved a Senate resolution of authorization for the bombing on an evenly divided 213 to 213 vote. The House also voted down a declaration of war against Yugoslavia, 2 to 427. However, the House also defeated a resolution calling for the withdrawal of U.S. troops from the war zone, 139 to 290.

27. There was one other point, however, mentioned in *Dellums*, though it is impossible to know how dispositive it would have been to Judge Greene. He noted that Congressman Dellums had not obtained the approval of a majority of Congress to bring his suit. 52 F. Supp.2d 34 at 1143. By contrast, in *Kennedy v. Sampson* the plaintiff senators and House members had obtained resolutions of each body in favor of going forward with the litigation.

28. 752 F. Supp. at 1148.

29. Arend and Lotrionte make this argument, analogizing legislators to board members in a corporation, who cannot assert a right of the corporation without the support of a vote of the board. Arend and Lotrionte, "Congress Goes to Court," 276. That specific analogy, however, is flawed in that shareholders can and do sue on behalf of corporations, having presented the chance for approval to the board and been refused, under the rubric of shareholder derivative suits—alleging the board's negligence in failing to assert the corporation's rights takes its action outside the business judgment rule.

30. The appropriations vote could not, logically, be a premise to deny standing, since it was a vote to replenish supplies. The bullets and bombs for Yugoslavia had already been spent at the time of the congressional vote. Further, as Judge Greene noted in *Dellums*, to vote against appropriating money for soldiers already committed to battle is very difficult. Hence, such a vote might not represent an honest expression of congressional will on whether the troops should have been so committed in the first place, which, constitutionally, is the right to which the members of Congress were entitled. Finally, the War Powers Act specifically provides that an appropriation vote is not an authorization for the use of force. 50 U.S.C. § 1547(a).

31. The opinions of the court of appeals were as follows: (1) Judge Silberman for the court, that *Raines v. Byrd* cut off all legislative standing so long as any possible redress was available through Congress. 203 F.3d at 20. (This ignored the fact that the only possible redress would require two thirds of each house, as discussed above.) (2) Judge Randolph, concurring, that there was no war in Yugoslavia. 203 F.3d at 28. (The well-pleaded complaint, however, alleged there was and that it could be shown by the defendant's own admissions. Secretary of Defense Cohen was quoted thus, in *Time* magazine, for example: "'We're certainly engaged in hostilities. We're engaged in combat. Whether that measures up to, quote, a classic definition of war, I'm not qualified to say.' William S. Cohen, the apparently underqualified Secretary of Defense, on whether or not we

are at war with Yugoslavia." *Time*, April 26, 1999, 19.) (3) Judge Silberman's separate opinion, that this was a political question since a court lacked standards to apply to ascertain whether there was war. 203 F.3d at 24. And (4) Judge Tatel, concurring with the court opinion, see (1) above, but disagreeing with Judge Silberman's separate opinion, stating that the political question doctrine did not preclude hearing the case. 203 F.3d at 37.

32. The First Circuit relied upon Justice Powell's concurring opinion in *Goldwater v. Carter* that a court should not decide "'issues affecting the allocation of power between the President and Congress until the political branches reach a constitutional impasse.' 444 U.S. 996, 997 (Powell, J., concurring)." *Doe v. Bush*, 2003 U.S. App. Lexis 4477 at 12. On this basis, the First Circuit held the members of Congress's suit in the second Persian Gulf war case to be unripe. Curiously, in *Goldwater*, the Senate had taken such a vote—in favor of Senator Goldwater's position. Justice Powell made no mention of this.

33. 50 U.S.C. § 1545–46. A remarkable part of the War Powers Act gives any member of Congress the right to bring a resolution under that statute, either to authorize military action or to compel the withdrawal of troops, to the relevant committee and then to the floor for a vote (even if the committee voted no). Congressman Dellums chose not to make use of this in his lawsuit, basing it entirely on the Constitution. Were a coherent rule on legislative standing to be adopted, the fact that Congressman Dellums could have obtained a vote on going to war, but chose not to, would likely preclude standing or ripeness.

34. Technically, a single senator could propose an amendment to a bill already on the floor. "Germaneness of amendments is not required in the Senate; except in four specific instances [not relevant here]." J. Schneider, "House and Senate Rules of Procedure: A Comparison," Congressional Research Service, April 19, 2001 (Document no. 30945). However, the motion to table an amendment would require fifty-one votes, cutting off the rights of the thirty-four. If the thirty-four attempted a filibuster of the motion to table, cloture could be invoked by sixty senators. Hence, thirty-four senators have no guaranteed way of obtaining a vote.

35. In *Edwards v. Carter*, 580 F.2d 1055 (D.C. Cir., 1978), the plaintiff members of the House also lacked the procedural means to obtain a vote (there, on the question of whether the Panama Canal Treaty effectuated a transfer of federal government property thus requiring approval of both the House and the Senate). The D.C. Circuit did not, however, require any procedural predicate, jumping over the district court's dismissal on standing grounds to rule against plaintiffs on the merits.

36. 521 U.S. at 829–30.

37. 307 U.S. 433 (1939).

38. Indeed, the class was superperfect, as one state senator who had voted for the U.S. constitutional amendment nevertheless opposed the process whereby it had been deemed ratified and joined the lawsuit.

39. 521 U.S. at 823.

40. 203 F.3d at 29.

41. 307 U.S. at 450.

42. There were forty Kansas state senators, and twenty-one joined the lawsuit, so the plaintiffs had a majority of the senate, which, presumably, could give an order to its employee, the secretary of the senate. Even if a supermajority were required to give such an order to the secretary of the senate, under the rules of the Kansas State Senate, that also remained a possibility, which would be enough to deny standing to the state senators under the D.C. Circuit's logic.

43. It is for this reason, I believe, that Judge Silberman in *Campbell v. Clinton* took the unusual step of writing a concurrence to his own majority opinion. That concurrence relied solely on the political question doctrine, which had not been developed at the time of *Coleman v. Miller* 203 at 24–25 (Silberman, J., concurring).

44. 521 U.S. at 823.

45. In most instances, the action would have to be brought against a cabinet officer, or other agent of the president, rather than officially against the president, since the "court has no jurisdiction of a bill to enjoin the President in the performance of his official duties," *Mississippi v. Johnson*, 71 U.S. (4 Wall.) 475, 501 (1867), cited in *Franklin v. Massachusetts*, 505 U.S. 788, 803 (1992). I thank Dean Jesse Choper for this point.

46. This distinction parallels the common law distinction between mandatory and prohibitory injunctions. The mandatory injunction was less favored in antiquity. See Bispham, *Principles of Equity*, 457: "An injunction may, therefore, be said to be either mandatory or prohibitory. A mandatory injunction is one that compels the defendant to restore things to their former condition and virtually directs him to perform an act. The jurisdiction of the court to issue such a writ has been questioned, but it is now established beyond doubt." (Citations omitted.)

47. "[L]egislators whose votes would have been sufficient to defeat (or enact) a specific legislative Act have standing to sue if that legislative action goes into effect (or does not go into effect), on the grounds that their votes have been completely nullified." 521 U.S. at 823.

48. 580 F.2d 1055 (D.C. Cir., 1978).

49. 656 F.2d 873 (D.C. Cir., 1981).

50. The issue arose in the impoundment controversies during the administration of President Nixon. *Train v. City of New York*, 420 U.S. 35 (1975). A statutory compromise was eventually worked out, so the Court never had to rule on the constitutionality, or workability, of ordering the president to make a specific expenditure.

51. This could be cured by a resolution authorizing the litigation, but that would only be a valid expression of congressional will until the next election.

52. The classic case is described in E. Snell, *The Principles of Equity* 512 (1920):

The incapacity of the Court to compel the complete execution of a contract sometimes limits its jurisdiction to compel specific performance. This principle is most frequently illustrated in cases of agreements to do acts involving personal skill, knowledge or inclination. Thus, in *Lumley v. Wagner*, where a lady agreed with a theatrical manager to sing at his theatre for a definite period, the Court refused to order her to sing; but, as the agreement contained a clause by which she engaged not to use her talents at any other theatre or concert room during the agreed period, the Court granted an injunction to prevent her from breaking this negative term. (Citation omitted.)

53. There can be instances where Congress is seeking a specific ministerial, nondiscretionary act from the executive, so well defined and limited that a court could order it done. When the General Accounting Office (GAO), an arm of the Congress, sues to obtain documents withheld by the executive branch, for instance, relief is an affirmative act by the executive, the handing over of the documents, but no exercise of discretionary judgment is required. Such an instance is currently brewing regarding records of the vice president's enrgy task force meetings. J. Gerth, "Accounting Office Demands Energy Task Force Records," *New York Times*, July 19, 2001. Cf. *Walker v. Cheney*, U.S. Dist. Lexis 23385 (D.C. Cir., 2002) and the parallel action, *In re Cheney*, 2003 U.S. App. Lexis 18831 (D.C. Cir., 2003), *cert. granted*, 124 S.Ct. 958 (2003).

54. 462 U.S. 919 (1983).

55. Id. at 931 n. 6.

56. Chief Justice Rehnquist, however, in dicta in *Raines v. Byrd*, lists giving the "Attorney General . . . standing to challenge the one-House veto provision" among his parade of horribles should the Court's limitation on standing be undone. 521 U.S. at 828. It is hard to see why this would have been so horrible, however, given that the attorney general did actually precipitate the *Chadha* litigation by putting Chadha in legal limbo, and the case that went to trial and Supreme Court adjudication included all the same parties as it would have had the attorney general sued Congress.

57. Bill of attainder problems might exist, although deportation is a civil, not criminal, proceeding. *United States v. Lovett*, 328 U.S. 303 (1946). However, the presence of an unrelated constitutional impediment should not save the *Campbell* court's construction of *Raines* from the logic that it would deny legislative standing in the one-house veto context. Simply substitute in the fact pattern that an arms contract had been terminated by a one-house veto for an individual subject to a deportation order and the bill of attainder problem disappears.

58. The rule I advanced above, that Congress be requesting a negative rather than an affirmative injunction, might still work to preclude congressional standing in the *Chadha* fact pattern. But that was not the distinction on which the Court relied in *Raines*; indeed, the *Raines* Court purported to grant standing to legislators in this kind of case: who voted to take an action (to lift the stay on Chadha's deportation), and that action did not go into effect. 521 U.S. at 823.

59. One example would be the president suing the Senate for not moving on his appointees. There is a textual commitment to the Senate to make its own rules regarding how it will proceed with matters over which it has authority. This is entirely symmetric with the fact that, even under the standing rule being advanced here, there will be occasions where actions by members of Congress will be denied for political question purposes. A suit to compel the president to send a name over for a vacancy, for example, should be a parallel case.

The political question doctrine knocks out private parties' suits as readily as it does those of legislators, or of a president. That is as it should be, because the issue itself should not be before a court, as opposed to the party being inappropriate to litigate the issue. Legislative standing rules, by contrast, do not knock out private plaintiffs. For example, the line-item veto was overturned in a private party action shortly after *Raines*. Judge Tatel, concurring in *Campbell*, opined that a soldier would have been able to bring the case that the members of Congress had brought.

60. This approach, as to legislators, is advocated in Arend and Lotrionte, "Congress Goes to Court," 279–80, 282.

61. 369 U.S. 186 (1962).

62. The political question doctrine, to the extent it is constitutional and not just prudential, would be retained under the analysis of whether a case or controversy existed.

63. 521 U.S. at 828–29.

64. Chief Justice Marshall ruled on a procedural point, that only a district court, not the U.S. Supreme Court, had the authority to issue the relief requested by Marbury.

65. Consider Justice Powell's claim that eschewing the role of supervision of interbranch disputes "has maintained public esteem for the federal courts...." I disagree. Taking on the role of supervising important interbranch disputes has, rather, enhanced that esteem. Was *U.S. v. Nixon*, 418 U.S. 683 (1974), simply a criminal discovery case? Or was it a resolution of a fundamental dispute between the executive and judicial branches? Did it bring honor to the Court or shame?

66. Such a resolution could be adopted under the authority of each house granted under Article I, sec. 5, clause 2, to provide for the rules of its own proceedings, and hence not require the concurrence of the other house or be subject to the president's veto. U.S. Const. Article I, sec. 7.

67. In *Raines*, Chief Justice Rehnquist recites a list of hypothetical cases whose adjudication by the courts, he believed, would follow from a more expansive rule on standing. He intends this list to shock the reader with the prospect of judicial intervention. 521 U.S. at 826–28. Yet my reaction, at least, was that judicial intervention in most of the cases cited would have been salutary for our country.

1. "[I]f their [the legislators'] claim were sustained, it would appear that President [Andrew] Johnson would have had standing to challenge the Tenure of Office Act before he ever thought about firing a cabinet member." 521 U.S. at 826–27. Yes—and our country might have been spared his impeachment and other excesses by the Radical Republicans. This is precisely the kind of example I would give of the harm from letting battle between the political branches substitute for resort to the judicial branch.

2. "Similarly in INS v. Chadha, 462 U.S. 919 (1983), the Attorney General would have had standing to challenge the one-House veto provision be-

cause it rendered his authority provisional rather than final." 521 U.S. at 828. This is almost precisely what did happen, however. The case only in its most technical sense was brought by Chadha against the INS. In truth, they were on the same side, and it was only the permissive intervention into the lawsuit by Congress (creating a true interbranch dispute) that saved it from dismissal under case or controversy grounds. 462 U.S. at 931, n. 6.

3. "By parity of reasoning, President Gerald Ford could have sued to challenge the appointment provisions of the Federal Election Campaign Act which were struck down in Buckley v. Valeo, 424 U.S. 1 (1976) (per curiam)." 521 U.S. at 828. This is a remarkable case to cite, because the eventual case was brought by an individual, who was also a legislator. What practical difference did it make that James Buckley the candidate brought the suit rather than James Buckley the U.S. Senator? Or does Chief Justice Rehnquist intend to find something worse about a president bringing the suit than a senator? As discussed above, and as is intimated by Chief Justice Rehnquist's choice of "horribles" to present, the rules for standing should be the same whether the case is brought by the executive or a member of Congress. Indeed, Chief Justice Rehnquist brought forth a series of four "horrible" instances, three of which dealt with allowing a president to sue, in order to demonstrate the folly of allowing legislators to sue in the case before him.

4. "[A]nd a Member of Congress could have challenged the validity of President Coolidge's pocket veto that was sustained in The Pocket Veto Case, 279 U.S. 655 (1929)." 521 U.S. at 828. This, of course, is exactly what happened in *Kennedy v. Sampson*. Senator Kennedy, a member of Congress, did, in fact, challenge the exercise of the pocket veto by President Ford. What harm the country suffered from that, in Chief Justice Rehnquist's eyes, is a bit hard to conceive. He doesn't identify any. There is no generally accepted recognition in the public consciousness of harm to our republic from this case being heard and resolved by the D.C. Circuit in 1974.

68. Professor Laurence Tribe tells us that Justice Stewart considered the Court's refusal ever to rule on the constitutionality of the war in Vietnam as the Court's greatest failure during his time on the Court. L. Tribe, "Justice Stewart: A Tale of Two Portraits," 95 *Yale L. J.* 1328, 1331 (1986).

69. The thirty-four senators who wanted the Taiwan treaty to continue in *Goldwater* would fit this description.

70. Letter from A. Lincoln to Herndon (February 15, 1848). 2 *Complete Works of Abraham Lincoln* 2–3, J. G. Nicolay and J. Hay, eds. (1905).

"In contrast to the English system, the Framers did not want the wealth and blood of the Nation committed by the decision of a single individual." The Constitution of the United States of America, Analysis and Interpretation 308, S. Doc. No. 103-6, J. Killian and G. Costello, eds. (1996) (collecting citations from the records of the Federal Convention and the *Federalist Papers*).

71. In arguing for some legislators' standing, I recognize that the political question doctrine will still apply and that, in the context of war, that doctrine might prevent a court from ruling on some challenges. During my time in the House, President Bush ordered the invasion of Panama, the insertion of troops in Saudi Arabia during Desert Shield, and then the expulsion of Iraq from Kuwait in Desert Storm; and President Clinton ordered the bombing of Sudan, Iraq, Afghanistan, and Yugoslavia. Desert Storm was specifically authorized by both houses of Congress; none of the other instances were. Asking a federal court to stop an ongoing war might be held to implicate the political question doctrine, as the D.C. Circuit held in *Mitchell v. Laird*, because of the intrusion into the president's commander-in-chief authority. If so, Desert Shield and Yugoslavia could still have been heard as, in each case, there was a substantial pre-war buildup of American and allied military forces during which Congress could, and did, take a vote. Even if the other instances could not have been adjudicated, at least these two could. Our country would benefit from an authoritative constitutional division of the congressional war-declaring power and the executive commander-in-chief power. This clarification has eluded us for the entire post–World War II era during which the president, in a departure from almost two centuries of precedent, commenced substantial military actions without congressional authorization. See J. Ely, *War and Responsibility* 10 and n. 54 (1993). Such a ruling would bind in future cases, whether or not there was time to get to court in those instances and, at the least, make it harder (and potentially impeachable) for a president to violate the proscription against commencing war on the will of one person alone.